TAKE THE BALL
AND RUN

D0185276

TAKE THE BALL AND RUN

A Rugby Anthology edited by

Godfrey Smith

Foreword by Cliff Morgan

PAVILION

For our grandson Max
who looks as if he well might

First published in Great Britain in 1991 by
PAVILION BOOKS LIMITED
26 Upper Ground, London SE1 9PD

This paperback edition published in 1995

Compilation, introduction and commentary
copyright © Godfrey Smith 1991

Designed by Roy Cole

A CIP catalogue record for this book is
available from the British Library.

ISBN 1 85793 764 3
10 9 8 7 6 5 4 3 2 1

Printed and bound in Great Britain by
Cox & Wyman Ltd, Reading

Contents

Foreword

On my Mother's knee I learnt that Bob Deans, the New Zealand three-quarter, did NOT score a try against Wales at Cardiff Arms Park in 1905 and that Rhys Gabe DID tackle him less than a yard from the try-line and that Deans tried to scramble over but the referee had spotted him! I have to confess that The Lord's Prayer and Nursery Rhymes, Hymn Tunes and the Welsh National Anthem came a close second, but even then, as a baby, rugby was closer to me than speech or action. The game, with its excitements and frustrations, its satisfactions and resentments, its inspiration and vanities, has dominated my life ever since.

Maybe Richard Burton was right when he wrote that 'rugby is a game of massive lies and stupendous exaggerations', for in truth it is the romance we all yearn for in a sporting world that so often appears to be on its head. It is the power of the written and spoken word – the story – that enriches and explains the beauty and the complexities of any game. To produce this book, Godfrey Smith has cast his enquiring net wide and his selection – sometimes from seemingly unlikely sources – will surprise and delight.

To an old has-been like me this collection of rugby writing evokes memories of a sunken past. When I started playing the game at Tonyrefail Grammar School, my games master, Ned Gribble, claimed that 'rugby is a game that sweats the vice out of you'. He taught not only the skills and the daring, but also that victory is never for all time and neither is defeat irreparable. It was when we Valley kids were in the second form that he told us the story of The Shoulder-High Chivalry of the Vanquished Welsh, relating how A. L. Gracie of Harlequins and Scotland was chaired from the field by the Welsh crowd after he had scored the tries that beat Wales at Cardiff in 1923. I am glad this act of sportsmanship appears in this book. My father was actually at that match, watching from what was then the Tanner bank, because it cost sixpence to stand there. He was also in Dublin in 1952 at the Ireland–Wales Triple Crown match, when he lost his teeth and he wasn't even playing.

What happened was this. From our own 25 yard line (metres had not then been invented) the Welsh wing and Olympic sprinter Ken Jones raced 75 yards, outstripping Ireland's wing, Phipps, to score a memorable match-winning try. Now my father, who was sitting in the back row of the Grandstand in the one seat we could purchase as a player in those days, leapt to his feet and shouted his joy and his top set ended up some 25 rows in front. He never found his teeth. Some years later I was telling this story on a radio programme in Ireland in the company of Tony O'Reilly, and when I had finished O'Reilly swore that he knew a man in Cork who was still wearing them!

In mapping and signposting and selecting, Godfrey Smith has added a little more joy to those who care for 'A Game for Gods' – just one extract from the novel *Magnus Merriman* by Erik Linklater. And there is P. G. Wodehouse: 'Tuppy and the Red-Haired Bounder' from *Very Good, Jeeves!*; 'The Lifelong Regret of F. E. Smith', by John Campbell; and from E. H. D. Sewell's *Rugger the Man's Game*, a preface by Charles Fry – C. B. Fry, whose sporting and academic achievements will never be equalled; a Cup Final with Southampton, Test Cricketer – and only injury stopped him getting a rugby Blue for Oxford.

The contribution of C. B. Fry, who died in 1956 at the age of 84, prompted in my mind thoughts of J. L. Manning, who for me was one of the finest journalists and most interesting people I have met. In his last broadcast, only days before he died, he looked back on his distinguished and campaigning life in sports journalism and produced a love poem written by C. B. Fry to his grandmother – his father's mother.

> Dear one, no capital save Love,
> may pay the toll of strife
> so mine, of now and every year
> would bring you back to life.
> No wintry woe shall ever dim
> The Golden joy you bring
> Your daffodils are here again
> And my perpetual spring.

The late H. B. Toft, England hooker, captain, selector, rugby writer for the *Observer* and scholar, once remarked to me: 'Rugby is different from all other games. We do not play strictly towards a goal. The approach is on a broad front . . . and this is what we should concentrate on, an effort to expand our game and our minds.'

Henry Toft, whose writing I admired so much, would have approved of 'Take the Ball and Run', for it is such an appropriate title for this anthology. Like the game itself it is so beautifully unpredictable. A master hand has produced many jewels to be wondered at and some rare flowers to be enjoyed. Take down this book.

Cliff Morgan, 1991

Introduction

I have just been looking at a pair of modern rugby boots. Compared with the dun and dubbined affairs in which I learned the game as a boy, they are miracles of high tech. With their cutaway back and soft fabric, psychedelic studs and smart black and red trim, the maker's name tastefully marketed on the side and soles, they seem to me very much to stand for the modern game.

Indeed, one look at a modern player will at once show you how the game has changed this half-century. His hair is long, and innocent of the short-back-and-sides with which our heroes played at Twickers in my youth; and though his jersey is skin tight – as of course it must be – his shorts are no longer the baggy garments of my youth, but minimal. The old scrum caps of your latter-day second-row forward have all gone, and instead your modern forward wears a sweatband (or more recently a rather ghastly piece of what looks like black plastic tape). However, he still wears no padding, in contrast to American football, and, once he starts to do so, I think the game will be on the rocks; for of course, the more padding you wear, the more damage you feel able to inflict on the other chap. It is one of the great glories of our game that you go into the tackle knowing you are as likely to get as to give.

The game itself mirrors the snazzier image of its gear. It has demonstrably grown quicker. You have only to look at the flickering black-and-white images of old newsreels to see that. When I was a boy (though it's hard to believe now) we were taught to catch the ball in the line-out, whip it down to calf height, turn our backs to the opposition and pass the ball to the scrum-half. If you were to do that nowadays, the ball would be halfway down the other end of the ground before you'd finished your drill. The tapped ball, which would have seemed sinfully casual to us when young, is now a normal skill.

Players have got bigger. All modern three-quarters in international games now play absolutely fit at heavier weights than pre-war forwards. What is more, they play what must surely be recognized as a much more exciting game. Unlike association football, which changes its rules seldom, rugby football is continuously evolving. One change alone has revolutionized the pace and interest of the modern game: the law that says that only kicks directly into touch from within your own 22 will earn you a line-out at the point where the ball goes out of play on the full. I have seen many a dour battle at Twickers in the 1950s and 60s which became stalemates under the old law.

For someone of my vintage, even the difference in points must have residually helped; four points for a try rather than the three points when I was a boy give just that slight edge to the running game; though personally I shall not be happy till the conversion counts for one point as in

American football. In the same way, the law allowing substitutes when players are injured has prevented many a game from becoming a mockery (though as we shall see in these pages heroic games have been won by fourteen men). And the more recent rule that allows play to go on while an injured player is restored speeds up the action still more. It is, incidentally, a pleasing novelty to see the rise of the female spongeman; I said recently in *The Sunday Times* that it would surely not be long before we saw one at Twickers. I was too late; the Cambridge team have already had one for the university game – with notable effect.

We have also seen, since my youth, the birth of women's rugby; last season a young woman called Maggie Waugh got married on Saturday morning, then turned out as hooker for the Sale women's rugby XV. The old song about the Marrying Kind of Maid clearly needs a new verse.

The actual *look* of the game, though speeded up, is not fundamentally different. The phallic echoes which surface when the ball is put into the scrum, and the overtones of childbirth itself as it squirts out, have not been overlooked in the late-night revelry which is an essential part of the game. The accident of the pig's bladder which was first used for a ball at Rugby school gave it that odd egg-shape; the first certain intimation we have of that shape comes in *Tom Brown's Schooldays* when the ball is *pointed* at the goal. Yet the shape of the ball has far more to it than that; it also lends the game its innate unpredictability. We say – and the Americans say – of any unhappy news: 'That's the way the ball bounces.' Their game and ours derive from the same oval ball.

Refereeing, I submit, has improved, and having in major matches what are in effect three referees, two playing as linesmen, has certainly brought swift retribution for foul play previously unpunished by the unsighted arbiter on the field. A referee of Clive Norling's class enormously helps the game's fluidity, and an experiment in wiring him for sound at the Bath–Toulon game last year greatly helped TV spectators to understand his decisions; if the idea becomes general it may well put an end to the balletic mime which referees have long had to use in the past.

Our game benefits too from being played in three dimensions. Soccer, it is true, is also played in the air; but not, at any expert level, in the high air. In rugby, the high ball, the Garryowen, or the up and under, is part of the majestic, the appalling and the unpredictable dimension of our game.

What is its future? Twenty years ago, when the Rugby Football Union was celebrating its centenary, various pundits were asked to gaze into the crystal ball and say how it would be in 2001. The great Dr Danie Craven himself predicted that some parts of the game – the ruck, for example – would be phased out, just as hacking was phased out a century ago. I think he is right. I hope, though, that we shall not give up the line-out, that untidy illegitimate child of rugby, as Danie has called it; replete as it is with every kind of chance for ambiguity and sin. Rugby League has done away with the line-out – to its own detriment, in my opinion.

The greatest single problem the game faces is that of money. The cardinal difference between rugby and association football at the top level has long been that the former is played for fun, and the latter for money. The result, for the followers of the round ball, has been demonstrably appalling. There has never yet, thank God, been any crowd violence at Twickenham, and this despite the enormous quantities of alcohol disposed of there. Last season, however, there were two cases in Wales of referees being attacked. I see that as a sinister pointer to the future.

The secretary of the RFU, Dudley Wood, has said that he is proud to be a Canute; in other words, that he is proud to stand out against payment for players even as the commercial waves wash over him. 'The old idea of a ticket tout being someone in a dirty raincoat making a few bob on the side,' he remarked recently, 'has long since been overtaken. We are talking about organised crime.' Yet when millions pour into the modern game, how can we reasonably expect the young men who create the bonanza not to share in it? We all know about the tenner in the boot; but how long the modern game will hold out against proper compensation for international players is anyone's guess. It was Gareth Edwards, no less, who remarked that while you were getting your ribs kicked in on the other side of the world, the bills from the electricity company were still coming in. For myself, I don't want to see our game go professional; but fear it is inevitable.

Still, money will not ruin the game, I submit, at its humblest levels; nor will it dispel its mysterious macho appeal; its weird compulsion as moments of muddy chaos suddenly flower into movements of intense beauty; those uninhibited and rabelaisian songs after the game; the lifelong freemasonry and friendships that flourish between people who only an hour before have been doing their damndest to knock each other's blocks off.

It is something of an enigma that a game so hypnotic in its thrall – 116 countries played it at the last count – should be so sparsely chronicled. Cricket has spawned a vast literature and an academy of elegant essayists all the way from Cardus to Arlott. Rugby has no such pretensions. Nevertheless, when we look into the matter more closely, we shall see that the standard of rugby writing has been rising steadily. Frank Keating is a flip Cardus if ever I saw one; Alan Watkins, doyen of political columnists, does rugby on the side but could clearly lead the field if he ever put all his mind to it; John Reason (as I hope we show in these pages) is a reporter of true clout; Michael Green is arguably the funniest chronicler of any sport that we can boast. Indeed, his scope is enviably infinite, for rugby is built over a subterranean river of humour that no other sport can match. I have included therefore a good smattering of rugby stories that have made me laugh and a sample of rugby songs from the several hundred sung after the game all over the world (and soon in Russia too: until they toured here recently, Russian players used to shower and dress at the recreation ground and go home; they're unlikely to do so after having sampled the pleasures of other rugby evenings). What is more, I believe there are greatly enjoyable scriveners of our game like my colleague Steve Jones, an old Newport No. 8 who now covers the worldwide game for *The Sunday Times*.

I have included examples of all their work in this anthology. It makes absolutely no claims to be thoroughgoing or scholarly, comprehensive or definitive. It is the fruit of one man's love affair over half a century with a game played in the mud with a piece of leather shaped like an egg: a game that will, the gods willing, always set the pulses racing – even though the ball be lofted into the upper air by psychedelically tinted boots.

As I write this, Twickenham is already girding itself for the World Cup. The dire predictions about the first such contest, held down under, proved totally wrong – it was a triumph. Philip Toynbee famously remarked that a bomb under the West Stand at Twickenham would end fascism in England for a generation; what you're likely to find there, in my experience, is not so much the fascist as the publicist. We're always being told that rugby needs more money; I wish it could do with less business cash and more ordinary punters. When I first watched rugby there forty years ago we always used to meet by an old oak tree in the charming east car park; that is now the headquarters block. The west car park, always the grandest, is now totally swallowed up on international days by debenture holders. That means that those of us who are not officials and not rich enough to run to a debenture are directed round to the north car park. Let us hope the RFU's plan to buy some more land from the school to its west matures. For the sheer showbiz magic of Twickers seems to grow each year.

We shall learn in this book that in the 1920s when Donald, the naïve young Scot in A. G. Macdonell's masterpiece *England their England*, goes to Twickers, he lunches off beer and bread and cheese. Such homely fare would hardly do in these lavish days of barbecues, *boeuf bourgignon* and bubbly. But perhaps we can put that down simply to the slow but steady rise in conspicuous consumption.

What is the secret that draws more and more people irresistibly to the game each year? Perhaps that sheer unpredictability is one element. It is not much of a betting man's game and I for one have never been able to predict the outcome of games in the Five Nations Championship with the slightest success. Who, for example, would have predicted that in 1990 Scotland would halt the previously unstoppable English and win the Triple Crown and the Grand Slam? And who, given their respective past records, would have taken Oxford to beat Cambridge last year? Rugby is full of such surprises; and it was only when perforce making a detailed study of past decades for this book that I realized with a start that Wales had hardly won a game throughout the 1920s and that the mighty All Blacks trail well behind the Springboks in the bloody tally of all their epic encounters.

It is indeed in the southern hemisphere that the worst examples of gratuitous violence have most marked the beauty of the game, and I have included John Reason's emetic account of what happened to Sandy Carmichael's homely mug on the 1971 Lions Tour because I think it points to obvious future dangers. I thought it right, too, to include Danny Hearn's own account of the crash tackle that broke his neck but from which he has made such a gallant recovery. I suppose we would all expect it to go hand in hand with our game, but I believe no one before has worked out a precise summary of how many awards for gallantry in war our internationals have won. The odds against such a small group of men winning four VCs would have been long; against Irish players winning three of them, longer still.

To whatever glory rugby aspires, its heart for me will always be at club level, and it is one of my greatest consolations that when I look out of the window in our Wiltshire village I can see the slightly sagging goalposts where Minety second XV do their muddy battles. When they founded the club ten years ago they sent me a letter inviting me to be one of their vice-presidents. They had, they went on, two claims to distinction: they were the smallest club in England and had the ugliest colours, since only pots of mauve and green paint were available when they first put up their clubhouse. If I did not wish to accept their invitation, not to worry: they had already been turned down by Princess Diana, Phil Bennett and the Duke of Beaufort. It is as one of the many proud vice-presidents of Minety RFC that I offer this modest expression of gratitude for all the fun the game has given me.

Godfrey Smith
Malmesbury
June 1991

The Sweet Thanks of Four French Tarts

Robert Sloman

We start with a piece specially written for this book by my old friend Bob Sloman, the only man, I believe, to have written a play in which a rugby ball is bounced on to the stage. It was called, as he explains here, The Tinker, and was filmed as The Wild and the Willing. Bob has written widely for television too and is the author of many Doctor Who scripts. I remember him first, though, as a tall and rangy No. 8 with a secret celebrity in his family. When, as young air crew cadets, we went to get certain items of equipment at our Lancashire base, we were required to pay half-a-crown each – no doubt later recoverable from HMG. When Bob came to pick up his stuff the Lancashire civilian on the other side of the table had a question for him: 'Art related to England skipper?' 'Yes,' said Bob, 'he's my father.' 'Right lad,' said the ardent Lancastrian, 'there'll be no half-crown for thee to pay.'

I never had the pleasure of meeting Bob's father – also called Bob – but he must have been quite a man. He kept a pub in Devon and would ask any new customer two questions: 'What do you do for a living?' and 'How much do you earn?' It says much for Sloman père's charm – and perhaps also his physical presence – that no one ever took affront. But then father had played for Plymouth Albion and for Devon in the 1920s, went north to Oldham, which he skippered, and toured with the rugby league Lions in 1924 and 1928. Bob junior played for Plymouth Albion too, and for Devon some twenty times between 1950 and 1956. Indeed, he went on playing until he was forty – but never turned professional like his father. I think his testimony about the game stands right in the centre of rugby experience, and I'm delighted to kick off with it.

Rugby. What a wonderful game, of infinite complexity, of infinite jest. The questions crowd in. Did the man who first called it Rugger also invent the word Twickers? Did William Webb Ellis realize that he was responsible for one of the great metaphors of life as well as a great sport when he picked up the ball and ran? Memories crowd in, too. I was playing for Plymouth Albion against the Leicester Tigers. Things were getting fraught in the pack. Boots, fists, blood and curses were flying about inches in front of my nose at number eight, so I stood up. As I did so, my opposite number did the same. 'I'm not putting my head in there,' he said, across the heaving, steaming backs. I agreed, so we paired for the rest of the match, standing out of the scrums.

During a county match at Exeter, Fred Hill, the Gloucester hooker, came around the front of the line-out and got a hand in the face from our scrum-half, Mo Andrews. He was in distress, so I went to him to give aid. When he removed his hand I was horrified to see an empty eye socket. I looked at the ground, fearful of what I might find staring up at me. He explained that he had lost his eye in the war. Our front row already knew this. The Woodgate twins, Bill and Eddie, took turns in flicking mud into his good eye as the ball came in. Bill said Fred always hooked with his hand anyway. Quarter was neither given nor asked among West Country packs. Forwards regarded the backs as unnecessary frills, employed mainly as decoration. They would stand about, adjusting their hairdos, gossiping about the cut of so and so's shorts, while the real game went on up front.

I played serious rugby for seven or eight years and then relegated myself to the reserves as family and the need to make a living intervened. From that moment I began to enjoy the game more than ever. At last the chance to go for the double reverse dummy scissors was possible. Most of the attempts resulted in the ball being left in the middle of the field for the opposition to scoop up and score, but it didn't really matter. When it came off the heady exultation more than compensated for the discomforts of playing low grade rugby.

So I carried on playing and found myself turning out every Saturday at the age of forty for the Newmarket All Blacks. The only resemblance we showed to the other lot was that we wore an all-black strip. We changed under hedges or in cars or in ramshackle Scout huts. From time to time we played with less than the obligatory fifteen and on one occasion with sixteen, unnoticed by the referee until the end of the match. On several occasions the referee didn't turn up and the game was played by consensus. It worked very well, and all the old jokes applied: 'Never mind the ball, get on with the game' . . . 'We were bloody lucky to get nil' . . . 'Is it finished, or have they declared?'

Two episodes stand out in the memory of this period. I had written a play, called *The Tinker*, which went on in London and which had been bought by The Rank Organization for a film. The title came from the well-known rugby song. Ralph Thomas, the director, telephoned me and asked me to organize a rugby match, which was to be used as background for the credits. When I asked the team to turn up, they all thought it was an elaborate practical joke, but came anyway. The film was made as *The Wild and the Willing*, for some incalculable reason known only to the Front Office at Rank. If you ever see it on television you will see the lads playing their hearts out behind the rolling credits. The opposition included such luminaries as Andy Hancock, who scored that immortal try for England against Scotland in a snowstorm, to win the game in the dying seconds. As a reward for our efforts and because, in those dear innocent days, payment was unthinkable, the film company presented the club with a new set of goalposts.

The second episode was more exotic. Newmarket had been twinned with the Paris suburb of Maisons-Laffitte, the great French racing centre. We were invited to send a team to play the locals. Amid much excitement the arrangements were made for Easter Sunday. We set off by coach on the Saturday and arrived to find that we were to be billeted in the homes of supporters and that four separate receptions had been organized in our honour. First came the civic reception, held at the Town Hall, then the Supporters Club, followed by the official club dinner. Finally, the team spilled over into the popular local cafés and dance halls. It was a long night. The next morning, pale and devastated, we met at the ground where the match was to be played in the afternoon. It was magnificent; a custom-built stadium in immaculate condition. The pitch was like a bowling green, with an athletics track around it. Two stands had a seating capacity of about ten thousand and we were informed that all seats had been sold. Somewhere along the line a PR man must have been economical with the truth. It was a thoughtful group which met in the palatial changing-rooms, complete with massage beds, physiotherapy rooms and medical units. I didn't have time to join in any discussion, since I was delegated to lunch with the president of the club. My schoolboy French had clearly been improved by the previous night's wassailing and I was the official interpreter. Off I went to a charming house to meet again the president, his attractive wife and a number of local dignitaries.

I would like to say that the meal was superb. It wasn't. I know the French are wonderful cooks, but they have several weaknesses. My idea of roast lamb is a well-cooked leg, covered with crispy skin. We had lamb which was stuffed with whole cloves of garlic and then waved over a candle for about thirty seconds. It ran with blood and I am not a great fan of garlic, especially when it is that obtrusive. But I had to eat it, or cause an international incident. There was only one solution – wash it down with draughts of the fortunately delicious wine. Things got a bit out of hand. I remember at one point, in an attempt to make a joke about my age and grey hair, that I referred to myself as the *éminence grise* of the team. It caused a stir. All might still have been retrievable had not the host, at the end of the meal, produced a dust-encrusted bottle of Armagnac, which I freely confess is a weakness of mine.

I was delivered back to the ground ten minutes before kick-off, to be greeted by my fellow players, who were so psyched up by the occasion and the surroundings that they didn't even comment on my condition. The captain gave a team talk just before we went on the field to the effect that we were representing England and that every man should remember Agincourt. They all played so much above themselves and their experience and ability that we won, nine points to six. I recollect little of the game, but after the match, during yet another reception in the three-storey clubhouse, I was approached by the president. He told me that in no small measure the victory was due to my tactical skills. It was noticeable, he said, that while everyone was running one way, I was running in the opposite direction, clearly to initiate some cunning ploy well beyond that of ordinary mortals. I accepted his observations with seemly modesty.

As a footnote to this bizarre tale, the evening was rounded off with a visit to the Moulin Rouge in Paris for a dinner and show. At about two in the morning my age was beginning to tell, so, along with other oldies, I went back to Maisons-Laffitte, to snatch a few hours before the coach left for the return journey. Many of the younger team members decided to stay in the Pigalle and go directly to the coach. At some time during the night two of them saw a small Algerian run up to a lady of the town, knock her down and steal her handbag. They, gentlemen to the last, set off in pursuit, but, because of their exertions during the day, were losing ground. Fortunately another two team members came out of a bar ahead of them and caught the miscreant. The girl was delighted, since the handbag was crammed full of notes. It was Easter and she had been busy. By now the police had become involved and she wanted our Galahads – all four of them – to go to the police station to make a deposition. They were reluctant to do so, as they could think of better things to do in their last few hours in Paris. However, she prevailed on them and they went with her. When it was all over, as a token of her gratitude, she rounded up three colleagues and our four stalwarts had their gratification free of charge. This story has a touch of Somerset Maugham about it. I can only say that every word of it is true. What a wonderful game.

Four Great Twickers Tries

Now we come to the heart of the matter – the try, which after all is what the game is all about. Yet, as we shall see later, the word try has quietly changed its meaning over the last century. What we now call a try was then called a touchdown, as it still is in the American game; what we now call a conversion was then called a try at goal. Whichever, it is the marvellous running through what looks like impenetrable defence and the scoring of what look like impossible tries that gives the game its unequalled delight. All our four tries here were scored at Twickenham by Englishmen.

Peter Jackson scored his great try for England against the Wallabies on 1 February 1958. Peter Robbins, who describes it, was playing at centre three-quarter that day and thus had a first-hand view of the action. Jackson's jinking was legendary. On a rare occasion when he was rested it was even suggested by one wag that he should appear on the sidelines performing on a trick cycle to entertain the crowds. He was nicknamed Nijinsky in his playing days, and it is due to him, as secretary of the English senior clubs, that the Courage leagues have been organized and run so smoothly.

The Wallabies were very anxious to beat England and would have earned at least a draw but for Jackson's dramatic try. Neither do I use the word dramatic loosely, for the situation had been building up wherein only a stroke of genius could rescue England.

Consider the fact that Horrocks-Taylor had been carried off fifteen minutes before half-time with Butterfield moving into his position. Australia had led at half-time through a penalty by Lenehan which Phillips cancelled out by a brilliant try in the second half. But then, six minutes before full-time, Curley, the Australian full-back, kicked a beautiful drop-goal for what looked like the winning score.

Critically at this point both teams became desperate, but their desperation took two entirely different forms. England began to pass the ball on every occasion. Marques, Thompson and Jackson were all just held on the line. Australia showed their panic by some blatant late tackling on the England three-quarters, especially on Butterfield. In addition Thompson had been brutally and needlessly kicked when on the ground, and these incidents incensed the crowd. According to Jackson, this heightened the tension and thus made his try even more sensational since the crowd were now without shame part of the England struggle.

With time running out, England launched a series of frenzied attacks. I was playing in the centre in the second half and had only one thought: that was to give Jackson the ball whenever and as soon as possible. Marques won the line out on the Australian 25, and on the left playing towards the south terrace. The ball sped from Jeeps along the line to Jackson, who received it just outside the Australian 25 with Phelps, Curley and the cover to beat.

Jackson says that Phelps did not come in cleanly enough to tackle him, and so he was able to hand off, using Phelps's head as a lever. This left Curley, who knew Jackson's liking for coming inside. Jackson vividly remembers that Curley shaped up to expect this inside jink, and he says that this was all he needed. To use his own words, he did a double shuffle to the right, and I believe that only he could have left such a vital decision to this last moment. Curley got a hand to him, and incredibly Phelps got back to retackle, but Jackson had already launched himself at the line.

I asked Peter Jackson what had been going through his mind in this hectic period. His prime thought was that, under Evans's encouragement and fine leadership, there must be a chink with so much pressure. When he got the ball his reaction was, 'At last I have space and time. Here is a golden chance.' He quickly erased any other thoughts from his mind and his brilliant rugby brain turned its attention to the local and away from the general situation.

Had Phelps not been so psychologically afraid, the game might have ended in a draw. Yet it was this very paralysing effect that Jackson had on defenders, coupled with his own genius, that gave England victory.

When the try was given the scenes were extraordinary. Cushions flew sky high. The crowd cheered in joy, excitement and relief. Jackson walked back to the half-way line feeling nothing but complete numbness, so drained was he emotionally and physically. We all felt numb in the dressing-room afterwards. There was total silence until our wonderful skipper, Eric Evans, said in that chirpy voice of his, 'Well, we beat 'em.'

from *Touchdown*

Richard Sharp was a blond Cornishman who had served as a commando in the Royal Marines, and it was no doubt this background that helped give him the strength to add to his innate powers as a brilliant stand-off half. He was capped fourteen times for England between 1960 and 1967 and played twice for the Lions against South Africa – the last Englishman to appear for them in that position till Rob Andrew did so against Australia in 1989. His elegant try against Scotland in the Calcutta Cup match on 16 March 1963 is described by another legendary stand-off – Cliff Morgan of Wales.

Richard Sharp said, 'Mike Weston really made that try. You see, the critical man in a scissors move is *not* the man carrying the ball. Just as in soccer, it's the player running *off* the ball who does the damage. That's what Mike did – causing the defence to hesitate a fraction and so give me the space I needed.'

Richard Sharp was not being modest. His assessment of that never-to-be-forgotten 22 seconds of magic was realistic.

It will come as a surprise to many that this move had been pre-planned. England had scored an almost identical try against France the season before, and Sharp and Weston believed in the scissors. Working on the hard facts that in a period when, more often than not, the defensive formation was flat, they decided that there were only a limited number of possibilities of attack from a set scrummage (from the line-out, attack was almost impossible).

It was the age of the selective and discriminating player. The fly-half could do one of four things: a high punt to catch the opposition full-back in possession; the long, rolling ball to the corner flag; the short chip over the heads of the advancing three-quarters – or the scissors. Sharp's effort against Scotland has become the classic example of that.

From the moment he received the ball the try was on. A flat Clarke pass taken at speed put Sharp a yard outside the back-row cover. He was immediately moving faster, for Sharp's real advantage was that he was even quicker over the second ten yards than he was over the vital first ten. At this moment his direction was somewhere along a line from the 25 yards mark on the right hand touchline, to a point 15 yards in from the other side.

Mike Weston ran wide with Sharp for several yards – and here is the secret of a perfect scissors. The supporting player has first to run with the carrier of the ball before switching inside. Weston's move inside and his call were perfection, and they brought confusion in the Scottish centre. That moment of hesitation gave Sharp only a split second, but that's all a great player needs.

Sharp didn't stop to ask the time of day, and he found his wing, Jim Roberts, up in support at his left elbow. Only one Scot was in the area – the full-back, Colin Blaikie – so it was a two-to-one situation and a certain score. It was at this point, with Blaikie in his sights, that Sharp straightened and leaned away from Roberts, in classical style, as he offered a pass. For a fraction of a second, Blaikie moved towards Roberts – a glorious dummy – and Richard Sharp had crossed the Scottish line.

Some who saw that try still claim that Sharp should have passed to Roberts, but to the trained eye it was plain. Sharp simply had to go it alone . . . 'I had no choice, for my mind was made up for me. Blaikie committed the cardinal sin of not going for the man in possession. I was almost on top of him when I realized that although he was physically in front of me, his mind was on Jim Roberts. The memory of that moment is still vivid. I know I did the right thing.'

So many things could have ruined that moment – had Sharp decided to pass to Roberts. The angle at which Roberts was forced to run to get up with Sharp might well have meant a forward pass. The pass could have been a bad one. Equally, Roberts could have put it down. But these things are conjecture, and the hard fact is that Sharp scored a winning try.

The real test of greatness is in adversity, and this try is proof. It was scored from a set scrumamge in a period when it was virtually impossible to move from a set-piece. And it was scored when England trailed by eight points to five.

In this glorious flourish Richard Sharp, like all the great professionals at a craft – like Sophie Tucker and Bob Hope – revealed a perfect sense of timing. This one move bore the hallmark of Sharp's class. From the moment he fastened on to that low, flat pass from Simon Clarke until he touched down – near enough to make the conversion by John Willcox a formality – it was all grace, pace and co-ordination. For a fly-half watching a fly-half, this try was the ultimate.

From *Touchdown*

Andy Hancock *played only three times for England – twice against France, and once against Scotland. However, his wonderful last-minute try in the Calcutta Cup match of 20 March 1965 is part of the folklore of the game: a run of 95 yards through sticky mud after slipping two tackles. As he says himself in John Pargeter's reconstruction, it still seems a dream.*

The remarkable thing about Andy Hancock's try was that when one saw it 'live', it seemed to go on for ever and ever. It was tremendously exciting and seemed to be prolonged by the constant threat that he might be caught, by the abortive Scottish tackles, and by the roar of the crowd which reached a crescendo as he dived over the line.

Yet when one watched it later on the television screen, it seemed to be all over in a flash – a case, perhaps, in favour of seeing a game *in situ* rather than from the comfort of home.

Remember the build-up? England, with only minutes to go, were losing 0–3, and Scotland looked like ending a losing sequence at Twickenham which had lasted since 1938.

A loose kick ahead by England had been caught by Whyte, a Scottish winger who, instead of finding touch, elected to run. But he ran inside and was enveloped by the England back row inside their 25. The ball shot out on the England side to Mike Weston, who takes up the story:

'When the ball came out I realized there was no winger on the left side, but someone was approaching me fast from that direction. I managed to draw him and get the ball away to Andy. But then I was tackled and I didn't see the try at all. When I got to my feet there were so many players in the way. It was really a case that we had to keep the ball in play. Time was running out, and it was just one of those things which came off.'

The story is completed by Andy himself: 'It was like a dream. I think it still is. The remarkable thing about it is that anyone in the same position would have done the same thing, but ninety out of a hundred would not have got away with it. Iain Laughland would have caught me, I think, if he hadn't slipped. And Stewart Wilson, too – though at that time Budge Rogers was shouting that he was with me, and that may have distracted him.

'So on I went again, but I firmly believe that had it been a dry ground, Wilson would have tackled me into the stand. As it was, I moved a little inside to leave myself room to go outside him. He slipped, and only half-tackled me.

'I think this held up the covering forwards for a fraction of a second, too. And finally Laughland just caught my ankles as I crossed the line. Having seen the try on television, I realize now that it was "on" for me to have gone round behind the posts. Looking back, I think I should have done that, and I shall probably always regret it. But as I say, I still think it was all a dream.'

From *Touchdown*

David Duckham *was another of those blond English three-quarters who glided through the opposition, as Vivian Jenkins once said, like a sleek white roadster. His finest hour came when he toured New Zealand with the 1971 Lions and scored eleven tries for them. He defended as brilliantly as he attacked, and played a key part in the historic game between the Barbarians and the All Blacks in 1973, which some connoisseurs still believe to be the best of all time. However, it was playing for the Baa-Baas against the Springboks on 31 January 1970 that he scored this marvellous try. It was a pity that the game had to be marred by the smoke bombs and the flour bombs, the tin-tacks on the field and the insults of the apartheid protesters. Probably it was as well that soon after this South Africa withdrew from the international rugby scene.*

In the end the Springboks were to win this match 21–12, but early on it looked as if the Barbarians would overwhelm them. In the third minute Rodger Arneil had scored a try from Gareth Edwards's pass on the blind side. Now, after ten minutes, the Barbarians were in another strong attacking position when they won a ruck near the Springboks' 25 and seven or eight yards in from the left touchline. Duckham, who was playing on the left wing that day, describes what happened:

'It wasn't a planned move. Edwards got the ball from the base of the ruck. He just looked left, we looked at each other, and as he threw the ball I ran on to it. I was able to get round their loose forwards; there were two or three who hadn't quite joined in. And then I went racing down the wing with only their fullback, Henry de Villiers, to beat.

'Because I went blind there was no support. Most of our forwards were engaged in the ruck, and the three-quarters were all lined up the other way because we were so close to the touchline. So once I'd gone I was on my own. I was looking round to the right most of the time, but I kept de Villiers in my sights out of the corner of my left eye.

'I didn't really know how I was going to beat him. I decided I must try and break through the tackle or just take him. To try and fox him I veered right out – it couldn't have been more than a foot or so away from the touchline. And then at the last minute, after committing him . . . well, I didn't sidestep him, I just did a swerve inside. I felt an arm across my thigh, but at the speed I was going it didn't make any difference.

I made for the line and put down at once because at least one of their centres was covering across. It was about halfway out and we missed the kick . . . I suppose it's the try that has given me the most satisfaction because – although obviously someone had to give me the ball – it was virtually an individual effort.'

From *Touchdown*

The Greatest International Try of All

Ross Macdonald

We all have a favourite try – sometimes the one we saw, sometimes the one we scored ourselves. Since the advent of television, we can all share in the majesty of those tries by Hancock and Duckham, Sharp and Jackson. We could all relish that extraordinary try scored by Gareth Edwards for the Barbarians against the All Blacks in 1973. However, that was not in an international; and the greatest international try of them all – though there are not all that many alive now who were there to see it – is still reckoned to be that scored in 1936 by Alexander Obolensky, a White Russian prince playing for England against the All Blacks.

Obolensky was a cosmopolitan figure who had learned his rugby at Trent College in America and the previous December had already scored a devastating try against the All Blacks in their game against Oxford where he was then a Brasenose undergraduate. The Prince of Wales, three weeks before he became King, was introduced to the teams and rather churlishly asked Obolensky what he was doing playing for England. He was indeed both the first Russian and the first prince to do so; and, alas, was destined to die in 1940 in a flying accident while serving with the RAF – the first international cap to be killed in the Second World War.

A blond meteor, Obo's main secret was a deceptive change of speed which allowed him to whistle past an opposing defender as if he had gone into overdrive. On 4 January 1936 he had already scored once against the formidable All Blacks, a feat that had a strong influence on the historic second try.

The New Zealanders were hammering at the England line. There Charlie Oliver was bundled into touch at the corner flag; half-back Tindill fed his forwards as a scrum broke up and lanky Hugh McLean made for the line, for England's Owen-Smith to force him into touch with a matter of inches to go.

Gradually England managed to push the New Zealanders back and there was a scrum in midfield. Behind the scrum the back-line stretched out – Gadney, Candler, Cranmer, Gerrard and Obolensky.

Obo stood waiting out there on the right wing, a couple of yards inside the England half. England got the ball. From Gadney to Candler to Cranmer. A break and Cranmer was off upfield. But the All Blacks were quick to scuttle back in defence and he was hemmed in. He passed infield to fly-half Candler. Again hemmed in. But Obolensky was there in support on his right. The All Blacks converged on his side of the field, since he was obviously going to try to repeat the 40-yard dash he had done up the touchline earlier to open England's score.

I was sitting in the Press box in the East Stand and was virtually behind Obolensky as he got the ball. I could see, as though through his eyes, the situation that confronted him. His opposing wing, Ball, had been drawn in to counter the Cranmer break, so it was indeed obvious to go up the touchline. But All Black full-back Gilbert, centre Oliver and colleagues were moving over to do their best to block that avenue.

I saw, at the same moment I'm sure that Obolensky did, a midfield gap in the defensive hedge. So, instead of doing the obvious, Obolensky set course infield for that gap. For a split second it seemed that all the All Blacks ahead of him were frozen there, each on his wrong foot, all realizing that they must now change direction. The black tide swung around but right-wing Obolensky was going like the wind for that part of the goal line that is the left-wing's preserve. Off balance, the defenders clawed at him as he flashed by. Mitchell, on the All Blacks' right wing, went after the unexpected visitor but was beaten by sheer pace. Gilbert essayed the full-back's traditional cross-field cut-off, but he had started off going the wrong way and couldn't catch the long-striding Russian. Obolensky rounded him to touch down on the opposite side to his first try.

Was it in fact the greatest international try of them all? I would cast my vote in favour, because it was something unique – a right wing wrong-footing all the opposition and running diagonally through them to score a left-winger's try.

From *The World of Rugby*

Hymns and Arias

Max Boyce

Max Boyce was born and grew up in the small South Wales village of Glynneath. One day he saw a second-hand guitar for sale in the local paper shop for four pounds – or near offer. He bought it for three pounds ten shillings and laboriously learned to play it. His first attempts at writing comic songs about his friends in the local cricket club made people laugh and encouraged him to write more. Today he is an international celebrity whose record albums have sold two million copies; but he still lives in Glynneath with his wife and children. His greatest thrill was to hear the Welsh crowd in Cardiff Arms Park sing one of his songs, 'Hymns and Arias', about the trip thousands of Welshmen make to Twickenham once every two years for the game against England. 'Cwm Rhondda' and 'Calon Lan' – the two greatest of all Welsh songs – had found a companion.

'Ar hyd y nos', Max explains for the benefit of those of us not born in the valleys, means all through the night – not Harry's got a horse. Here it is.

We paid our weekly shilling for that January trip:
A long weekend in London, aye, without a bit of kip.
There's a seat reserved for beer by the boys from Abercarn:
There's beer, pontoon, crisps and fags and a croakin' 'Calon Lan'.

And we were singing hymns and arias,
'Land of my Fathers', 'Ar hyd y nôs'.

Into Paddington we did roll with an empty crate of ale.
Will had lost at cards and now his *Western Mail*'s for sale.
But Will is very happy though his money all has gone:
He swapped five photos of his wife for one of Barry John.

And we were singing hymns and arias,
'Land of my Fathers', 'Ar hyd y nôs'.

We got to Twickers early and were jostled in the crowd;
Planted leeks and dragons, looked for toilet all around.
So many there we couldn't budge – twisted legs and pale:
I'm ashamed we used a bottle that once held bitter ale.

And we were singing hymns and arias,
'Land of my Fathers', 'Ar hyd y nôs'.

Wales defeated England in a fast and open game.
We sang 'Cwm Rhondda' and 'Delilah', damn, they sounded both
    the same.

We sympathized with an Englishman whose team was doomed to
   fail,
So we gave him that old bottle, that once held bitter ale!

He started singing hymns and arias,
'Land of my Fathers', 'Ar hyd y nôs'.

So it's down to Soho for the night, to the girls with the shiny
   beads;
To the funny men with lipstick on, with evil minds and deeds.
One said to Will from a doorway dark, damn, she didn't have
   much on.
But Will knew what she wanted, aye . . . his photo of Barry John!

'Cos she was singing hymns and arias,
'Land of my Fathers', 'Ar hyd y nôs'.

A Welcome in the Valleys

Richard Burton

*Richard Burton the actor was born Richard Jenkins in 1925 at Pontrhydy-
fen, a small Welsh village in the Rhondda Valley, the son of a miner and a
barmaid. He left school at fifteen to work in the local co-op, and then,
because he wanted to play rugby, he became a cadet in the local air training
corps. One of the officers there was Philip Burton, who was to adopt him.
'In appearance,' says the* Dictionary of National Biography, *Burton was
'sturdily built, with the body of a rugby half-back, long and solid in the
trunk, but with short legs'.*

*Burton's love of rugby is manifest from the very first sentence of this
delicious memoir; and equally open is his manly admission that he was
often economical with the truth about it. He went to Oxford on a RAF short
course in 1943, but it is not true, as he let it be known, that while there he got
a wartime Blue; indeed it would have been a little difficult, since he was
there only from April to September. It is also hard to see how he could have
played rugby against a Cambridge college, as he claims here, in the summer
term. He wanted, he confessed later, to go back to Oxford to get a First and
a Blue; instead he went on the stage with the consequences we all know.
Whether he would have got a Blue is a moot point; but the testimony of
Bleddyn Williams to Burton's potential as a player is on the record and, as
Burton confesses, is the only notice he ever kept. We don't know either
whether he would have got a First; but this piece suggests he could
certainly have made his living as a writer.*

It's difficult for me to know where to start with rugby. I come from a fanatically rugby-conscious Welsh miner's family, know so much about it, have read so much about it, have heard with delight so many massive lies and stupendous exaggerations about it and have contributed my own fair share, and five of my six brothers played it, one with some distinction, and I mean I even knew a Welsh woman from Taibach who before a home match at Aberavon would drop goals from around forty yards with either foot to entertain the crowd, and her name, I remember, was Annie Mort and she wore sturdy shoes, the kind one reads about in books as 'sensible', though the recipient of a kick from one of Annie's shoes would have been not so much sensible as insensible, and I even knew a chap called Five-Cush Cannon who won the sixth replay of a cup final (the previous five encounters, having ended with the scores 0–0, 0–0, 0–0, 0–0, 0–0 including extra time) by throwing the ball over the bar from a scrum ten yards out in a deep fog and claiming a dropped goal. And getting it. What's more I knew people like a one-armed inside half – he'd lost an arm in the First World War – who played with murderous brilliance for Cwmavon for years when I was a boy. He was particularly adept, this one, at stopping a forward bursting through from the line-out with a shattering iron-hard thrust from his stump as he pulled him on to it with the other. He also used the mis-placed sympathy of innocent visiting players who didn't go at him with the same delivery as they would against a two-armed man, as a ploy to lure them on to concussion and other organic damage. They learned quickly, or were told after the match when they had recovered sufficiently from Jimmy's ministrations to be able to understand the spoken word, that going easy on Jimmy-One-Arm was first cousin to stepping into a grave and waiting for the shovels to start. A great many people who played unwarily against Jimmy died unexpectedly in their early forties. They were lowered solemnly into the grave with all match honours to the slow version of Sospan Fach. They say that the conductor at these sad affairs was noticeably one-armed but that could be exaggeration again.

As I said, it's difficult for me to know where to start so I'll begin with the end. The last shall be first, as it is said, so I'll tell you about the last match I ever played in.

I had played the game representatively from the age of ten until those who employed me in my profession, which is that of actor, insisted that I was a bad insurance risk against certain dread teams in dead-end valleys who would have little respect, no respect, or outright disrespect for what I was pleased to call my face. What if I were unfortunate enough to be on the deck in the middle of a loose maul . . . they murmured in dollar accents? Since my face was already internationally known and since I was paid, perhaps overpaid, vast sums of money for its ravaged presentation they, the money men, expressed a desire to keep it that way. Apart from wanting to preserve my natural beauty, it would affect continuity, they said, if my nose was straight on Friday in the medium shot and was bent towards my left ear on Monday for the close-up. Millions of panting fans from Tokyo to Tonmawr would be puzzled, they said. So to this day there is a clause in my contracts that forbids me from flying my own plane, skiing and playing the game of rugby football, the inference being that it would be all right to wrestle with a Bengal tiger five thousand miles away, but not to play against, shall we say, Pontypool at home. I decided that they had some valid arguments after my last game.

It was played against a village whose name is known only to its inhabitants and crippled masochists drooling quietly in kitchen corners, a mining village with all the natural beauty of the valleys of the moon, and just as welcoming, with a team composed almost entirely of colliers. I hadn't played for four or five years but was fairly fit, I thought, and the opposition was bottom of the third class and reasonably beatable. Except, of course, on their home ground. I should have thought of that. I should have called to mind that this was the kind of team where, towards the end of the match, you kept your bus ticking over near the touchline in case you won and had to run for your life.

I wasn't particularly nervous before the match until, though I was disguised with a skull-cap and everyone had been sworn to secrecy, I heard a voice from the other team asking 'Le ma'r blydi film star 'ma?' (Where's the bloody film star here?) as we were running on to the field. My cover, as they say in spy stories, was already blown and trouble was to be my shadow (there was none from the sun since there was no sun – it was said in fact that the sun hadn't shone there since 1929) and the end of my career the shadow of my shadow for the next eighty minutes or so. It was a mistaken game for me to play. I survived it with nothing broken except my spirit, the attitude of the opposition being unquestionably summed up in simple words like 'Never mind the bloody ball, where's the bloody actor?' Words easily understood by all.

Among other things I was playing Hamlet at that time at the Old Vic but for the next few performances after that match I was compelled to play him as if he were Richard the Third. The punishment I took had been innocently compounded by a paragraph in a book of reminiscence by Bleddyn Williams with whom I had played on and off (mostly off) in the RAF. On page 37 of that volume Mr Williams is kind enough to suggest that I had distinct possibilities as a player were it not for the lure of tinsel and paint and money and fame and so on. Incidentally, one of the curious phenomena of my library is that when you take out Bleddyn's autobiography from the shelves it automatically opens at the very page mentioned above. Friends have often remarked on this and wondered afresh at the wizardry of the Welsh. It is in fact the only notice I have ever kept.

Anyway, this little snippet from the great Bleddyn's book was widely publicized and some years later by the time I played that last game had entered into the uncertain realms of folk legend and was deeply embedded in the subconscious of the sub-Welshmen I submitted myself to that cruel afternoon. They weren't playing with chips on their shoulders, they were simply sceptical about page 37.

I didn't realize that I was there to prove anything until too late. And I couldn't. And didn't. I mean prove anything. And I'm still a bit testy about it. Though I was working like a dog at the Vic playing Hamlet, Coriolanus, Caliban, The Bastard in King John, and Toby Belch, it wasn't the right kind of training for these great knotted gnarled things from the burning bowels of the earth. In my teens I had lived precariously on the lip of first-class rugby by virtue of knowing every trick in the canon, evil and otherwise, by being a bad bad loser, but chiefly, and perhaps *only* because I was very nippy off the mark. I was 5 ft 10½ in in height in bare feet and weighed, soaking wet, no more than 12½ stone, and since I played in the pack, usually at open side wing-forward and since I played against genuinely big men it therefore followed that I had to be galvanically quick to move from inertia. When faced with bigger and faster forwards, I was doomed. R. T. Evans of Newport, Wales and the Universe for instance – a racy 14½ stone and 6 ft 1½ in in height – was a nightmare to play against and shaming to play with, both of which agonies I suffered a lot, mostly thank God, the latter lesser cauchemar. Genuine class of course doesn't need size though sometimes I forgot this. Once I played rather condescendingly against a Cambridge college and noted that my opposite number seemed to be shorter than I was and in rugby togs looked like a schoolboy compared with Ike Owen, Bob Evans or W. I. D. Elliot. However this blond stripling gave me a terrible time. He was faster and harder and wordlessly ruthless, and it was no consolation to find out his name afterwards because it meant nothing at the time. He has forgotten me but I haven't forgotten him. This anonymity was called Steele-Bodger and a more onomatopoeic name for its owner would be hard to find. He was, I promise you, steel and he did, I give you my word, bodger. Say his name through clenched teeth and you'll see what I mean. I am very glad to say that I have never seen him since except from the safety of the stands.

In this match, this last match played against troglodytes, burned to the bone by the fury of their work, bow-legged and embittered because they weren't playing for or hadn't played for and would never play for Cardiff or Swansea or Neath or Aberavon, men who smiled seldom and when they did it was like scalpels, trained to the last ounce by slashing and hacking away neurotically at the frightened coal face for 7½ hours a day, stalactitic, tree-rooted, carved out of granite by a rough and ready sledge hammer and clinker, against these hard volumes of which I was the soft-cover paper-back edition. I discovered some truths very soon. I discovered just after the first scrum for instance that it was time I ran for the bus and not for their outside-half. He had red hair, a blue-white face and no chin. Standing up straight his hands were loosely on a level with his calves and when the ball and I arrived exultantly together at his stock-still body, a perfect set-up you would say, and when I realized that I was supine and he was lazily kicking the ball into touch I realized that I had forgotten that trying to intimidate a feller like that was like trying to cow a mandrill, and that he had all the graceful willowy-give and sapling-bend of stressed concrete.

That was only the outside-half.

From then on I was elbowed, gouged, dug, planted, raked, hoed, kicked a great deal, sandwiched and once humiliatingly taken from behind with nobody in front of me when I had nothing to do but run fifteen yards to score. Once, coming down from going up for the ball in a line-out, the other wing-forward – a veteran of at least fifty with grey hair – chose to go up as I was coming down if you'll forgive this tautological syntax. Then I was down and he was up and to insult the injury he generously helped me up from being down and pushed me in a shambling run towards my own try-line with a blood-curdling endearment in the Welsh tongue since during all these preceding ups and downs his unthinkable team had scored and my presence was necessary behind the posts as they were about to attempt the conversion.

I knew almost at once and appallingly that the speed, such as it had been, had ended and only the memory lingered on, and that tackling Olivia De Havilland and Lana Turner and Claire Bloom was not quite the same thing as tackling those Wills and Dais, those Twms and Dicks.

The thing to do I told myself with desperate cunning was to keep alive, and the way to do that was to keep out of the way. This is generally possible to do when you know you're out-classed, without everybody knowing, but in this case it wasn't possible to do because everybody was very knowing indeed. Sometimes in a lament for my lost youth (I was about 28) I roughed it up as well as I could but it is discouraging to put the violent elbow into the tempting rib when your prescience tells you that what is about to be broken is not the titillating rib but your pusillanimous pathetic elbow. After being gardened, mown and rolled a little more, I gave that up, asked the Captain of our team if he didn't think it would be a better idea to hide me deeper in the pack. I had often, I reminded him, played right prop, my neck was strong and my right arm had held its own with most. He gave me a long look, a trifle pitying perhaps but orders were given and in I went to the maelstrom and now the real suffering began. Their prop with whom I was to share cheek and jowl for the next eternity, didn't believe in razor blades since he grew them on his chin and shaved me thoroughly for the rest of the game taking most of my skin in the process, delicacy not being his strong point. He used his prodigious left arm to paralyse mine and pull my head wthin an inch or two of the earth, then rolled my head around his, first taking my ear between his fore-finger and thumb, humming 'Rock of Ages' under his breath. By the end of the game my face was as red as the setting sun and the same shape. Sometimes, to vary the thing a bit, he rolled his head on what little neck he had around, under and around again my helpless head. I stuck it out because there was nothing else to do which is why on Monday night in the Waterloo Road I played the Dane looking like a Swede with my head permanently on one side and my right arm in an imaginary sling intermittently crooked and cramped with occasional severe shakes and involuntary shivers as of one with palsy. I suppose to the connoisseurs of Hamlets it was a departure from your traditional Prince but it wasn't strictly what the actor playing the part had in mind. A melancholy Dane he was though. Melancholy he most certainly was.

I tried once to get myself removed to the wing but by this time our Captain had become as, shall we say, 'dedicated' (he may read this) as the other team and actually wanted to win. He seemed not to hear me and the wing in this type of game I knew never got the ball and was, apart from throwing the ball in from touch, a happy spectator, and I wanted to be a happy spectator. I shuffled after the pack.

I joined in the communal bath afterwards in a large steamy hut next to the changing-rooms, feeling very hard-done-by and hurt though I didn't register the full extent of the agonies that were to crib, cabin and confine me for the next few days. I drank more than my share of beer in the home team's pub, joined in the singing and found that the enemies were curiously shy and withdrawn until the beer had hit the proper spot. Nobody mentioned my performance on the field.

There was only one moment of wild expectation on my part when a particularly grim sullen and taciturn member of the other side said suddenly with what passed shockingly for a smile splitting the slag heap of his face like an earth tremor,

'Come outside with us will 'ew?' There was another beauty with him.

'Where to?' I asked.

'Never 'ew mind,' he said, 'you'll be awright. Jest come with us.'

'O.K.'

We went out into the cruel February night and made our way to the outside Gents – black-painted concrete with one black pipe for flushing, wet to the open sky. We stood side by side in silence. They began to void. So did I. There had been beer enough for all. I waited for a possible compliment on my game that afternoon – I had after all done one or two good things if only by accident. I waited. But there was nothing but the sound of wind and water. I waited and silently followed them back into the bar.

Finally I said: 'What did you want to tell me?'

'Nothing,' the talkative one said.

'Well, what did you ask me out there for then?'

'Well,' the orator, said. 'Well . . . us two is brothers and we wanted to tell our mam that we'd 'ad a . . .'

He hesitated, after all I spoke posh except when I spoke Welsh which oddly enough the other team didn't speak to me though I spoke it to them. 'Well, we jest wanted to tell our mam that we had passed water with Richard Burton' he said with triumphant care.

'Oh 'ell!' I said.

I went back to London next day in a Mark VIII Jaguar driving very fast, folding up and tucking away into the back drawer of my subconscious all my wounds, staunched blood, bandaged pride, feeling older than I've ever felt since. The packing wasn't very well done as from time to time all the parcels of all the games I'd ever played wrapped up loosely in that last one will undo themselves spill out of the drawer into my dreams and wake me shaking to the reassuring reaching-out for the slim cool comfort of a cigarette in the dead vast and doomed middle and with a puff and a sigh mitty myself into Van Wyk, Don White and Alan Macarley and winning several matches by myself by 65 points to nil, re-pack the bags.

From *Touchdown*

There's Beautiful

Alun Chalfont

Now for the testimony of Alun Chalfont, Chairman of the All Party Defence Group in the House of Lords, but in his younger days, as Alun Gwynne Jones, a fleet-winged stand-off half for Newport before the war, Wasps after it, and winner of a Berkshire County Cap. It was in February 1971 that he saw the epic one-point Welsh win at Murrayfield.

Years and years and years ago, when I was a boy, when there were wolves in Wales, and birds the colour of red flannel petticoats whisked past the harp-shaped hills . . . No one but the Rimbaud of Cwmdonkin Drive could spin the swooping hiraeth-tongued prose to evoke the nostalgia of Edinburgh last Saturday. Any Welsh rugby game is an occasion of high drama; an international is a perceptibly more emotional experience than Handel's *Messiah* sung on a mountain top by a choir of ten thousand voices; and when Wales defeat Scotland at Murrayfield by 19–18, scoring the winning point two minutes before the end of the game – well, *there's* excitement for you boy.

Rugby football is as essential an ingredient of a Welsh childhood as 'Cwm Rhondda'. Dr Teddy Morgan's great try against the All Blacks in 1905 is a part of the racial memory – still described in every loving detail to boys themselves scarcely as big as rugby balls in Neath and Aberavon and Llanelli. Before they can recite the Lord's Prayer they can tell you how Dicky Owen's reverse pass started the movement that beat invincible New Zealand by one try to nothing. Before they built the new stadium in Cardiff, small boys were taken like pilgrims to see the piece of turf on which Morgan grounded the ball. Wilfred Wooller, who captained Wales at rugby and Glamorgan at cricket (something like being Prime Minister *and* Archbishop of Canterbury) swears that in the last war two New Zealand soldiers came to Cardiff to cut some grass from the spot and send it home to their families.

Every Welshman has his own private hoard of rugby memories:

Vivian Jenkins dropping a goal from the half-way line or Claude Davey tackling his opposing centre three-quarter like a man demolishing a building – you could feel the impact in the stands. But there have not been many days like last Saturday. The grass at Murrayfield was green and firm – perfect for the arts of half-back play which are to rugby football what the cadenza is to a concerto. There were about fifteen thousand Welshmen in the crowd and when they sang 'Land of my Fathers' it was like the war song of Dinas Vawr.

One of the keys to the game was quite clearly going to be the set scrummage. At Cardiff the Welsh pack had pushed England all over the place with a tactical plan of classical simplicity. Whenever England put the ball into the scrum, Wales made no attempt to hook it – they just shoved, all eight of them. It was a trick that could only come off once, and the Scottish counter to it was just as simple. Whenever the Welsh pack shoved, the Scottish forwards wheeled. With the battle forward virtually a stalemate, the game became what rugby football should be – a running handling game of superb courage and skill. The first exchanges were ominously conventional – two penalty goals to Scotland and one to Wales. Barry John's for Wales was neat and inevitable; Peter Brown's for Scotland were outrageous. He simply put the ball down, looked at it briefly as though it were something offensive on the pavement, and then turned his back on it. When everyone thought he was on his way back to the dressing-room he suddenly turned and as though to take the ball by surprise rushed at it with a sort of exasperated lunge. Still, he got three points a go, so no Scotsman was disposed to be too purist about it.

There followed an hour of perfection for anyone who cares for rugby football. The Scottish forwards showed all the majestic arts of line-out play; their half-backs cut into the Welsh defence like knives; the three-quarters tackled everything that moved; and at full-back Ian Smith bravely caught towering Garryowens and kicked with elegant precision. But all that was just not enough to beat a Welsh team that played with irresistible magic and flair. Gareth Edwards and Barry John, at half-back, were in virtuoso mood. From the scrum Edwards threw a pass so long that if John had let it go it would have disappeared over the stand. But John never let it go. He had fly-paper on his hands and room to move and he showed fifty thousand people something that they have a right to expect only once in a lifetime – a great gamesplayer and a superb athlete on a day when everything goes right. He slid through the Scottish defence like a lizard, his changes of pace and direction barely perceptible from the stand, marked only by the strange phenomenon of men in blue shirts appearing to melt away from him when they were actually vigorously engaged in trying to knock him flat.

The scoring was like a carefully written script; the lead changed hands six times. There were beautiful tries by Taylor, John and Edwards for Wales; defiant replies by Carmichael and Rea for Scotland. Two more absent-minded goals by Peter Brown, and with five minutes left Scotland led by 18 points to 14. It was then that Gerald Davies, the fastest man on the field, got the ball with the target in his sights. He was over the line before the Scottish cover could move and John Taylor calmly kicked the conversion to win the match and an eternal place in the Welsh pantheon.

Princes Street Saturday night was like a rehearsal for *Under Milk Wood*. Organ Morgan had a few too many and fell flat on his face outside the George Hotel; there was a fight on Waverley Station and somebody got locked, accidental, in the gents. A small party of urban guerrillas in red and white knitted caps, and scarves down to their bandy legs and leeks on their jackets went up to Edinburgh Castle where they offered to take on the whole bloody kilted garrison, with or without a ball. Somebody threw a leek at a sentry and missed. There's beautiful it was, boys.

From *The New Statesman*

The Last Place to be a Wallaby

Godfrey Smith

I thought readers might enjoy my own account of the stupendous encounter between the Australians and Pontypool. Certainly the sound of the weird chanting from the great mound where all Pontypool stood shrouded in mist, like some unearthly Wagnerian chorus, still lingers in my mind – as does the memory of McBain's bald head protruding from the undulating chaos of the scrum like Triton, demi-god of the sea.

Pontypool is celebrated for two things – its park and its pack. The park is arguably the prettiest place in Wales where rugby is played; the pack the hardest. No one is ever neutral about Pontypool. You either hate them or you love them. They like to tell the story of a famous Welsh player who had only two ambitions. One was to play for Wales; the other was to beat bloody Pontypool at Pontypool Park. He has achieved the first; not, so far, the second.

The man behind the Pontypool legend is, in his own rugged person, a living legend; Ray Prosser, 55, the club's coach these fifteen seasons. He does not believe in imparting his distilled wisdom through what he calls effing long words like effing marmalade or effing corrugated. Instead, he uses lots of effing four-letter ones. Yet let no one believe Pross has no sense of humour. On tour with the Lions, his particular pal was an England second-row forward called Marques who had learned his rugby at Tonbridge and Cambridge. Pross, then a dumper-driver by calling, used to wear Marques's bowler and carry his umbrella. As he explained: 'We effing ex-blues must stick together.'

It was Pross who fashioned the famed Pontypool front row, hymned in song by Max Boyce ('Up and Under Here We Go') and renowned wherever rugby is played. Its components were three Pontypool citizens who shared many of the earthy qualities of their great mentor. They were Bobby Windsor, who stood just 5ft 9½in tall and weighed 15st 2lb; Charlie Faulkner (5:10, 15:12); and Graham Price (5:10½, 15st exactly). Graham, born in 1951, is the youngest of the fearsome triad; Bobby was born in 1948, Charlie God knows when. His age varied according to the year. He was probably 34 when he first played for Wales. Today he coaches Newport, and turns out for them still if a regular prop is injured. As Pross would say, a coach doesn't have to produce an effing birth certificate.

When Pross began to coach Pontypool, their record was mediocre. He turned them into an awesome machine. Since their defeat by the Wallabies three years ago they have won 75 of their 77 home games; and when they faced the Wallabies again last Wednesday, were unbeaten this season.

It would be idle to deny that their triumphs were built on massive forward power and nine-man rugby. This mincing-machine philosophy did not appeal to some of Pontypool's opponents. Llanelli scratched their fixture, and have only just resumed.

London Welsh have cancelled, too, and so have Bristol. Worst of all, according to Graham Price, no less a celebrity than that prince of fly-halves, Barry John, recently described Pontypool as a cancer on Welsh rugby. 'For some at Pontypool,' writes Price in his book, *Price of Wales*, 'the remark was tantamount to a demand for the re-introduction of capital punishment.' The *fons et origo* of all this aggro is unquestionably Pontypool's tight, rugged and uncompromising forward play. As the old story goes:

'They've found Lord Lucan.'

'Where?'

'In a very good hiding place – playing on the wing for Pontypool.'

Nor does the Pontypool style export well. On a club tour of the United States in 1979, skipper Jeff Squire led his team off just before half-time in a game in San Francisco as a protest against the refereeing. 'I think it is important to say,' remarks Price laconically in his book, 'that American players and officials were not ready for our type of rugby.'

The Australians, however, were. Three years ago the Wallabies gave Pontypool a fearful drubbing, beating them 37–6. (There was an English referee, but still . . .) So when the Eighth Wallabies came back to Pontypool with wins against all four home countries already under their belt, they knew Pontypool would be intent on revenge.

When the Aussies ran into the murky cauldron, they were already heroes back home. Australians do not like to read about defeats (who does?), and the Grand Slam had marvellously taken their minds off the drubbing their boys were taking from the West Indian cricketers. They had received a telegram from the Australian prime minister, and all in all, said their manager, Charles Wilson, the team's triumph had caused rather more furore down under than the winning of the America's Cup.

The Pontypool front row has of necessity been re-fashioned, but Graham Price is still there, noble head much stitched and scarred, one ear now an honourable cauliflower, the other showing vegetable tendencies.

It must be a cruel culture shock for Aussies to come twelve thousand miles from their languorous climes to Pontypool. On the great mound, virtually the whole male population of Pontypool stood shrouded in mist on Wednesday, like some unearthly Wagnerian chorus. To their haunting chant of 'Pooler, Pooler, Pooler,' they willed Pontypool on to one of their great rolling mauls and an historic try under the posts. But back came the Aussies with a try of their own that was a mirror image. Both were converted: 6–6, anyone's game.

Now it settled to a war of attrition, the ball punted heavenwards in a salvo of up-and-unders. It was rugby Pontypool style right enough. The lead swung back and forth, all through penalties; at half-time it was 15–15, and still anyone's game.

In the second half, the Aussies began to dominate the line-outs, but the Pontypool pack were masters of the set-pieces, and at one heart-stopping moment actually shoved the Aussies back ten yards, boots sliding away in the mud like roller-skates. And the Aussies were taking the brunt of the physical toll; Holt went off with a damaged elbow, Lillicrap with a damaged ankle. McBain, the hooker, should have gone off, too, but he played on, increasingly out of touch with the action. Twice his prematurely bald head protruded from the undulating chaos of the set scrum like Triton, demi-god of the sea. Two more penalties, one apiece; 18–18, and still anyone's game.

The Aussies tried all they knew now to run the ball. The Pontypool backs laid them low with kamikaze tackles, and those over-elegant dummies and scissors fizzled out in monstrous rucks. Then there was a towering kick by Black, the Aussie centre, which plummeted down just outside the Pontypool posts. The Australian pack submerged Peter Lewis, the Pooler full-back, for a last-minute try. The score was 24–18, and thus, with Price's face a mask of red from yet another gash, it all ended.

Afterwards, Pross was charming and philosophical. The best side won, was all he would say. No complaints. The Aussie coach, Alan Jones, seemed as melancholy as Pross was serene. 'Was it a game?' he asked rhetorically. He'd lost count of the penalties. His men, Jones affirmed, were physically and mentally exhausted. Indeed, his dressing-room looked like a casualty ward.

In a Pontypool caff, four fans ate pies, drank tea and summed up: 'We were robbed. That last try was offside. The English referee, of course.' They sat in a melancholy gloom till one said: 'I'll tell you what though boys. They'll know they've been in a game.'

From *The Sunday Times*

The Pontypool Front Row

Max Boyce

*To follow that we have another view of a Welsh institution in Max Boyce's
tribute to the celebrated Pontypool Front Row – Charlie Faulkner, Bobby
Windsor and Graham Price – who went on to represent Wales and the
British Lions. Up-and-under here we go!*

Now I'll tell you all a story
About some lads I know.
Who're known throughout the valleys
As the Pontypool Front Row.
It's got a little chorus
And that chorus you all know.
So tell me are you ready?
Up-and-under here we go!

CHORUS
Up-and-under, here we go.
Are you ready, yes or no?
Up-and-under here we go:
It's the song of the Pontypool Front Row.

Now they made a film in London,
It was censored double-X.
The sort of film that frightens one,
Not one of lust and sex.
Mary Whitehouse saw it
And now they'll never show
A film called *Up-and-Under*
Starring the Pontypool Front Row!

We had trouble in Uganda
With President Amin.
So they sent an envoy out there
With a message from the Queen.
To stay that execution
But Amin answered 'No!'
Till a card was sent from the Viet Gwent –
The Pontypool Front Row!

They've had trouble on the railways
With some of soccer's fans.
I've seen them on the terraces
Throwing stones and cans.

They've stopped the soccer specials;
It's a waste of time I know,
'Cos in the end they'll have to send
For the Pontypool Front Row!

There's a programme on the telly,
I watch it when I can,
The story of an astronaut,
The first bionic man.
He cost six-million dollars,
That's a lot of bread I know,
But Wigan offered more than that
For the Pontypool Front Row!

The Making of Gareth Edwards

Bill Samuel

The remarkable story of how Bill Samuel discovered Gareth Edwards is told in his enchanting book Rugby Body and Soul. *It was described by Steve Jones of The Sunday Times as one of the two best rugby books he'd ever read, the other being Michael Green's* The Art of Coarse Rugby, *of which more later. It is a fascinating story on many levels – in its insight into a kind of Welsh life that is now all but gone; in its stark evocation of the contrast between Wales and England; in its expert account of how a gifted, athletic boy was turned into a player of genius. If Gareth did anything else at Millfield except train three times a day seven days a week, there is no evidence of it; but he made good friends among the la-di-das without ever losing an ounce of his Welshness. Millfield polished him but Bill Samuel gave him the groundwork. And what a groundwork! Where else but in Wales would a schoolmaster teach the twenty different kinds of kick you need in rugby football?*

By the time Gareth Edwards came to school in 1961, [aged 14] I was thoroughly committed to teaching rugby football. Whereas normal teachers would be on the lookout for well-behaved and well-dressed boys, my observations would be of a different kind. My prime occupation would be to hazard a guess at what position on the rugby field would suit each new boy (whether he had played rugby or not did not matter). By the time I had seen them working in the gym and on the rugby field a few times, I was confident that I could place them in their correct team positions for the rest of their playing days.

One of my first rugby duties every year in September was to discover which boys wanted to appear in the Swansea Valley District Rugby Union Under Fifteen Trials. As usual, I placed a plain piece of paper on the rugby notice-board inviting the boys who were eligible, and thought themselves good enough, to place their name, position, weight and height on the notice board. In due course, I took the list down and noticed that Gareth's name was above the rest. He claimed he was a centre, eight stone five pounds, and five feet three inches. 'He'll never make the team,' I thought.

The following Saturday morning, with other members of the Committee, I was on the touch-line observing the trialists in action. It was a very good trial, with plenty of exciting talent on view. The three-quarters were big boys. It was quite evident that Gareth was Lilliputian in comparison and in imminent danger of being hurt. Without any prompting from me, he was told by a wise master to come off the field. He had showed plenty of spirit but his withdrawal had obviously disappointed him. He came towards me very dejectedly.

'Paid â becso, boi bach. Daw dy dro di eto,' ('Don't worry, lad, your turn will come again.') I said. 'Go and shower. You can come home with me. My car is the red Mini over there,' I said, pointing to where it was parked.

A few hours later I went to my car. He was not there. The following Monday, during morning break, I saw him with his friend, David John, in the school corridor, both eating oranges. I called him over.

'You owe me an apology, don't you?' I asked.

'What have I done wrong, sir?' he asked with surprise.

'I offered you a lift on Saturday. Why didn't you come to say that you were going home?'

'I felt so ashamed. The boys had been running around me as if I had been standing still. When I tried to tackle, they brushed me aside as if I wasn't there. I did not realize that rugby was a big boys' game.'

'Why did you elect to play centre?'

'My rugby hero is Bleddyn Williams, the great Welsh centre. I want to be like him.'

'It's like a Pembrokeshire Corgi wanting to be a sheep-dog. It can't be done. At this moment you are too small to play in midfield.'

'That's what I thought. I think I'll concentrate on soccer.' I was taken aback at this seemingly well-rehearsed answer.

'Concentrate on soccer! Not giving in already, boy, are you? Let me remind you that rugby is the game of this school.'

He bowed his head.

'Are you familiar with the Bible, and in particular, the Book of Proverbs?'

He looked at me with his mouth agape, astonishment written all over his face.

'"If you are weak in the time of crisis, you are weak indeed",' I said with a big smile.

The quotation relieved the tension and he began to chuckle.

'While you dashed home on Saturday, I stayed to watch the trial through. It's a good job I did because I saw a position which is tailor-made for you. A position you will fill within a month if you listen to me.' I could see the intense curiosity on his face. He could not refrain from blurting out, 'What position is that, Mr Samuel?'

'Have you ever thought of yourself as a scrum-half?'

He pondered for a moment. 'I've never played in that position before, sir.'

'Well, you are never too old to learn, are you? We can start from scratch. I'll make you into one. We have produced many a Swansea Valley scrum-half in our school, you know. We'll start this afternoon in the games-lesson, and stay behind for an hour after school. Mark my words, you'll be playing for the District within a month.'

'Thank you, sir. I'll do my best.'

'That's the idea. You can't do better than that.'

As we went our separate ways, he said, 'Sorry about the lift last Saturday. It won't happen again, sir.' With that he gave a huge whoop as he hopped, skipped and jumped down the corridor, with David John in his wake.

That afternoon we started. 'Roll the ball against the goalpost, and on the rebound, pass off the ground to me. Your feet should be wide apart and your outside foot indicating in which direction the ball is to be passed. Keep your back flat and extend your arms and finally flick your wrists as you pass the ball. The rule states you should stand one yard from the scrum and put the ball in at a level between your knee and ankle.' A new scrum-half, and the same annual routine.

He took to the position as a duck to water. Within a month he was the proud and regular scrum-half of the Swansea Valley Schools. He had been hooked and was destined to spend his leisure time practising to play eventually, or so I thought at the time, for Cwmgors, his village club . . .

Gareth's introductory season with the Swansea Valley Schoolboys was not startling. He did not reveal any promise at all. He was just a small, run-of-the-mill schoolboy scrum-half.

However, if he was not a good rugby player, he was certainly a brilliant gymnast. His greatest asset was his uncanny ability to learn new physical movements without any trouble at all. He was the star performer in the group, when the Tech.'s gymnastic team gave a display on BBC Wales TV. I remember a St David's Day Eisteddfod when we used to hold an inter-house 'walking on hands for the longest distance' competition. In previous years the competition had ended inside the hall, but when Gareth's turn came, I had to open the door for him to continue hand-walking the corridor and outside to the yard, whereupon I had to stop him. When he re-appeared in the hall he received thunderous applause.

During the next three years, in addition to gymnastics, he shared with his classmates a very rigorous programme of circuit, target and weight training. The rivalry was intense and the performances were really extraordinary. Physical education was acknowledged as a very important subject in the school and accordingly end-of-term marks were given on a parity with the other subjects – the only school in Glamorgan to operate such a system. He also practised gymnastics as an after-school activity on Monday evenings for the purpose of competing in the Urdd National Eisteddfod.

When the summer of 1962 came, I prepared for the athletics season. I could not teach cricket because we had no facilities; consequently, I concentrated on athletics, without a doubt the finest training for prospective rugby players. I used to recommend those who had ambitions in cricket to the many village cricket clubs available in the area, with the result that none of them missed the experience of playing the game.

The old county of Glamorgan believed in athletics. Even the Director of Education, Trevor Jenkins Esq., was enthusiastic in his support. He used to come and judge one of the events in the county championships. Every child who was prepared to make an extra effort was awarded a county certificate if he achieved certain standards in the athletic event of his choice. These certificates were highly respected tokens of achievement. Athletics is a multi-sport where it is possible for a child to derive pleasure from either running, throwing or jumping. It is a fundamental and satisfying sport which offers no easy options. It is also a tough sport, which produces speed, strength, stamina and suppleness, the ingredients necessary to produce the best quality rugby players.

When I had completed my first athletics-lesson with Gareth's class, I was thoroughly exhilarated by their attitude. During the course of the lesson, I had been impressed by a number of them and invited them to stay after school for special tuition and practice.

I was occupied in teaching a particular boy when I noticed Gareth, with his kit-bag in one hand, and his satchel in the other, running in the direction of the school. 'Hey,' I said. 'Where do you think you are going? Come here!' He reluctantly stopped, dropped his bags, hesitated, and came trotting over to me. 'I thought we had agreed that you were to stay for extra practice.' 'But I can out-jump anybody in my class, sir,' he said sheepishly. 'And so you can. The boys who stay behind with me are not aiming to be champions of their class, or Gwaun-cae-gurwen, boy, but champions of Wales. I don't like boys who admire themselves. Be off with you.' I turned on my heel and left him there, staring ruefully at the ground.

I did not know the sequel of that little episode until years later, when Glan, Gareth's father, told me. 'Oh, yes, he came home fuming and in a sorry state. "That Mr Samuel has a down on me. I could out-jump them all in my class and he asks me of all people to stay for extra practice. He called me something like a big-head. I don't like him and I'm not going to school tomorrow".'

Glan was naturally distressed at his unhappiness and so was Mrs Edwards. 'Go over to Cwmgors and see that bugger,' was her reaction, according to Glan. Fortunately, Glan did not agree to his dear wife's request for retribution; had he done so, he would have been surprised to discover that I was not at all the ogre his son had supposed me to be. In fact, he would have found me in a state of excitement, for his son had shown signs of possessing rare ability which I had hoped to develop in the after-school practice.

By nature I happen to be rather direct in my dealings with people. A weakness, perhaps, but a quality that Gareth Edwards very quickly came to comprehend as vital in our future relationship. Another quality which I could claim to possess is that I forgive easily; consequently, on the following morning, I sent for him. When he came, he appeared melancholy, tense and forlorn.

'Do you think you can borrow some kit during today's lunch-time, Gareth? I want to test you in the long-jump pit.' The relief on his face was a joy to see. 'Oh yes, sir, I'll borrow from one of the second-year boys. They've got a games-lesson today.'

'See you at twelve-fifteen, then.' He was there on time, dressed for the occasion. I gave him some warming-up exercises and measured his run-up for the event. 'Remember,' I said, 'to hit the jumping-off board as hard as you can to get as much height as possible; do a cycling motion and reach as far forward as possible with your feet.'

I could see the determination written on his face as he accomplished his trial-jumps. His results were extraordinary. Still not satisfied, I took him to the gymnasium and tested his ability at the vertical-jump test, and when he recorded a jump of thirty inches I knew that I had a potential super-athlete on my hands. I kept that secret to myself . . .

When Gareth returned for his second year he was a changed young man. His athletics, as far as I was concerned, were in the distant past, for it was the rugby season once again.

'It does not matter where you go, if you play rugby, you are assured of making friends. Be it University, College, factory, or staying in your village – rugby is an universal brotherhood,' I used to say to them in class when the rain had intervened to stop our rugby-lessons. The free-periods would always involve talks about the many facets of rugby. All would listen and make a contribution to the theme . . .

There are over twenty different kinds of kick in rugby football, not all of them easy. The one I wanted to teach Gareth was the kick in defence from a line-out near the goal-line and under extreme pressure. It is a very difficult kick, which only a few of the current international scrum-halves can accomplish properly. Gareth had arranged for his friend, David John, to stay behind to help us with the practice.

'It is your job, David John, to throw the ball to me while I am standing in the line-out as a second-row forward,' I said in a convincing tone. 'As soon as I pass it to you, Gareth, at scrum-half, I become a loose-forward whose job it is to stop you from kicking the ball into touch. Got it? Right! Throw the ball then, David John!'

We did the practice twice. On each occasion I smothered Gareth's attempts at kicking into touch and made sure that I roughed him up a bit.

'Not much shape in this one kicking the ball, David John,' I said. David John refused to comment. It was no use asking him whose side *he* was on.

'Are you ready? Let's have it again.'

Before the ball was thrown, I had a look at Gareth. There was a mixture of anger and determination on his face. He was on the verge of losing his temper. I smiled at the prospect. We remained motionless until David John spurred us into action. The ball was in Gareth's hands before he knew it, and while he was in the process of kicking the ball I was on him like a ton of bricks, just enough to test his reaction.

I helped him to his feet as he released a torrent of expletives. 'That's not fair! You did not give me a chance,' he cried.

'Hold on now, boy. Don't lose your temper. That's a bad sign,' I replied in a firm tone. 'Let me play scrum-half so that I can show how it's done.'

Suddenly his whole attitude changed. His personal tirade against me finished. The chance he wanted for revenge had been offered to him. His whole being expressed his resolution; he was going to knock Bill Samuel for six. Fourteen stone or not, it did not matter.

David John was taking more than a passing interest in the exchanges. I heard him whisper, 'Bwr e lar' ('Knock him down'). Both of them were ready.

The ball was thrown, caught, and passed to me by Gareth and at the same time, with nostrils aflame, he came thundering towards me. Too late; the ball had been kicked and was sailing sweetly down the touch-line to land in touch forty yards away. Gareth stopped in his tracks, and his face broke into a smile. 'Oh, is that the way you do it?' he said, with a big laugh.

He would then be anxious to experiment and practise the art himself. This he would do for weeks on end and when he had achieved a standard of competency, I would take him to the left-side touch-line and encourage him to practise kicking in the same situation with his left foot. All his practices were for real. On other occasions, after certain practices, I would say, 'Oh, Gareth, that's it. Let's do the kicking-at-goal practice before we go home. Twelve times this time.'

'Oh, come on, Mr Samuel, must I go through that practice again?'

'The sooner the better. I want to go home too. My dinner will be on the hob by this time.'

We would collect all the rugby balls and drop them near where one of the corner-flags would be. He would then proceed to dig a hole with his heel and then place ball after ball, and kick each one at the nearest single goalpost, whilst I gathered and kicked them back. When he had hit his target a dozen times he would call it a day.

His talent was manifesting itself all the time. He was completely unaware of the change that had occurred in him. It was too good to be true. Did I have a prospective rugby-star on my hands, as well as a brilliant gymnast and athlete? While I was planning things for him to do, I discovered that Swansea Town were showing an interest in signing him as an apprentice. I had been told that he was the star soccer player of the village team. I was quietly pleased, because he was developing skills which would be invaluable to him as a rugby player. He did not confide in me, or provide me with information regarding the rumour. His whole attitude changed. He became furtive and independent. Whereas before he had been forthcoming, cordial and fun-loving, he became truculent and less conspicuous in his physical activities. The situation had to be resolved, because the glamour of soccer was like a magnet to him and his loyalty to the school was making him unhappy.

During one of Gareth's uncommunicative days I spoke to him. 'Do you think it would help if I spoke to you and your parents about your prospects in soccer?'

He was taken aback at the proposition, but he wisely agreed to a meeting. It was my first visit to 53, Colbren Square, the cosy home of Mr and Mrs Glan Edwards. Sitting comfortably around a bright coal fire, drinking cups of tea, we discussed at length the choice they would inevitably have to make. Mr and Mrs Edwards had no real opinions on the matter, wanting the boy to make sure that he chose the right option.

'I have no objection to Gareth becoming a soccer apprentice,' I assured them. 'It would suit Gareth perfectly. No more schooling. An idyllic existence.' I warmed to my theme as Gareth stood transfixed, ready to listen to every word.

'Ever since I have been in the Tech., I have seen excited boys going on trials to some of the top clubs in the country. Not one of them made the grade. I am a qualified soccer coach and referee. What would Manchester United do if I recommended a promising boy to them? Not only would they thank me, they'd send me a cheque as well, providing the boy was any good. Name your club, Gareth. I'll fix a trial-period for you.'

'What would *you* do, Mr Samuel, if he was *your* boy?' intervened Mrs Edwards, with the concern of a proud and caring mother.

'I am sorry, Mrs Edwards – he must make that decision for himself. I can write on his behalf to Manchester United, Arsenal, Spurs. Or, he can work for his "O" Levels to become a PE teacher, and play rugby for Wales.'

'Play Rugby for Wales, indeed! He'll be lucky to play for Cwmgors,' they both scoffed.

'You mark my words,' I said, having foolishly expressed my inner thoughts.

As anticipated, they opted as thousands of Welsh parents had done before them, for security. Mrs Edwards, in deadly earnest, said, 'He'd better pitch-in in school from now on. It's up to him now.'

'It's up to him.' The words echoed in my ears as I walked homewards. I could not help thinking, 'Aye, and up to me too! Fancy scoffing at my prophecy of Gareth playing for Wales. I must be careful or people will think I'm daft.' . . .

In the meantime, my brother-in-law, Tom, married to my sister,

Dilys, who farmed at Porthyrhyd Farm, not far away from the Gwen-draeth School, told me about a new schoolboy rugby phenomenon. 'They haven't seen his like,' said Tom to me. 'He has caused great excitement in the area with his extraordinary rugby talent. All he does is kick the ball. Touch-kicks, drop-kicks, punts, Garryowens, kicks to the wing, kicks ahead, cross-kicks and kicks for goal. He's a master. The only time he passes is when he is in the opponents' twenty-five, but almost invariably it will be a drop-goal, or a kick to his wings and usually they are spot on. Very rarely does his team lose. He is a one-man band – well worth seeing.'

Tom was not prone to exaggeration, but in this case I thought he had stretched it a bit, but he was right. The boy performed exactly as was predicted. He kicked and kicked, and two of his kicks ahead resulted in tries being scored, and he then kicked the goals with unruffled ease. It was a fascinating performance, but surely it did not help the cause of the three-quarters?

'I've talked to them about it,' said Ray Williams (Llanelli and Wales), Gwendraeth's rugby master, 'but they are happy to be on the winning side, such is his dominance.'

'There's no need to change him, Ray,' I said. 'He's a genius. Tie yourself to his star. He's got a glorious future.'

That was the first time that Barry John and Gareth Edwards appeared on the same pitch. Barry caught the eye that day, but Gareth signalled his presence very much in the minor key by scoring a try.

Barry's singular method of kicking for position in the opponents' twenty-five was not acceptable to the Schools' Selectors, who thought that his play was contrary to the spirit of schoolboy rugby. I had taken Tech. boys to the Final Trial before, but with Gareth it was different. It would take a very good boy to topple him. He had been chosen to play in the second half and by that time the players had been juggled to make the Reds into what was considered to be the eventual Welsh team. The writing was on the wall. The Reds won the vast majority of possession from scrums and lines-out, leaving Gareth clutching at straws. His dreams died in the depths of despair.

I was so disappointed I did not have the courage to commiserate with him when the trial was over. Nor did I have any objections to the scrum-halves who were in favour. The best of luck to them, but I felt very strongly about the treatment meted out to him.

However, when Gareth came to me after changing, I said, 'You did not get much chance, did you?'

'Much chance! You must be joking,' he expressed his emotions bitterly. 'What's the point of a trial, if everyone does not get a fair chance to show what he can do?'

'Perhaps you should go to a fashionable grammar school. Not a small insignificant place like the Tech.'

'Dim diolch! No thanks!'

The Glamorgan County Rugby XV recognized him as a player who could play anywhere. He emerged as the man of the match when he played full-back for them against Munster. That was his finale in rugby terms, as far as the Tech. was concerned. He had appeared in the Final Trial of the Welsh Secondary Schools Under-19 Group at just over sixteen and a half, which was in itself an achievement, for after all, he had played only one game of senior schoolboy rugby in his short career as a player.

That summer Gareth excelled himself in athletics and created a new Welsh record for the 200 yards hurdles at Aberystwyth . . .

It was very encouraging to see the Edwards family in Aberystwyth, sharing in Gareth's achievement. Little did they dream at that time that very soon he would be the toast of Wales.

In the summer of 1964, he was long-jump and 200 yards hurdles champion of Glamorgan and Welsh schools and also Welsh Games champion in the 110 yards hurdles. He was recognized by the *Western Mail* as the most promising athlete in Wales and was awarded a special trophy at Thomson House, by the Hon. Anthony Berry. His award by the *Western Mail* had wonderful repercussions as far as the future generations of young Swansea Valley sportsmen and women were concerned.

. . . Gareth began to experience and enjoy local fame.

'Who is he, then?'

'The son of Glan, who drives buses in his spare time, and Annie Mary who sews. They live near Eic, you know.'

'He is a nice boy. Said hello to me the other day. Very good at jumping the sticks, they say.' . . .

Time was running out; his days at the Tech. were rapidly coming to an end. We had come a long way together, and he trusted me absolutely. I had a feeling at one time that if I asked him on a Friday evening after school to run around Wales and be back by Monday morning, he would be sitting by the school gate, panting, waiting for me to arrive at school, and would ask, 'Beth nesa, syr? What next, sir?'

I was loath to see him go, because I knew that the next two years were vital in his development. He could either enter one of the two local Grammar Schools, or seek an apprenticeship with the NCB. I was not happy with either choice, for I had a feeling – a premonition if you like – that there was a school somewhere that would allow him to train three times a day, seven days a week, and follow on from the work I was doing with him.

One day, as I sat alone in the Tech. staff-room, I happened to pick up a copy of the *Daily Express*. It must have been Providence that guided me to find within its columns a story about a working-class girl who, because of her brilliance in athletics, had gained a special place at the most expensive fee-paying public school in the United Kingdom. The girl's name, of course, was Mary Bignal, and the school, Millfield, in Somerset. It triggered off a wild idea. Surely what had happened to Mary could also happen to Gareth? A member of staff came into the room and I asked him to read the story about Mary. He did so and with a shrug of his shoulders asked, 'Well, what about it?'

'Don't you think Gareth would qualify?' I asked in earnest.

'Mae eisiau mynd â dy ddŵr di i Herbert's boi,' he said. My spirits sank immediately. Herbert was a local herbalist who prescribed a cure once he had analysed your urine!

I pondered about the prospect for days. With tongue in cheek, I quietly sought my wife, Velda's, reaction, and to my surprise she said that no harm would ensue from sending an exploratory letter. After many attempts at composing a letter, I finally managed one which had as its theme 'a sports scholarship at Millfield'. I addressed the letter to the Head-master, without even knowing his name. Within four days a reply came through the post. It was from a name which was not unknown to me – R. J. O. Meyer, Esq., MA, the former distinguished cricketer, Captain of Somerset County Cricket Club and the then Headmaster of Millfield School. They did not provide sports scholarships at Millfield, he outlined in his letter, but he was always interested in helping any boy or girl of great ability who was not having the chance of developing his/her talents to the full. With the letter he had enclosed a thick colourful brochure which in itself was frightening because of its superior quality.

I thumbed briskly through the pages, searching frenziedly for the details of the fees and was relieved to discover that, even though they were formidable, it was possible that Mr and Mrs Edwards could, with a generous Bursary from the school and a little sacrifice, cope with sending their son to Millfield.

Alas! that impression was instantly dispelled when I examined the paragraph more closely, for it said 'per term' and not 'per year' as I had thought initially. My spirits sank. I knew that, however generous the Bursary, we could never possibly entertain the difference in cash. I decided to ignore the contents of the brochure and instead I concentrated on submitting to the Headmaster a list of Gareth's achievements to date. They were very impressive . . .

Within a few days a reply came – 'Gareth Edwards sounds a natural for Millfield'. At the time, that was a big boost for my ego, for to my mind the Headmaster was handling requests like mine every day. I read the letter the second time, and came across something disturbing. 'You might tell them that the Headmaster has offered to find half the fees, and ask whether they, the Edwards family, would consider finding the other half'. If that was not possible, would I write or contact the monied people of Wales for them to consider providing financial support for a young Welsh sportsman to achieve his ultimate potential and to represent Wales.

The impact of this suggestion did not fully register for a long time. When it did, I realized it was asking me to beg. I did not relish the idea one bit. Nowadays, there would be no guilt-complex attached to such a proposition. It would be called 'sponsorship'. I have never liked the word 'begging', in fact, I loathed it. I have seen many broken-down miners and soldiers destined to a life of penny pinching: broken men playing the accordion, trumpet, or mouth-organ, begging from people who had nothing to give, who, in turn, with compassion in their hearts, could only offer a cup of tea and a piece of cake. The realization that I would have to write and speak to monied people for the sake of pursuing an impossible ideal sickened me. I asked myself why should I care? The boy knew nothing of my troubles on his behalf and probably did not even share my ambitions for him. Why not allow him to stay in Gwaun-cae-gurwen where I could still keep an eye on him?

The following day I decided on a tactic to see whether I could resolve my problem. As usual at break-time he was in the school corridor. 'Can I have a word with you Gareth, please?' I said.

He came very quickly with a questioning look on his face.

'Which of the two grammar schools are you going to next year, Pontardawe or Ystalyfera?'

'I don't know. Both of them demand four 'O' Levels before I can join the Sixth Year, and that's a bit of a hurdle in itself.'

'You have no other plans?'

'If I fail, I suppose I'll have to seek an apprenticeship somewhere.'

'Would you like to go away?'

'What do you mean, sir?'

'Well, you are a first-class gymnast. The Army PTI course will take you. A police cadet?'

'The Forces don't appeal to me really and anyway I'm too short for the police-force.'

'The Army Apprentices offer good trades you know. Or a rugby-playing public school?'

'A rugby-playing public school? A rugby-playing public school! You must be joking,' and he laughed at the absurdity of the suggestion. 'Me, a miner's boy, who lives in a council-house, in with those la-di-das? I honestly can't imagine that,' he continued.

'Well, you never know. Let's hope that you get your 'O' Levels. Make sure that you pass in my subject.'

As I walked away I realized what a blithering idiot I was. The boy had no aspirations, he was happy as he was. All the fantasies that existed for him were purely of my own making. He had no ambitions of which I was aware. I realized that whatever was going to happen to him in sport and education would be of *my* volition. *I* was his ambition. During the next few days I wrestled with my problem. I did not want to saddle Mr and Mrs Edwards with financial suicide and I wanted to assure them when the occasion arose that the right thing was being done for their boy. To snatch him from his happy working-class home, and place him into the most expensive public school in Britain could have woeful, as well as happy and profitable repercussions.

Perhaps writing a few letters to the monied people of Wales – the Miners' Welfare, NCB, Glamorgan Education Authority, BBC, etc. –

would do no harm. After all, people with money usually take care of it and are loath to part with it. How do you write to millionaires? Are there any in Wales? I did not know. What if Gareth did not make the grade? That was ridiculous. He would make it all right.

The next time I spoke to Gareth it was in earnest. I told him of my plans. 'There are reasons why I think you should go. You need a platform in an established rugby school to show your talents. You will certainly get a Welsh Senior Schoolboy Cap. You need an opportunity to develop your potential. You should represent the English Schools in hurdling. You can consolidate your 'O' Levels and gain admission to do PE at Cardiff.'

While I was speaking, I could see that he was flabbergasted at my suggestion. 'I want you to promise me that you will do your best, and that you will never let anybody down.'

'Don't worry, Mr. Samuel.'

'Tell your parents I'll see them tonight.'

As always it was cosy in the Edwards' household. My meeting with them was going to be a difficult and sensitive one; money matters usually are. I informed them both of the developments which in the end meant that they would have to pay half the fees.

'That's impossible,' said Glan. 'We can't afford that, we'd be in debt for the rest of our lives.'

I had to agree with this. Miners earned very poor wages in those days.

'Mr Meyer wants me to try to get some money from the monied people. If I succeed, are you prepared to make some financial sacrifices on his behalf?'

Quite naturally they were apprehensive, but they agreed to allow me to negotiate for terms which would be acceptable to both parties. That night I could not sleep. I was composing letters.

'Dear Sir,

I would like to draw your attention to the extraordinary sporting talent of . . .'.

I wrote to Mr Meyer, informing him of my disappointment in being unable to procure financial support for Gareth. I received assurances from him, by return of post, that he would endeavour to find a sponsor. He also suggested a date for us to visit Millfield.

In company with Gareth, sister Gloria and brother-in-law, Clive, we made our first journey to the small village of Street in Somerset. As we came near to our destination, I realized that our conversation throughout our journey had been in Welsh. I urgently reminded Gareth that when we got to the school it would be common courtesy to speak only in English.

The school was not as opulent as I had expected. The classrooms were ex-army huts which were dispersed around the stately Millfield House. As befitted a headmaster well-known for his cricketing prowess, the school was extraordinarily well blessed with facilities for that game. Mr Meyer turned out to be a tall, distinguished, good-looking middle-aged man, who greeted us warmly. As we walked around the school, Gareth became tongue-tied. When he did speak it was invariably in Welsh, which I translated. He was completely overawed with the situation. I felt I had to apologize, 'I am sorry that Gareth and I speak to each other in Welsh; we cannot help it, really, because it is our natural language. From now on both of us will make an effort, won't we, Gareth?'

'Don't worry one bit,' he said. 'We teach sixty-four languages here, and Welsh is one of them. I am glad to hear that it is alive and kicking. Carry on, I am enjoying it.'

His reaction impressed me, and so did his philosophy when he said, 'The British Empire has gone to the dogs. We must seek excellence in our brilliant young people to be assured of future glory. That is why I am keen on helping your young man.' We got along splendidly and in private conversation we discussed the question of fees.

'I must be honest: I am here to safeguard the financial interests of Mr and Mrs Edwards. I am not prepared to encourage them to go into debt,' I said quite frankly.

'The boy *must* come to Millfield. I am impressed with him.'

'Well, I'm sorry, there is no-one in Wales prepared to help him,' I said sadly.

'Leave the matter with me. In the meantime try to find out what the Edwards can afford.'

We shook hands, bade farewell and journeyed homewards. Gareth was in a state of great exhilaration as he talked endlessly about the day's happenings. I was occupied in wrestling with financial problems as I pretended to be asleep. By the end of the journey I had arrived at a formula which I thought was fair and reasonable for the Edwards to pay. It transpired that both supported me to the hilt even though it would entail financial sacrifices on their part.

'We have great faith in you, Mr Samuel. You do what you think is right for Gareth,' said Glan with calm assurance.

Although both were supportive of my idea, I still wonder if they had moments of regret during Gareth's days at Millfield, for Mrs Edwards sewed into the small hours as a dressmaker, whilst Glan had to drive buses in his spare time.

In August I received a letter from Mr Meyer. 'Let him come if you are all keen.' The message still rings with the same excitement now as it did then, over twenty years ago. All my worries vanished with the glad tidings. My plans were about to be realized. Gareth would have his stage after all.

'It is only because I got a little help from an Englishman whose grandmother was Welsh that I can help to finance Gareth for a year, which ought to be two. Your own enthusiasm, of course, has done even more to bring me to my decision,' wrote Jack Meyer after what seemed to me to be years of negotiation. Gareth was speechless when he saw the letter and realized the gist of its contents.

'It's great, Mr Samuel! How can I ever thank you for what you've done for me?'

'My reward will be your success. The door is ajar. As you go through it, make sure that on your return your head will go through it as well.'

'Oh, I won't be like that. That's for sure.'

'Many men have forfeited their principles at the rustle of a few fivers.' I realized I was lecturing again. 'By Christmas you'll be speaking with a tight upper lip, like an Oxford don. You will want to forget the language of the Waun collier.' He laughed loudly at the notion.

'That's one thing they won't do,' he said, with natural conviction.

When I went back to school in September it was a strange experience not to find him there. He had provided me with expectation, excitement and success for the last three years. I was not despondent at his departure, though, there would be plenty of boys with spark to come in his wake. Perhaps there could be one better?

I remember Mr Thomas, the Headmaster, mentioning in the school assembly one morning, that he had received a letter from Millfield in which Gareth had conveyed his thanks to the staff for helping him along the way. Mr Thomas enjoyed the tribute. He made the staff and children laugh when he mentioned that, 'Mr Samuel not only taught him PT and scripture, but he looked after his body and soul.'

Gareth was seventeen when he went to Millfield. Mr Sid Hill, the biology master, who hailed from Morriston, in the Swansea Valley, was the master in charge of rugby there. He was a former Swansea University player. Sid was of the opinion that Gareth could make a better contribution to the team by playing as a full-back. He was not wrong in thinking of alternative positions for him to play, for he was good enough to play for Wales in any position. It did not take long for Sid to discover that the nearer Gareth was to the ball, the more dangerous he became. He was extraordinarily gifted as a goal-kicker and broke the school's goal-kicking record. He would have done so at international level too, but for his easy-going manner. How Wales could have benefited from his kicking, especially in the matches against New Zealand at the Arms Park! Both games could have been won by consistent kicking.

When Gareth had been interviewed for entry into Millfield he had been told that it would be expected of him to be tolerant of young people with different talents. They were to help each other in learning different skills, whether they were artistic, scientific, or sporting. I was somewhat amused when Gareth informed me that he had been testing and measuring in PE and that many of his new friends were doing schedules on circuit, target and weight training. That was over twenty years ago. It was only recently the WRU became aware that such systems existed.

In those days Millfield did not play inter-school rugby in the second term, they concentrated on Sevens at the end of the Spring term. All

schools who play Sevens to a high level gather at the prestigious Roe-
hampton Schoolboy Seven-a-Side Tournament in March. In 1965, Millfield, in brilliant style, emerged winners and Gareth was deemed the best
player of the Tournament. John Reason of the *Daily Telegraph* ear-marked
him as the next golden boy of Welsh Rugby.

Gareth was encouraged by Mr Meyer to stay on for an extra year.
Mr and Mrs Edwards unhesitatingly supported the idea, which was a
brave and unselfish thing to do; the fees remained formidable.

In his final term at Millfield he became the British Schoolboy
Champion in the hurdles, breaking the record in the attempt, and also
beating the eventual great Olympic English hurdler, Alan Pascoe.

When Gareth finished at Millfield, Mr Meyer wrote to me, 'Gareth,
alas, has moved on, the better I hope for his days at Millfield. I doubt if I
shall see his like again, for of all the top-class performers in various fields
of school activity, he was on his own.' By this time I was confident that
Gareth would emerge as the best Welsh scrum-half of all time.

From *Rugby Body and Soul*

The Day Gareth Was Dropped

Max Boyce

*Some idea of the awe in which Gareth came to be held at the zenith of his
career can be gathered from this song by the Bard of Glynneath.*

It was the day of the England–Wales rugby international in 1978 at
Twickenham. A Welsh supporter who was without a ticket was standing
outside the ground in the pouring rain. He called up to some English
supporters inside the ground, 'What's happening? What's happening?'
and was ungraciously told that all the Welsh team with the exception of
Gareth Edwards had been carried off injured.

Some five minutes later there came a great roar from the crowd and
the Welsh supporter called out again, 'What happened, what happened,
Gareth scored, has he?'

This next poem inspired by the same blinding faith was written at
the time when Gareth, seemingly like good wine, was improving with age.

A man came home off afternoons and found his child in woe
And asked him, 'What's the matter bach, pray tell what ails you so
Your little eyes are swollen red, your hands are white and shaking.'
Oh! Dad,' he said, 'I've got bad news, my little heart is breaking
Gareth Edwards has been dropped, 'twas on the news just now
The Welsh selectors must be mad, there's bound to be a row.'
His father said, 'Now, dry your eyes and don't get in a state
Let's be fair mun after all – the man is seventy-eight!'

The Shoulder-High Chivalry of the Vanquished Welsh

A. L. Gracie

The match between Scotland and Wales at Cardiff Arms Park in 1923 is always known as Gracie's game. In it, Leslie Gracie, the Scottish skipper, scored a superlative try in the last minute of the game and was carried off shoulder-high by the sporting Welsh crowd. I should like to believe that could still happen today; but would not like to put too much money on it. In scoring at the Westgate Street end Gracie almost ran over the dead ball line as he tried to get under the posts. A small boy was struck in the mouth by Gracie's boot and lost some teeth. He had no complaints; he said he was a Scottish boy. The E. H. Liddell who also scored that day was the same gifted athlete who was to run for Britain in the 1924 Olympic games and to be immortalized in the Oscar-winning film Chariots of Fire. *Gracie was the son of a missionary; Liddell was to die a missionary in a Japanese prison camp.*

Wales: B. O. Male; T. Johnson, R. A. Cornish, A. Jenkins, Rowe Harding; J. C. M. Lewis (captain), W. Delahay; T. Parker, T. Roberts, D. G. Davies, Gethin Thomas, A. Baker, S. Morris, G. Michael, Llew Jenkins.

Scotland: D. Drysdale; E. H. Liddell, A. L. Gracie (captain), E. McLaren, A. Browning; S. B. McQueen, W. E. Bryce; J. M. Bannerman, J. C. R. Buchanan, L. M. Stuart, D. S. Davies, J. R. Lawrie, D. S. Kerr, D. M. Bertram, A. K. Stevenson.

When asked to write about the finest game I ever played in, I brightly consented, but when I got down to the job I wondered what was really wanted. Unfortunately, more by good luck than good judgment, it happens to be the one in which I met with the most personal success. You can understand, therefore, that I tackle the task with diffidence, and why I should be reminded of the line – 'Ye little stars! hide your diminish'd rays.' Forgive me, therefore, if I instinctively choose that grand game between Wales and Scotland on 3 February 1923, at Cardiff Arms Park.

If only the subject had been 'The Most Dangerous', or 'Exacting', or 'Amusing' game, the personal element would have been eliminated, and I could have told you about the game in France within range of the enemy's long-range guns – one in particular when my battalion borrowed C. N. Lowe from a neighbouring unit and he helped us to overwhelm a French Army XV by scoring several tries himself; or, a Scottish trial at Glasgow when relentless icy rain numbed the fingers and dulled the brain, and the ground was so atrocious that we changed our clothes at half-time; or that comic game against France at Inverleith when I noticed a rotund French forward shadowing me relentlessly, who told me afterwards that he had been instructed never to let me out of his sight or get off the mark! It was in this game that a very famous French wing threequarter was seen to produce an apple and start munching it in disgust because no passes were coming his way.

It was early on a cold wet Friday morning that I joined the remainder of the Scotland team at Paddington Station. It poured with rain all the way down, and I remember wondering whether Cardiff Arms Park would live up to its notorious reputation for a big match, and, if so, how our young team, particularly the forwards, would fare against a strong Welsh pack on a slippery ground. As captain, I felt a tremendous responsibility, and inwardly, I confess, a certain nervousness. I had read that Scotland had not won at Cardiff for thirty-three years. Moreover, since the commencement of the series in 1883, we were one behind, having fifteen successes against sixteen for Wales, and no fewer than eleven of the Welsh victories had been gained in Wales. What chance had we of breaking the Cardiff tradition and of making the match score 'all square'?

I admit my main apprehensions lay with the forwards. True the Welsh pack had not covered itself with glory at Twickenham a fortnight earlier, but it was potentially 'great', and I felt that on their own 'mud heap', and encouraged by thousands of their compatriots, they might give our forwards a thin time. Scotland had a very young and virile pack, and it was in the loose rather than in the set scrums that I expected them to shine. This reliance on mobility was not misplaced, for, as the game progressed, our young giants gradually wore down the Welshmen, and had it not been for the sustained, superlative, superhuman efforts in the open of Stuart, Buchanan, Lawrie and Bannerman, Wales would surely have won the day. As for the outsides, I felt we should be able to hold our own, for surely, man for man, we were considerably faster and, given a fair share of the ball, our main problem would be to find ways and means of breaking through a sterling defence, which included the then greatest defensive wing-player in the four countries, 'Codger' Johnson.

Those were the thoughts running through my mind when our train arrived at Cardiff. On the platform I was faced by an army of enthusiastic reporters who wanted my opinion of the Scottish chances. I blurted out something to the effect that we had a well-balanced side and were out to win – the usual hackneyed, stereotyped reply anyone might make – but when asked how the wet and heavy ground expected for the morrow would affect my side, I courageously replied, with a certain amount of misgiving, that 'our forwards are used to that sort of thing and will fairly revel in it, as most grounds in Scotland are on the heavy side'. Actually I had only played on three Scottish grounds, Inverleith, Hawick and Galashiels, and, in fact, they had been remarkably dry and fast! Some of my facetious friends assert that I have never been to Scotland except to play football, but here let me allay the fears and doubts of every such ignoramus by telling him that at the age of three I was brought all the way back from Ceylon to see my grandparents and other relations in Ayrshire, and as a schoolboy have vivid recollections of seeing the *Lusitania* sailing down the Clyde on its maiden voyage, when spending a summer holiday near Dunoon! But I am digressing.

That afternoon the Scottish team went to Cardiff Arms Park for practice, but it was waterlogged and we went on to the ground of the Welch Regiment. We resigned ourselves to a game on the morrow under the worst possible conditions, but eventually had a pleasant surprise, as we found the turf fairly good. A small army of men and several fire engines had worked wonders during the morning.

From the dressing-room we could hear the crowd singing their national songs and this did not improve our nerves, but the generous welcome from the 45,000 spectators as we ran on to the field was stimulating. I believe the gates were closed long before the kick-off, and that there were a few minor casualties through the collapse of some supporting railings.

Clem Lewis, the Welsh captain, had won the toss and for the first half Scotland defended the town end. This period was comparatively tame and a direct contrast to what followed after the change-over, when thrill after thrill followed in rapid succession . . .

The only score in the first half was a penalty goal by Albert Jenkins for an offside infringement. That was early on and except for several unsuccessful attempts at dropped goals by Jenkins and Arthur Cornish, a wonderful smother tackle of Liddell by Johnson which saved a certain try, and a terrific Welsh onslaught on the Scottish goal line for several minutes just before half-time, I can recall nothing of note. Wales had a slight territorial advantage and certainly got the ball in the tight scrums more frequently, but their threequarters could make no headway, so deadly was the Scottish tackling. I was very glad to see Sammy McQueen shaping up so well in attack and defence – the greater experience of Clem Lewis, his opposite number, giving no advantage. Further, Dan Drysdale, playing his first big match in Wales, was rising to great heights and supplying that confidence to the rest of the team which comes from a full-back's faultless fielding and accurate kicking. While the Welshmen were hooking better, the Scottish forwards' versatility, brilliant wheeling and dribbling more than compensated. Incidentally, how refreshing it would be to see more wheeling and dribbling in present-day football. Why don't the powers that be legislate to keep those wing forwards pushing until the ball is out?

So at half-time Wales led by three points, a penalty goal to nil.

On changing ends Scotland had the benefit of a slight breeze. This second half, I have been told by Welshmen whose International experience goes back to the great days of Rhys Gabe, Gwyn Nicholls, Ronnie Trew, Dick Jones, Teddy Morgan and Dicky Owen, produced more good football, more spectacular movements and more excitement than any game since Wales beat New Zealand in 1905, when Teddy Morgan scored the only try of the match. I did not see the Wales v. New Zealand game of 1935 and from all accounts it was magnificent from every point of view, but even it can hardly have produced the dramatic finish and the sustained anxiety right up to the last moment that characterized the game I am describing.

It was not long after the restart that Scotland drew level with an unconverted try by Eric Liddell. Luckily J. C. R. Buchanan, that sterling forward, was up on my left when I was faced by Male, the Welsh full-back. I passed to him but he was tackled almost immediately and could only throw out a ground pass. This was so well timed that Liddell, zooming along the horizon, picked up the ball at full speed without the slightest check and ran over in the left corner.

It was after this reverse that the Welsh forwards, urged on by the crowd, lashed out at us with devastating attacks. For a period – it seemed years – they lived in our twenty-five. Wave after wave swept down and first Drysdale and then McQueen saved brilliantly. Once, also, I fell on the ball at the feet of those inspired Welsh forwards led by Tom Roberts and paid the penalty of bad technique by getting my nose broken and a boot on the right thigh which to this day has left me with a lump the size of an egg. It was my fault entirely – I should have known better than to fall facing a rush – but it was well worth it, for another dozen yards or so and the ball would have been over the line!

Wales were not to be denied, for soon after Rowe Harding, the reigning Welsh amateur sprint champion, picked up in the loose near the half-way line and, swerving first to the right and then to the left, brilliantly evaded all would-be tacklers till faced by Drysdale just in front of our left-hand goal-post, where he passed to Clem Lewis, who scored in an easy position for Jenkins to place a goal. Wales now led by 8 points to 3 with another twenty minutes or so to go.

From now on, except for one or two abortive raids by the Welshmen, Scotland took the upper hand. Our forwards rose to the occasion magnificently. Lawrie, Bannerman, Buchanan and Stuart – if I must name individuals where all were so splendid – gained or regained twenty to thirty yards by massed dribbling. I have never seen the like of it since and it was fitting that after a break through by McLaren, our youngest forward, L. M. Stuart, should have had the honour of touching down for a try after working the blind side from the ensuing scrum. Again there was no conversion – Browning, usually so accurate, had evidently left his kicking boots behind – and I'm certain all Scotland's supporters feared, as indeed all the players must have done, that that kick would be the deciding factor.

Thus the score became 8–6 in the Welshmen's favour and remained so for nine of the remaining ten minutes.

It was during this last period that the Scottish attacks became more concentrated and persistent than ever before. And the thrills – those few minutes were full of them! Undaunted by the failure of the kick every man jack in our team was fighting with a fervour born of the prospect of a victory which could still be snatched at the last moment, while the Welshmen were grimly determined to hang on to their slender lead for the remaining minutes. I can imagine what Clem Lewis was thinking – 'If we can only hook the ball in the scrum and keep out these man devils by touch-finding!' But Bertram was doing his stuff; he was beating the Welsh hooker all the time and the ball kept coming out of the Scottish scrum with unfailing regularity.

'Wee' Bryce became more inspired, if that were possible, and gave us threequarters chance after chance. McQueen acted as a splendid link, but could we score? – No! First Browning on the right was brought down a yard from the line, then McLaren narrowly missed a drop at goal. Then I was within an ace of scoring from a lovely return pass of Browning's almost on the line, and again, immediately afterwards, on the other wing I managed to get through but foolishly kicked ahead, only to be beaten by Male for the touch. Still we could not score. The Welsh tackling, to use a Welsh epithet, was 'stupendous' – Cornish, Jenkins, Johnson and Male offered an impenetrable defence. It was like trying to bash a way through the Hindenburg Line without an artillery bombardment. Time was drawing on – getting desperately close to the finish, but how near we did not know. The shouting and cheering of the vast crowd was deafening, but somehow it helped us, although it was meant for the defenders. Some of us were dazed from having passed through the fiery furnace of the Welsh forward fury earlier on and were undoubtedly playing as we never played before, and well above form – inspired, as is quite possible, from some hard knocks which subconsciously had the effect of making the recipient throw discretion to the winds and take risks which normally he would not take.

In this way it so happened that Fate decreed that I should be the one 'to find a gap in the enemy wire'. There was not a moment to be lost – Bryce had whipped out the ball to McQueen from a scrum just outside the Welsh twenty-five. The latter very cleverly threw me a long pass over McLaren's head as he saw McLaren was well marked, and this just gave me the chance. Running slightly diagonally to the left to go between Arthur Cornish and 'Codger' Johnson, I saw in a flash that the latter was in two minds – whether to go for me or run between me and Liddell and prevent me passing to the latter. Liddell had scored once and Johnson was mindful of that. Moreover, up to now, I had always passed to Liddell when the ball went towards the left wing and an Olympic record-breaker in the making had to be watched! But as I went on, the way opened up for me and the tactics to be adopted were as plain as a pikestaff. Whether I dummied anyone or not I do not remember but I was just able to swerve round my opposite number, and doing so I saw I had Male on the wrong foot, and all I had to do was carry on over the line. But here I nearly spoilt everything. The dead-ball line at Cardiff is desperately near the goal-line and in trying to touch down near the posts I recklessly ran along this dead-ball line, only inches off it, till the close proximity of Cornish and Jenkins made me decide to drop the ball, although short of my objective. Dan Drysdale took the kick and, by goaling, converted the one point lead into three. Thus ended 'the finest game I have ever played in', the final score being Scotland 11, Wales 8.

All those who took part in the match, Scots and Welshmen alike, must retain many poignant memories from the galaxy of thrilling episodes. The relentless tackling, the constant attacking and counter-attacking by forwards and backs alternately, and the delirious excitement of the crowd urging on their men to withstand the onslaught of the Scots during those hectic ten minutes towards the finish, when we literally lived in their quarter, and finally rushed and counter-rushed to a standstill, culminating in my fortunate try in the nick of time.

Even in the moment of defeat the Welsh crowd forgot their great disappointment and, be it recorded to their everlasting credit, gave a truly remarkable display of sportsmanship and proved the genuineness of their feelings, by swarming on to the ground and selecting me, as captain, for the signal honour of being carried shoulder-high off the field. Moreover, their applause did not end there. As our team passed through our hotel many people interrupted their teas to stand up and cheer, and at the station the platform was several deep with enthusiasts who came to see us off. Even the poor little boy spectator who was sitting near where I scored and had some teeth knocked out by my boot was reported to have said that he did not mind, as he was a Scot himself.

All this is typical of the Welshman. Rugby is bred into his very bones and such is his appreciation of good play that he is no partisan; he is, if anything, more generous with his praise of foe than of friend.

My final memories of that great day were handing over a mud- and blood-spattered Scotland jersey to someone in the changing-room, who asked for it as a souvenir for the Mayor of Swansea. I consented and, mark you, I was later presented with a new one free by the Scottish Union! Then there was the journey back to London and the celebration dinner on the train (a great pity the Welsh and Scottish teams never used to dine together in those days when playing in Wales), when the Union rose to the occasion and stood us champagne. Few of us felt like eating, all of us felt dead-beat – at least all but one, for the indefatigable Bannerman sang Gaelic songs to us most delightfully.

From *The Game Goes On*

The Broken Heart of Jack van der Schyff

Reg Sweet

It has always seemed to me that to turn the whole issue of winning or losing a great game on a single kick at goal is to put an intolerable burden on the man who has to take it. If it goes over, as it did when John Taylor landed his seemingly casual conversion in the Scotland–Wales game Alun Chalfont has described, well and good. If it veers sickeningly outside the posts, then the memory may haunt the hapless kicker for the rest of his days. The picture of Jack van der Schyff's bowed head when his kick failed in the 1955 Test is surely one of the most poignant ever taken.

British Isles: A. Cameron (Scotland); A. C. Pedlow (Ireland), J. Butterfield (England), W. P. C. Davies (England), A. J. F. O'Reilly (Ireland); C. I. Morgan (Wales), R. E. G. Jeeps (Northampton); W. O. G. Williams (Wales), B. V. Meredith (Wales), C. C. Meredith (Wales), A. R. Higgins (England), R. H. Thompson (Ireland, captain), R. H. Williams (Wales), J. T. Greenwood (Scotland), R. J. Robins (Wales).

South Africa: J. H. van der Schyff (Griqualand West); J. J. N. Swart (South West Africa), D. J. Sinclair (Transvaal), K. T. van Vollenhoven (Northern Transvaal), T. P. D. Briers (Western Province); C. A. Ulyate (Transvaal), T. A. Gentles (Western Province); A. J. J. du Plooy (Eastern Province), C. M. Kroon (Eastern Province); A. C. Koch (Boland), C. J. van Wyk (Transvaal), J. A. du Rand (Northern Transvaal), J. T. Claassen (Western Transvaal). Referee: Mr R. Burmeister.

Drama, sheer and stark, built up to a climax which was very near unbearable within the torrid, sprawling bowl of Ellis Park. The crowd, eventually to be numbered at 96,000, was the biggest ever to have watched a Rugby Union international. Heroism there was, and also heartbreak: for this was surely the rugby Test of all Tests, perhaps the greatest ever played. It was a constant round of triumph overtaking disaster, of fights against the odds. One side looked to be assured of victory, and suddenly it was no longer so . . . and yet it stood again on the brink of triumph in the final seconds of the match, only to lose by the odd point in 45. Inspiring play by inspired players made this test what it was and at the end there were no quibbles.

Down 11–3, the Lions came back to lead 23–11. This first test of the series, so it seemed, was theirs for the taking. But the artistry was not yet at an end and sortie after Springbok sortie closed the gap relentlessly until, in the final fateful minute, there on the winter-browned turf of Ellis Park, stood the loneliest man in all South Africa: the tall and rangy full-back, Jack van der Schyff, charged with goaling the conversion kick that would win the Test . . . or lose it.

The photograph of Van der Schyff as he turned away, shoulders hunched and head bowed while the kick veered away to the left of the posts to give the Lions victory, has rightly become one of the most celebrated in the annals of the game. Poignantly it set the final seal upon the Test match that had everything, the international that went deservedly to a team which fought it out so gallantly with only 14 players in the second half.

We may not see its like again; and because of that the memory will be even sweeter.

The Lions came to Ellis Park with a tour record and a reputation which had made it very clear that they would contest this series strongly. In 12 matches they had lost to Western Transvaal and to Eastern Province; but the major games had been won against Western Province, Transvaal and the Free State, the latter two in brilliant exhibitions of attacking rugby by respective margins of 36–13 and 31–3. South Africa fielded half a dozen of the survivors of the series against Australia and with the retirement of Hennie Muller the captaincy had devolved upon the experienced and imaginative Stephen Fry.

Of the hundred haunting memories of that August afternoon, the first of all remains the crashing roar of the biggest crowd the game has known as the teams ran out – the Lions piped on by Ernie Michie, a reserve second-row forward, resplendent in kilt and full regalia; and the renewed thunderclap of expectant cheering, 96,000 voices strong, which was hardly ever to let down until the final whistle, and the battle was joined on the signal of referee Ralph Burmeister.

There were no tedious preliminaries, no feeling of the pulse; straightway the Springboks, as if conscious of the fact that the British Isles were, if anything, fractionally the favoured side, pitched in at the line-out play and, with Colin Kroon clearing well from the short throw, away went Van Wyk with Fry at his side to open up a gap within the first two minutes. They were checked and then sent back, but Van der Schyff now placed a raking kick deep into the British quarter and the nuggety Jeeps, the only uncapped player in the British side and therefore playing in his first international, turned and twisted and dodged his way out of all manner of impending trouble to save and clear the ball.

Ten minutes gone, and neither side could point to any clearly-cut advantage. Then, suddenly, almost on half-way, big Rhys Williams reared and collected and twisted in a line-out, and with the perfection born of long experience delivered the ball to Jeeps. The Lions were away.

Cliff Morgan ran into his pass at pace and at once was going even faster. Phil Davies, in the classic style, straightened the run and gave to Butterfield. The pass was not entirely accurate but Butterfield, with the aplomb of a Cinquevalli, retrieved it from somewhere behind his right ear, brought it forward with not the slightest suggestion of a fumble and with his pace unchecked, and made straight for van der Schyff at full-back before sending Pedlow scurrying the final fifteen yards for the opening try.

The angle was wide and Cameron was unable to goal – and South Africa, within minutes, were level and then ahead. First there came an infringement at the line-out, with a Lion offside as he sought to effect a breach. From thirty yards or so and an unpropitious angle, 'Big Jack' never really looked like missing. Neither did he falter after Ulyate, making the initial running at out-half, brought the play back for his forwards and Retief, Claassen and Du Rand handled before a maul developed in which a British forward played the ball in an offside position.

Six-three now, and the Lions took a hand. Phil Davies probed the outside gap against Van Vollenhoven and burst past his defence, and away went O'Reilly on the right. Gentles corner-flagged to converge upon him as van der Schyff did, and together they pulled him down with seven yards to go. Then it was Pedlow on the opposite wing, and again van der Schyff was there to bring his man to earth. With less than a quarter of the match elapsed, this Test had already exploded into a succession of thrills of the rarest order.

Half an hour had come and gone when the Springboks rushed into an impressive lead. Twenty yards from the British line, Kroon heeled fast and cleanly. Gentles went quickly around the blind-side and Fry, moving wide, ran with him. Now he had the ball and successfully he drew the defence upon him – then slipped the ball swiftly to Briers, on the wing, who sprinted the last fifteen yards for the corner flag and the try. And van der Schyff, carrying the ball back thirty yards, proceeded to goal from the touchline with a nonchalance which suggested that he did these things for fun.

For the Lions, at any rate, an 11–3 deficit at this stage was beyond a joke. At once they called in the threes again and O'Reilly was hauled down within a few yards of the corner. Then Jeeps hurried Morgan on his way as Meredith heeled quickly when 55 yards out, and Morgan was hardly one to stop to ask the time of day: with the defence in travail he left most of it behind as he cut through, then gave Jeff Butterfield his head . . . and Butterfield, swerving to the inside as he went, left the remainder of the defence well beyond the reckoning as he ran through to score at the posts. A fine try, and a straightforward kick for Cameron; and now it was half-time, 11–8 to the Springboks and anything could happen. Held in the set scrums, South Africa had established a useful lead through Du Rand and Claassen from the line-out play. The tempo had been admirably fast and open.

On the Lions' side, however, one niggling doubt had now arisen. Reg Higgins, doughty blind-side wing-forward, had hurt a knee in the first half of the match. During the break he had been given further attention. And now, as O'Reilly once more struck out for the corner flag with little Tommy Gentles covering grandly to pull him down, Higgins was again in trouble. From a line-out he slumped to the ground and was carried from the field on a stretcher.

At this stage of a test match, particularly a test match such as this, it was a cruel setback. Higgins had in fact made his last appearance of the tour. Robin Thompson, leading the pack – and the side – from the second row of the scrummage now reduced to seven, faced the supreme test of ability to captain a test team with the odds stacked heavily against it.

Perhaps he saw it as a challenge. In any event, came the very next scrum and the all-Welsh front row, in which Courtenay Meredith and Billy Williams propped Bryn Meredith, had the ball back fast. Jeeps to Morgan it was and Morgan, with a twinkle of the feet, had come and gone. The old stalwart 'Basie' van Wyk had made a desperate effort to reach him and van der Schyff had not a hope in the world of getting across as Morgan brushed through the defence on the outside and then angled in again. It was all pace and co-ordination and perfection of judgment, as fine a try as you could wish to see.

When Cameron goaled, the Lions, for the second time, were in the lead. And suddenly, as it must have seemed to a harassed South African defence, the flood gates burst. Morgan, the inevitable Morgan, stabbed a punt toward the corner flag and away streaked O'Reilly with an eye to the main chance. Van der Schyff grasped for the ball on the bounce, then grabbed for O'Reilly, who was there and then was not. A yard or two from the corner, no more, O'Reilly fell to weight of numbers. But the fair-haired Jimmy Greenwood, from the side of the scrum, was at his shoulder: and as the ball rolled clear it was Greenwood who tapped it forward and across the Springbok line, and fell upon it happily. Angus Cameron, perhaps by way of showing that one Scot was as good as the next when it came to building up a test match lead, converted from the tricky angle. Within 10 minutes the 11–8 deficit had become a lead of 18–11. And there was more to follow.

Greenwood, as much as any among Robin Thompson's surviving seven in the pack, was revelling in this. Now he covered behind a loose mêlée, gathered and kicked ahead . . . and the hapless van der Schyff, who had started so well but fallen suddenly upon evil times, got under the ball but failed to clutch it to him. O'Reilly, long legs pounding like a pair of pistons, was up to him and in possession and across the line before the consequence of Van der Schyff's misjudgment became obvious.

And Cameron, with precise angling of his goal-kick from almost on the touchline, made it 23–11, a lead which now had made the Springbok chances look remote indeed.

About thirty minutes still to go. Twelve points to be made up, or thirteen to win. In terms of test match rugby, it had begun to look impossible. But Stephen Fry, himself peerless as an instigator of the surprise attack off the loose and often apparently profitless ball, was at it again. And his team, rocked back upon his heels as it had been under the three hammer-blows which had lost it fifteen points in a little more than ten minutes, now responded well.

Butterfield, carving a way infield through the loose, was pulled down by Du Rand and lost the ball. Gentles pounced upon it and away went Ulyate. Van Vollenhoven entered the picture, running into a gap as he took the pass – and knocked it on! The forwards had a 'go', passing crisply one to the other until Claassen, with the line in sight, failed to hold the ball and the chance was lost. Then Van Vollenhoven shaped to cut the defence and Davies pulled him down decisively. The door, it seemed, was locked.

Gentles, behind the pack, tried something fresh. He shaped as if to run, then kicked across the line of the scrum for a point just infield from the corner flag. Cameron had been drawn across and for once was out of position. Even as he turned to race back and check the threat it was Swart, cracking on the pace from the left-hand touchline, who was first on the scene and up to the line and over.

Van der Schyff missed the kick, and time was running perilously short. Three minutes only, and not a second more, remained when Chris Koch pounced upon the ball in loose play, some twenty yards from the British line: and dodging and weaving, side-stepping too, for this was no ordinary front-row forward but one of the finest the modern game had known, Koch made grimly purposeful tracks for the target ahead of him and then, as he reached the line, flung himself across it.

This time van der Schyff goaled. Mr Burmeister had checked his watch. It seemed to be all over . . . but here, with the match as good as gone and done with and ready for post-mortems, here out of the blue came another Springbok thrust and Sinclair, in the centre, was straining every fibre as he hunted for an opening. He was held, but Gentles and Stephen Fry were there – and Briers, on the outside. And Briers, as Fry moved him quickly away, beat two defenders on the touchline and scored, as near as made no difference, six yards infield from the corner flag.

It was, of course, fantastic. Like so many other features of this incredible Test match, it simply had no right to happen. As if someone had thrown a switch, the 96,000 lapsed into silence. Two points now would earn a win, and van der Schyff's kick was obviously to be the final action in this match of matches. Wherever the sympathies lay, the suspense was hardly bearable . . . and as the Springbok full-back turned away in deep dejection while the kick flew high and to the left, the excited crowd burst across the barriers and mobbed the players.

First Butterfield, then Morgan and O'Reilly, were hoisted shoulder-high and carried from the field. On the merits of the case, it might have been more fitting had the honour been accorded to those seven gallant forwards; or to every player on the field, if it came to that.

In Test match rugby we might never see the likes of this again.

From *Pride of the Lions*

Did Deans Do It?

William Scott

We have already heard from Alun Chalfont how small Welsh boys not much bigger than a football themselves were taken to see the historic piece of turf on which Doctor Teddy Morgan scored the great try in the epic first encounter between Wales and the All Blacks in 1905. On that day Wales had not been beaten at home for six years. The All Blacks had 27 consecutive victories behind them. Did Deans score the equalizing try? Even some Welsh players thought he did, and was dragged back the vital six inches. Some say the Welsh crowd was unnaturally quiet, as if they knew a wrong decision had been given. Yet the truth of the matter is Deans did not score because the Scottish referee, John Dallas, ruled that he did not – and said so again in his last will and testament.

The rugby argument which dwarfs all others is the one concerning the 'try' by Bob Deans in 1905. It ranks with cricket's body-line and boxing's Dempsey–Tunney 14-second count among sport's most protracted controversies.

> The scene: Cardiff Arms Park.
> The match: Wales v. New Zealand.
> Date: 16 December 1905.

It was the 28th game of the All Blacks' tour. They had won all the preceding games (points for: 801; points against: 22), so their invincible record was at stake. Forty thousand turned up to watch this first-ever fixture between a Welsh side and New Zealand.

The teams:

Wales: Winfield; Llewellyn, Nicholls (capt.), Gabe, Morgan; Cliff Pritchard (extra back); Bush, Owen; Joseph, C. Pritchard, Harding, Williams, Travers, Hodges, Jones.

New Zealand: Gillett; McGregor, Deans, Wallace; Hunter, Mynott; Roberts; Gallaher (rover, capt.), McDonald, Seeling, O'Sullivan, Newton, Glasgow, Tyler, Casey.
> Referee: J. D. Dallas (Scotland).

The first half brought several surprises for the All Blacks. When the first scrum went down they were disconcerted to find that Wales had adopted their seven-man scrum, the formation that had been so successful in their triumphant journey through England, Scotland and Ireland. Then they found that Wales had a 'rover' too, in the person of Cliff Pritchard, to harass their inside backs, just as Gallaher had been doing to their opponents throughout the tour. The All Blacks learned (and have had it underlined in red ink for them many times since) that the Welsh are keen students of tactics – something upon which the other Home Countries do not place such stress.

And in the thirtieth minute Welsh tactics paid off. Scrum-half Owen had always served Bush, while Cliff Pritchard, on the other side of the scrum, had been entirely ignored. At a scrum within striking distance of the All Black line the Welsh captain gave the signal and Owen went right, with Bush, Nicholls and Llewellyn ready for the ball. The All Blacks took the bait and were wrong-footed when Owen passed across the scrum to Pritchard. He drew Deans and passed to Gabe, who handed on to Teddy Morgan. Morgan, with the overlap, flew past Gillett to score near the corner. The try was unconverted, but Wales were leading 3–0.

That was the score at half time and as the second half progressed it looked as though the Welshmen were going to be able to hold on to their lead. In desperation the New Zealanders launched attack after attack as they sensed the possibility of their unbeaten record being shattered. But nothing they did could penetrate the Welsh defence.

Billy Wallace, who already on the tour had scored more than 200 points in tries and place-kicks, was on the right wing for the All Blacks that day. He felt that something just had to be done, so when he fielded a Welsh kick-ahead on the touchline near halfway he set off infield, weaving his way through the oncoming Welshmen. It was the sort of diagonal run which Obolensky was to repeat against the All Blacks thirty years later, but with a difference. Wallace was confronted by the full-back, Winfield, and passed to centre Bob Deans, who had raced up in support. Deans headed for the line and dived for it as he was tackled.

With what result? There are numerous versions.

This is the telegram Deans sent to the *Daily Mail* on the day after the match: 'Grounded ball six inches over line some of Welsh players admit try Hunter and Glasgow can confirm was pulled back by Welshmen before referee arrived.'

J. A. Buttery, describing the match for the *Daily Mail*, wrote:

> It was now that Wallace, chafing under the prolonged inaction which the Colonial three-quarter line had endured, rushed with the desperation born of despair into the thick of the fray. Gathering the ball from an opponent's toe, he tore his way through every obstacle, and in a trice was speeding down the field, with Deans on his flank. It looked an absolutely certain try. Winfield went for Wallace a dozen yards from the line, but ere he could reach him the ball had been passed out to Deans. He, too, was collared, but not before he had grounded across the Welsh line, though the referee – whose decision is bound to be accepted in such matters – declared that he had been 'held up', and ordered a scrum instead of a place-kick.

The All Blacks manager, G. H. Dixon, in his book, *The Triumphant Tour of the New Zealand Footballers, 1905*: 'Deans dived over and grounded the ball well over the chalk mark. He was at once dragged back. That this was an absolutely fair try there is overwhelming evidence, and it was most unfortunate that the referee should not have been on the spot to see what actually occurred.'

Reporter for *The Sportsman*: 'I was within six yards of the spot when the New Zealanders scored the disallowed try. It was the unanimous verdict of a goodly number of Welsh supporters next to me, and also my own, that no fairer try has been scored on the football field.'

W. J. Wallace, in his memoirs:

A line-out had been formed on our side of half-way, and from a long throw-in the Welsh forwards gained possession. Freddy Roberts was just in front of them, and in order to beat him they kicked ahead, but just a little too hard. I was on the wing on the touchline and I dashed in, scooped up the ball and cut across the forwards before they could lay a hand on me. I then made diagonally across the field until I came in front of Nicholls. In order to beat him I turned and straightened up and when he came at me I side-stepped him and slipped through between him and Gabe so that I had a clear run through to Winfield, the full-back. Meanwhile Bob Deans had scented the possibilities of the situation and had run his hardest to come up in support. As I neared Winfield I was undecided whether to kick over his head or sell him the dummy and then I heard Bob calling out: 'Bill! Bill!' I feinted to pass and could have gone through on my own, for Winfield took the dummy, but rather than risk any mishap at this critical stage I threw Deans out a long pass which he took perfectly and raced ahead.

But he made a slight mistake here, for instead of going straight ahead he veered in towards the goal posts. Teddy Morgan, the Welsh wing threequarter, was coming across fast from the other wing and Bob was becoming a little exhausted. Bob saw Teddy Morgan in time and altered his course to straight ahead and just grounded the ball six inches over the line and about eight yards from the goal posts as Teddy dived at him and got him around the legs. But the try had been scored.

Some of the Welshmen quite openly stated that the result was wrong. Morgan told an associate at Guy's Hospital that Deans had scored a fair try and he still sticks to that through the passing of the years. In 1924 at the dinner after the Welsh match he was sitting alongside Cliff Porter and confirmed that Deans' try was a fair one. Cliff got him to write it on a menu card. If the man who collared Bob Deans says that Bob scored, what more evidence is needed?

But did Morgan in fact tackle Deans? Gabe, in the book *Fifty Years of the*

All Blacks, claims that *he* did: 'When I brought Deans down I thought that he had scored, but when I found him struggling, I sensed that he had not, and I, with Cliff Pritchard, pulled him back.'

Perhaps Morgan, if he didn't actually tackle Deans, was on hand for the pulling back. Suffice to say that when Referee Dallas did arrive (he was no match in fitness and speed for men such as Wallace and Deans), he was confronted with confusion on the Welsh line. It would be unfair to accuse the Welsh players on the spot of having created that confusion. But by the same token no Welshman worth his salt would, in such a situation, make any move to clarify things for a belated referee.

So it was that the record books read: Wales 3, New Zealand 0 – the only defeat New Zealand was to suffer in 64 matches in the British Isles before defeat number two at the hands of Swansea in 1935.

Final word, perhaps, on the 1905 incident is this: When Deans was brought down, this was not greeted by the tumultuous applause that would be expected from a Welsh crowd acknowledging a brilliant saving tackle. The crowd was glum, in keeping with the opposition having pulled the game out of the fire. It could have been that *they* thought Deans had achieved those vital six inches.

From *The World of Rugby*

JPR, the Threes, and the Sevens

Now for a set of cameos – glimpses of a wide range of players, some heroic, some not, but every last man imbued with the same passion for the game. We start with the strange little story Carwyn James tells about JPR's three sets of seven stitches because it is so Welsh and perhaps impenetrable to English minds, accustomed over long years to being dazzled by the alchemists from the valleys.

JPR is a man after my own heart, simply because he is never less than completely honest and forthright in his views. He follows the advice given in Shakespeare's *Hamlet*: 'To thine own self be true'—a remarkable philosophy which is usually alien to politicians, even rugby politicians.

Longfellow's lines also come to mind:
—I shot an arrow in the air,
—It fell to earth I know not where.

JPR knows his little patch of earth well; it is in Bridgend, Wales, where his roots are firmly embedded despite his London Welsh connections. He has never been afraid, unlike so many other public and rugby figures, to shoot his arrows from well behind the shoulder. And to rub shoulders with him has always been for me a unique privilege, so I'm delighted that in this autobiography John has decided to put on record his views on the current scene as well as his views on a decade or so of a golden era of Welsh and Lions rugby, successful, though not without blemish.

He played an important part in the success of the 1971 and the 1974 Lions tours. Knowing him, I think that even in the hour of success he was always aware of the chinks in his own armour. Like a forest animal he was blessed with a sixth sense for the presence of danger, an element which he often sought, and loved. Fearless. Uncompromising. The competitor of competitors. Early on he won the Junior Wimbledon. The following year he lost and I for one shall never forget the anguish as he hid his face with his two hands to conceal the disappointment which he felt so bitterly. The champion had lost. He had let his parents and his younger brothers down, he had let Wales down, or so he felt. But the true champions always come back and so did J. P. R. Williams, the very same young lad who was even then playing rugby for his country with Phil Bennett, Derek Quinnell and Allan Martin, at the start of an illustrious career.

The private views of a well known person, I find, are always fascinating. With JPR this is particularly so, for his courageous, extrovert displays are a front for a sensitive nature. Welshmen, and this is a weakness in us as a nation, are given to please. To outsiders we may appear charming but somewhat insincere, but I don't think you'll find JPR guilty on this count.

When he was awarded the honour of being chosen as Rothman player of 1976–77, I wrote at that time of the Twickenham match: 'John Peter Rhys Williams, a doctor himself, had seven stitches inserted to patch a facial injury. He had gone on to the field with seven others, acquired in a previous match. To Welshmen along the centuries the figures three and seven are nothing if not mystical. The figure of Williams in the distance, long hair flying in the wind, may remind us of Pwyll, Prince of Dyfed, riding majestic and mysterious in the mists of the Mabinogi; but a closer look reveals the stark realism of a warrior fully committed to battle. And at Twickenham, that day, in the cold January air, rivulets of blood congealed below his high cheek-bones. What a sight he made on television immediately after the match! The gory, victoriously happy sight of a man who had scored two winning tries – both initiated from a wheeled scrummage!'

And the figure seven struck again. Pinned down at the bottom of a ruck in the first few minutes of the All Blacks match at the Brewery Field, his unprotected face was trampled upon by a vicious prop. Before leaving the field to have another seven stitches inserted he paused and gave instructions to his men. A lesser mortal would never have returned to the field of play. Characteristically, he did.

Bridgend, Millfield, London and Old Deer Park, every famous rugby stadium in the world, the joys and tribulations of long tours, Wimbledon, hospital wards, famous players, fifty caps culminating in the captaincy of his country; and like a thread running through the fascinating tale which he tells, there is always the influence of his family and his charming wife. I found JPR's story compulsive reading and so will all Welshmen, all rugby fans and players, and all who share a love of sport.

Foreword to *JPR*

The Majesty of King John

John Reason

Next, a glimpse of the majestic Barry John, master of the fingertip tackle. It was not, as John Reason explains, that Barry couldn't tackle; it was just not his métier. Yet of course he could when he had to, and I was there the day that he laid low the huge French skipper Benoît Dauga. The sixteen-stone café proprietor from Montgaillard and the eleven-stone boy from Gwendreath collided with an almighty crash, and Barry had to go off, his nose bleeding profusely. A French doctor gave it a tweak which clicked it back into place, cotton wool was pushed into his nostrils to staunch the flow, and he was back in the game. Did it affect his play? Well, he told me afterwards, it had interfered with his breathing a bit; but once back on the field he had got totally involved in the action 'and was ready to do something just as daft again'. He went on to score a penalty goal and a typically magical try.

The factor which made the Lions' win so remarkable was its efficiency. The forwards had the better of their opponents but they did not crush them and their loose forwards hardly came into the game in attack. It was just that whenever the Lions won a good ball, they used it so well that they scored. It is rare indeed for a team to make so few mistakes from so much ball and so much running.

This efficiency found its supreme expression in the play of Barry John. He scored 19 points in the match and played with such an air of aloof and remote disdain that it was easy to understand why the Lions had taken to calling him the 'King'. When moving with the ball he was all feint and swerve and insinuation. When kicking it out of the hand, he flighted and floated the ball into just that square yard or two of the field where it would cause most embarrassment. When place-kicking at goal, he achieved a success ratio of nearly 80 per cent. This made even Bob Hiller look like a hit and hoper.

In four matches in New Zealand, Barry John had scored 66 points, which was within seven points of Malcolm Thomas's record for a British Lion in that country. The 'King' was making New Zealand pay for every drop of sweat and every drop of blood he had spilled on the ill-fated Welsh tour of 1969, and it was clear that he had only to avoid injury to break every scoring record for tours of New Zealand.

His cool on the field was enough to chill a polar ice-cap and it was as unshakeable. I have never seen a player with more deign in his game. Perhaps Toscanini, in his quietest moments on the conductor's podium, may have equalled Barry John's ability to exercise the maximum of control with the minimum of movement; perhaps not. There was one moment in the second half against Wellington when John Dawes skipped back in defence and threw a rather hurried ball to Barry John on the 25. The 'King' stood quite still for what seemed like seconds, just as a matador stands above the bull before he kills it, and then calmly kicked the ball to touch.

It was a moment which looked very much like arrogance, but afterwards Barry John gently dissociated himself from any such display of exhibitionism. 'As a matter of fact,' he said mildly, 'I was wondering whether to chuck the ball back to Syd.'

With so many players named John in the team, the captain was usually referred to rather irreverently by the shortened version of his first christian name, which is Sydney.

Barry John did not tackle too many people. When the players watched the film of the Wellington game afterwards, and the 'King' was seen quietly avoiding such sordid confrontations, he said, 'You can't beat these finger-tip tackles.' In all the games he played in New Zealand before the first Test, Barry John was never caught on the ground with the ball. He *could* tackle, if he wanted to; no one who saw this frail bit of sinew stop the 6 ft 5 in Benoît Dauga head-on five yards from the Welsh line in Paris would ever be in any doubt as to his defensive capabilities. It was just that he chose not to use them much in New Zealand. He was content just to conduct the orchestra, and he did it with such fastidious precision that he made even the coughs from the audience sound like music.

From *The Victorious Lions*

The Zap! Zap! Zap! of David Campese

Evan Whitton

Now we have the international debut of an Australian illusionist called David Campese. Seen here playing on the wing against New Zealand in the Bledisloe Cup, he was as often seen through the 1980s as a full-back of world class.

The heavy thinkers of New Zealand rugby nearly went off their brains trying to describe the little number that David Campese (rhymes with easy), unveiled for the stupefaction of his opponents. Was it a goose step? A Hesitation Waltz? A minuet? What?

What he did was throw a foot out, and then bring it back before it touched the ground. The idea was to anchor his opponent for an instant before Campo blasted off round him. So it was feint like nothing seen before, and it blew poor Stu Wilson, 27, veteran of sixty-nine first-class matches for the All Blacks, and billed as the best right wing in the world, right out of the water.

We may suppose that Campese was only selected for that tour because ten leading players declined to make the trip, and I figured the Wallabies were superior to the All Blacks in only two positions: outside half Mark Ella and full-back Roger Gould. Fortunately, the new coach,

Bob Dwyer, had reverted to that method of ensemble play invented by the 1905 All Blacks and adopted by the 1927 Waratahs, but largely forgotten since and the Wallabies, against all expectation, got up in one of the three Test matches.

Campese, a full-back by inclination, was played on the left wing in the internationals. He beat Wilson on the outside a couple of times and scored a try, admittedly from an offside position, in the first; put Gary Ella in for a try and scored one himself in the second: and spectacularly took the advice of the great Welsh coach, Carwyn James, in the third.

James, lately and sadly dead in an Amsterdam bath, had noted that the All Blacks are made to be side-stepped; Campese produced three stunners in a row. They all but retained the Bledisloe Cup for Australia. He fielded Stu Wilson's attempted drop at goal out from the posts and stormed upfield to his right. Left wing Bernie Fraser barred his way. Zap! Outside centre Steve Pokere menaced him. Zap! Inside centre Billy Osborne, the Wanganui Express, flew at him. Zap!

These sidesteps, all off the right foot, and executed without any apparent loss of pace, carried Campese almost to half way, and over to the left, and left behind twelve All Blacks. But he had also left the referee, portly Scottish schoolteacher Alan Hosie behind, and had lost contact with Mark Ella, who had initially followed him out to the right, and who might have been expected to finesse any remaining defenders.

Campese finally passed left to Andrew Slack, and Hosie, wallowing ponderously some eighteen yards behind, blew him on suspicion of a forward pass. Campese will go to his grave firm in the belief that the pass was valid by 'one or two centimetres', and I am inclined to think that had the try been awarded and Australia thus gone to a lead of 15–6 with fifty minutes remaining, they may have hung on for one of the great upsets in rugby history.

We needn't go on whining about this decision, or at least not for as long as New Zealanders have about the try the 1905 All Blacks were not awarded against Wales. But those sidesteps, the most prodigious, I imagine, since Prince Obolensky, cutting back from the right wing, spreadeagled the All Blacks at Twickenham in 1936, will live long in the memory . . .

It seems to me that Campese is a great player, but not yet a good one, if that makes sense. It may be a question of concentration. He can wipe out a club team on his own, but he is a bit sloppy in delivering the coup de grace of the final pass.

However, with his kick inside off the right foot, if I were an up and coming young openside breakaway, I'd be looking to make my reputation by simply going straight down field and waiting for Campese to arrive. I'd figure to score a lot of tries, providing that he thought a little about giving me the ball properly.

From *The National Times (Australia)*

I, Charles Fry

C. B. Fry

*C. B. Fry was unquestionably one of the most gifted all-round sportsmen of
all time. At Oxford he won a Blue for association football and that winter
gained a full international cap for England against a touring side from
Canada. He once held the world record for the long jump. At thirty he
achieved a remarkable double by playing for Southampton in the final of the
FA Cup on Saturday and scoring 82 for London County against Surrey at
the Oval on the Monday. Yet, as he tells us, he much regretted that he had
not been to a rugby school. He did, however, manage to fit in ten games for
Blackheath between 1894 and 1897, scoring two tries, and it is also true that
only a last-minute injury stopped him getting a fourth Blue as a rugby wing
three-quarter. The trouble with being a sporting superstar is that you cannot go on doing it for ever. Fry's later life was something of an anti-climax –
though he was offered the throne of Albania. Nor, as we can see, did the
munificent gods endow him with modesty.*

Once on a day, pre-Hitler, my Editor having regarded me for years as an
amateur in everything but Cricket, suddenly found out that I had played
Rugger for Oxford University, the Barbarians and Blackheath. So he said
would I do Blackheath v. Cardiff at the Rectory Field next Saturday. So I
said, certainly.

So my pre-Hitler motor-driver Jimmy Brooks (now mending and
wiring Spitfires and last heard of over the air in lunch-time war workers,
introduced as 'Public Nuisance No. 1,' he being an accomplished revue
artist in the style of Max Miller) — Jimmy, I say, drove me to Blackheath. He
also 'phoned my copy to the *Evening Standard* and drove me home.

We left the field in reverent silence. But after half a mile he said:
'Excuse me, Sir. . . .'

'Well, Mr. Brooks,' said I.

'Well, Sir,' said he, 'now I call it a man's game, this Rugby Football.'

Now Jimmy Brooks had spent 1914–15 in the Flanders trenches, had
seen life in the Halls and, with me, any number of Soccer Cup-ties and
League matches.

So I cross-examined him, as one whose opinion counts.

It transpired that (a) this Rugby is pretty well a free fight and tough at
that; (b) further, that the scragging was pretty well all-in wrestling; (c)
further, did I see the Cardiff chap make a swallow dive at full speed and
fling the Blackheath chap, also going full speed, at least ten yards head
over heels? And (d) that in this game a man could run full bat without
having to palter. And (e) all this, all this, Sir, with no one losing his temper
so as you'd notice it.

Now if I, Charles Fry, who spent most of my football years playing

Soccer for the Corinthians and for Southampton in League matches and Cup-ties, say that I liked Rugger better than Soccer and found it a finer game, all I do is to give a personal opinion, liable to paradox.

But Jimmy Brooks is, I assure you, a good cross-section of observant quick-witted democratic experience. That is why I give the story.

For myself I would say that being a wing three-quarter who could take a pass and leg-it pretty well in even time for the 100 yards, naturally I liked Rugger. The game is so full of plot-interest and drama.

True, I never compassed the swallow dive at the ankles of a full-speed opponent: I never got lower than the thighs. But as I began at the neck when first I played for Wadham I don't call that so bad.

The chief interest of this is that I was at a Soccer school and even played for England at Soccer, so I must be rated a not altogether despicable convert.

And I do wish to this day that my Public School had played Rugger instead of Soccer.

Still, I hold that anyone who is of any use at the one game can be of some use at the other, so be he genuinely means to learn. My one regret is that one had not the sense to go off to Cardiff or Newport in the winter vacation from Oxford and persuade them to let one play in their second or third fifteen so as to learn how to behave in the mud by way of falling on the ball with eight short-legged sturdy forwards charging down from a two yards' distant horizon. For nothing quite like this happens in Soccer.

Now Association Football is a fine, a glorious game. But it has, through no fault of its own, become overlaid with a massive counterpane of laws, bye-laws, and regulations, so that an old-timer were he to take the field in a miraculous second youth would scarcely know his way about, and could scarcely move in the field without being whistled to order and penalised for an offence, civil or criminal.

We cannot but admire the organisation of their huge public entertainment by the Football Association and the League Managements. It is on the whole remarkable for ability and scope. But the game as a pure game has, one feels, been swamped by its aspect as a public entertainment. This at least in its higher walks of play.

Rugby has on the whole kept its pristine freedom as a game played for its own sake, and this is an aspect which our Author is entitled to add to his heraldic escutcheon of praise.

So much then in support of our Author's title to his title.

His title to authority needs really no substantiation because in the course of this interesting and enthusiastic book it appears to the reader that, except in the intervals of pulling the legs of captains and committees of County Cricket, and of watching Test matches, he has avowedly devoted his life to his 'Man's Game' ever since he himself helped to raise the Rugger of Bedford School to the high standard for which it has ever since been famous.

They tell me that in his school days our Author, a three-quarter weighing 14 stone, and fast off the mark at that, was the terror of visiting teams and, in the case of other school fifteens, a nightmare before the match and a backache after.

His brief career for the Harlequins is outside my ken and hearsay, but I can guess he would be remembered.

His lore of the game is pretty well unrivalled, even on the count of the extent of his critical experience. He may safely be backed to produce his facts and argue his case against almost anybody, though there is a large barrister named G. D. Roberts, KC, whom I would much like to pit against him in open court. Just to see.

Still, you can judge for yourself, distinguished reader.

All I can say is that having drunk delight of battle with my peers (and superiors) far on the ringing plains of many games, I do not care how much praise is given to Rugger, nor how many converts accrue to our Author from other field-games such as he may rank as lesser.

But there is always Polo. Remember that. Polo, too, is a Man's Game.

Preface to *Rugger, the Man's Game*

The Lifelong Regret of F. E. Smith

John Campbell

F. E. Smith was one of the brilliant group who put Wadham on the map at Oxford in the 1890s. He was there with another future Lord Chancellor, John Simon, a future editor of The Economist, *F. W. Hirst, and the amazing C. B. Fry. Yet, with all the glittering prizes that he won, F.E. had one lifelong regret – that he had not won a Blue for rugby.*

Part of F.E.'s popularity at Wadham derived from his prowess at rugby. He was always a keen games-player and a good performer at any sport he took up. Practically the only game he never seems to have played was cricket. He became a sturdy centre-half in Fry's college soccer team, 'with a capacity for work that made up for his rugby man's disinclination to treat a ball as spherical and susceptible of accurate treatment'. He was also a good three-mile runner, and later in life a first-class tennis-player. But rugby was his first and at this age his best game: according to his own account he had captained Birkenhead Park, presumably while at Liverpool, 'with two of my brothers in the scrum with me'. Rugby required less finesse and more hard physical courage than other games: F.E. loved the very mud and sweat of it, the masculine exhilaration of sheer exertion. He was a great believer in the maxim *Mens sana in corpore sano*: he both acted on it himself and preached it to others.

No young man who does not take care to harden his body, to exercise his muscles, to promote by judicious exercise his intestinal and perspiratory functions, can hope to address himself to his work with the keenness and vigour of his more athletic rivals. What is more, even if by sheer force of habit he reaches the age of, say, thirty without taking reasonable exercise, he will certainly find after that age an increasing staleness and liability to illness.

Once, when Sir John Masterman asked F.E. the secret of his success at the Bar, he simply rolled up his sleeve and bared his powerful forearm.

In 1893–4 F.E. captained the Wadham rugby XV to victory in the inter-college championship – a remarkable achievement for a college of only eighty members. At the end of the season the team, which included Fry and Simon (but not, to his chagrin, Hirst) travelled through to Cambridge to play the Cambridge champions, Caius, and beat them by a try to nothing. (His son claims that F.E. scored the winning try, but Simon does not confirm this too-perfect detail.) This was the high point of F.E.'s rugby career, marred only by an outbreak on the way home of the sort of vandalism that used to be called youthful high spirits; years later F.E. claimed that he had done his best to dissuade his team from wrecking the railway carriage. 'That journey', he told the Oxford University Athletic Club, 'cost me the most miserable twenty pounds that I have ever been compelled to borrow.'

He only narrowly missed winning a Blue that year. He was convinced that he had been denied only by a prejudice in favour either of Fettesians or of beefy forwards possessing more bulk than brain – though *Isis* blamed an ill-timed injury. The evidence of his contemporaries, however, suggests that F.E. had not quite the skill to make up for his relative lack of weight: guts and vigour were his qualities. The disappointment was one of those wounds to his pride that never healed. 'To the end of his life', Sir John Masterman has written, 'his language about the University officials who left him out was a lesson in opprobrium.' And Simon tells of F.E. raging to a friend of his about the 'putrid forward' who had kept him out of the team, before discovering that he was talking to the very man. The lack of a Blue spoiled his record as an all-round man.

From *F. E. Smith*

Now for two Frenchmen, of whom each in his different way illustrates the sheer joie de vivre *laced with Gallic rigour which has made the French so fizzing and formidable a rugby power: the Abbé Henri Pistre, and the little Napoleon Jacques Fouroux, who, by the way, fell out with Albert Ferrasse and did not become president of the French rugby federation as predicted.*

The Priest with a Passion

Alex Potter and Georges Duthen

High on the list of France's rugby characters – if not at the top – is big, jovial Abbé Henri Pistre, parish priest of the village of Noailhac (population 600), near Castres, southern France, who loved the game to passion point, yet renounced it. As great match-winning or match-saving feats have places in the game's history, so should the story of this renunciation, and of how the abbé did not quite lose his beloved.

In 1921, Henri Pistre, then twenty, was a seminarist in the old cathedral city of Albi. Soon his army period would begin and his superior, hearing that young men who won a *brevet militaire* (pre-service fitness test) would not be displaced for training, encouraged his charges to prepare for it.

Doing this, Henri Pistre, whose sports opportunities had so far been thin, found that he had been an athlete without knowing it. With no preparation, and *wearing a soutane*, he jumped 5 ft 5 ins. In running kit he soon covered the hundred metres in a fifth of a second outside evens.

On sports fields he spent energy as spendthrifts spend money. And he was built like a rugby forward. So it is hardly surprising (writes Maurice Colinon in *Pionniers en Soutane*) that in a week or two his army captain, being an old player, said: 'Pistre, on Thursday you play rugby.'

Pistre played; in the pack; and as though possessed by a demon. Moreover, this novice performed as though the game was not new to him. So well, in fact, that next day the captain convoked him. 'Pistre, I speak to you now not as your captain, but as an official of the Albi Rugby Club. I *ask* if you will join us.'

The seminarist-now-soldier was soon playing in Albi's first XV, one of the best in France. He blossomed into a great player, and was heading for a cap, when he was demobilized and returned to the seminary. Several clubs tried to capture him. 'Leave your studies, play for us, and we will get you a good job. And you'll be an international. Sign here . . .' Pistre, however, continued his studies, and played when he wanted to play. And the passion grew.

Then the blow came. He learnt that while a seminarist might play rugby, a priest should not. So with superb stoicism he gave it up. He was ordained in Albi Cathedral. Many of his playing friends were there, but only the young men who were ordained with him saw, at the disrobing afterwards, the colours – yellow and black – of Albi Rugby Club. He was wearing a club jersey for the last time.

That was in 1923 and friends of the abbé say that, ever since, the Church and rugby have struggled for possession of him, with the Church always winning, though often with little to spare.

The abbé, however, is allowed to write on the game, and his articles have leading place in the quaintest of sports journals, the weekly *Courrier Sportif du Tarn* (Tarn is his county). Sometimes he writes with a vigour you cannot help associating with old suppressed longings to spend his strength in a pack. It is nearly thirty years since he began writing for the *Courrier Sportif du Tarn*. The paper, born in 1777, was then in very poor health, with a temperature as high as its circulation – just over a hundred. With the abbé's contributions on his lost love, it rose handsomely, and is now about fifteen hundred.

We sports writers could get a free copy but we are happy to pay for ours, for it is a reminder of serener days (its make-up hasn't changed since it was born) and the rugby writing is rich and pure. 'You can talk of rugby in many ways,' wrote journalist Yvan Audouard in *Paris-Presse*. 'You can be enthusiastic, even lyrical, with praises, audacious with epithets, violent with denigrations, technical with analyses . . . The Abbé Henri Pistre is all these . . .'

All these, and more. He called the drab (3–3) draw between France and England in Paris in 1960 a game of smother-ball. 'We don't go to stadiums to see the ball systematically buried. What are undertakers for?' When France beat Ireland in Paris (23–6) two months later and connoisseurs complained that play was too adventurous, he wrote: 'It was gay. A fig for those who called it mad. When our rugby, rid of its old inferiority complex, spreads its wings in the spring sunshine, may we not call it joyful? Why give its young and smiling face a monocle?'

After an extra dull game: 'Is this dingy labour all that we can offer the Youth of France?' And this: 'What we need in our rugby is a freshness, a brightness and a grace. I hear that Moncla [France's captain] shouted to his braves: "Look out – we're playing in the old style!" Bravo, Moncla! That alone shows you have the makings of a great captain.'

The abbé suspected certain super-critics of having 'a refrigerator where their bladder ought to be.' He liberally uses phrases such as: 'He clung to the ball as though it was a glass of absinthe or a piece of lobster.' And: 'How could he shine as a forward? It was like expecting a duck to do a trapeze act.'

To hide his identity when he began to write, the abbé took the extraordinary step, for a Roman Catholic priest, of inventing a wife for himself. Thus, in one of his reports: 'Splendid weather, a good crowd, an excellent cigar, and my wife in very agreeable mood.' In another article he referred to the imaginary wife as 'Virginie, my gentle dove'. But his style of writing – its imagery and virility – soon led to identification. No one in France writes on the game quite like Abbé Pistre.

When the French national XVs were getting poor results a few years ago, he wrote: 'Our players eat too much. What can men with paunches do against the bread-boards they send us from Britain?'

But his pen got him into trouble, even in France where, some Europeans say, the libel laws are made of velvet. In a report of a match in

1952 between Castres (the regional team he firmly supports) and Narbonne, he let fly with ink at a referee, saying (among other things):

'His perfumed luggage included a tiny hunting-horn [presumably in place of a whistle] but not the lorgnette indispensable to one so short-sighted. At a welcoming hostelry he refreshed himself after his long journey and bright-eyed and rosy-cheeked, stepped confidently on to the field, to be greeted with cries of: "Scoundrel! Knave! Hooligan! Bandit! Give us victory, or tonight you'll hang on a lamp-post." Terrified, the sounder of the hunting-horn lost control. His lofty brow sank almost to the ground, as though he were looking for daisies or buttercups in the December slush . . . His brainbox was as empty as the purse of a mendicant friar.'

And the abbé added a postscript:

'I have till now stubbornly defended referees. I have stood by the short-sighted, the short of breath, the clumsy, the unlucky and the partial . . . I cannot support the stupid.'

The referee sued for libel, and lost. He appealed and it looked as though the abbé had lost. For technical reasons, three further appeals were heard at long intervals, and the result hung fire for six years.

Said the abbé: 'If I lose, I'll be logical to the end. It's my body they'll have. To prison I'll go. I have no money for damages.'

Said his friends: 'If you go to prison, we'll bring you tasty foods and venerable wines.'

Till 1960 we were never clear how the affair ended; so we wrote to the abbé, who characteristically replied: '. . . So you followed what was called the judicial marathon. For six years that referee held with all his teeth to my old soutane. There were not, in this affair, grounds for punishing a cat, let alone for fleecing a priest. I had to pay 20,000 francs [old francs, thus equivalent to about fourteen guineas] and more. Friends helped me . . . You see that the blow has not broken my pen.'

The concluding words refer to the lively way the abbé continues to write on the game.

He has countless rugby friends. When he was established as a priest some of them gave him a dinner service wrapped in the colours of the Albi Club. The service is proudly used when he entertains rugby friends. He founded a rugby team in the village of Noailhac. It failed to last, but one of the players turned the abbé's grief to thankfulness by joining the church choir.

When he was a priest at Castres in 1932 and the town xv was faltering, he became coach. For two seasons, in the evenings by lamplight, he put the local braves through their paces on an old artillery ground.

From Church duties on Sundays he often cycled furiously to the Castres stadium to watch the day's match. Greeted with: 'Have you come straight from church, Monsieur l'Abbé?' he might say: 'Yes, mon ami; I didn't see you there.' Nowadays he drives to the Castres ground. If there's a traffic block, gendarmes wave him on. He's part of the establishment. He is respected on all of the rugby grounds of France. 'My soutane and hat at first aroused curiosity,' he said. 'Then they were tolerated, then liked. I have been applauded by miners. Miners applauding a priest! That's something to boast about . . . Providence made me a rugby player and that permitted me, later, to do good as a priest.'

He was made a Chevalier of the Legion of Honour by the French Government a few years ago, chiefly for services to rugby.

The Abbé Pistre sees most things from the rugby angle. When he goes to Paris, sports journalists like to take him to games other than rugby. Of a tennis champion he said: 'That fellow would make an excellent three-quarter.' Of a boxer: 'His right hook reminds me of that of a prop forward with whom I once came into close contact.'

Of soccer and billiards: 'They satisfy my mind. Only rugby captures my heart.'

From *The Rise of French Rugby*

The Rigorous Reign of Jacques Fouroux

Steve Bale

He stands only 5 ft 5 in yet he is head and shoulders above the giants that are his to command in the French rugby team who play England at Parc des Princes this afternoon. As Little Corporal and Little General – both sobriquets are sometimes applied to him – Jacques Fouroux is unchallenged as the fount of power and authority.

The Napoleonic coach upsets many in French rugby but anyone who enjoys the patronage of the man who matters, Albert Ferrasse, president of the French rugby federation, is inviolable. However much people despise the old dictator, they still vote for him: in 1988 Ferrasse (and by extension Fouroux) polled 98.8 per cent in the last presidential election.

A figure that would once have been commonplace in eastern Europe represents an unassailable power base. 'Ferrasse is like Caesar controlling his empire by putting into position people who owe him favours,' a Federation observer said. 'Whether these people have any talent themselves is another matter.' Walter Spanghéro, Fouroux's first French captain and no friend of his old comrade, puts it more witheringly. Federation committee men, he said recently, 'are Pink Floyds who know nothing about rugby and are only there for the slap-up meals.' This pusillanimity is all Ferrasse requires.

As Monsieur le Patron has often said that he regards Fouroux as the son he never had, the coach is as entrenched as the president. Few except Ferrasse say they actually like what Fouroux has done to the French team, the triumph of brawn over brain, but fewer still risk the wrath of Ferrasse by daring to speak out against it.

Those who do – the distinguished and successful coaches of Toulouse and Toulon, Pierre Villepreux and Daniel Herrero, to name two – are officially vilified for their presumption. Both are proponents of the bygone French virtues, the flair and unpredictability which breathed *joie de vivre* into European rugby. Although their clubs are habitually France's best they are lucky ever to have more than one or two representatives in the national team.

Villepreux grew so frustrated with Fouroux's unshakeable resolve to develop enough muscle-power to emulate the All Blacks that he went off and helped coach England, treachery that earned him a stinging rebuke from Ferrasse. Herrero, a bizarre figure with hippy hair, red bandana and occasionally bare feet, so upset Fouroux that Ferrasse publicly wished defeat on Toulon in last year's French Championship semi-final. They won.

For the president, an attack on Fouroux is an attack on Ferrasse and in the autocracy of the federation this is unacceptable. Even if more people were prepared to speak out it would make no difference because the future is as predictable as the charmless French style has become. Fouroux will coach France until the 1991 World Cup and then, if Ferrasse is good and ready, assume the presidency (he is already vice-president). It is a carve-up, as indeed is the succession to Fouroux, and it could not happen anywhere else.

Fouroux was a very small back but his rugby life has been dominated, as player and coach, by very large forwards – and his obsession with the All Blacks. Aged 42, he is from the Armagnac region of south-west France, from Auch, capital of the Gers department, where he is a successful businessman. He played for Auch and Cognac as well as La Voulte, the club from which he won all his 27 caps.

His fame goes back to 1967 when, at 20, he did so well for a regional selection that the All Blacks rated him the best scrum-half they encountered on tour. But Max Barrau was France's well-established scrum-half and it was another five years before Fouroux became an international.

Even then he was making enemies. Walter Spanghéro, a once-great No. 8, who remains a figure of profound respect in the game, said only last week: 'He still holds it against me because when I was captain and had some influence I preferred Max to him.'

Indeed, Fouroux's career was always a struggle to prove himself. For nine years he alternated with Richard Astre until eventually, in an oddly typical Gallic compromise, they were made joint captains on France's 1975 tour to South Africa. It did not work – and certainly did not satisfy Fouroux, since Astre played in both Tests.

Fouroux's *jour de gloire* did finally arrive in 1977, when he led France to only their second Five Nations Championship Grand Slam, an achievement which profoundly affected his subsequent thinking. France's triumph was founded on the power of their pack.

Flair had been fair enough in the old days but not any more – certainly not in an era when the Welsh forwards were, annually, the biggest Championship obstacle. These days he has three cronies from that side – Roland Bertranne, Gérard Cholley and Jean-Pierre Bastiat – as co-selectors.

When Fouroux became coach in 1981 France proceeded immediately to a third forward-dominated Slam. The pattern for the Eighties – and now the Nineties – had been set. There was a famous victory over New Zealand at Nantes in 1986, another Slam in 1987 and at least a share of the Five Nations' title in each of the past four seasons. It is a formidable record but Fouroux remains deeply dissatisfied.

'If we add rigour and realism to our traditional qualities of flair and invention we can become world-beaters,' he once said. 'My role as coach is to help players of exceptional ability and intelligence exploit fully their potential. I have to blend together a diversity of styles and mentalities into one team effort.'

This was his view immediately before the 1987 World Cup final, when France had beaten Australia in a classic semi-final and were about to be overwhelmed by New Zealand. That 29–9 final defeat in Auckland has been the genesis of much that has followed. 'When you meet people who beat you nine times out of ten you are confronted with an insoluble problem,' Fouroux said admiringly.

His solution was to become more All Black than the All Blacks, bludgeoning opponents into submission before unsheathing the more traditional rapier. With any other country it would be loudly applauded; with France it just seems a dreadful waste.

In any case, given that its aim is to beat New Zealand again, it has not worked. The test of the Fouroux philosophy came when France toured New Zealand last summer. They lost both Tests and All Black hegemony was confirmed. It was almost as shattering as the World Cup final had been. 'They want to beat us by imitating us but they don't even understand our game,' Grant Fox, the NZ stand-off, derided.

Meanwhile, the relationship between Fouroux and his players was beginning to deteriorate. His powers of motivation roused the French to their 1986 defeat of New Zealand, but his technical expertise is limited. This is hardly surprising, because when Ferrasse appointed him Fouroux had no coaching experience. Resentment was inevitable.

Fouroux in turn settled on Pierre Berbizier, his present captain, as his own coaching successor. Then 18 months ago Fouroux himself had a recent ex-player – Daniel Dubroca, his 1987 Grand Slam captain – foisted on him as assistant and decided he had had almost enough. But when Ferrasse asserted his authority, Fouroux quickly agreed to coach on.

The New Zealand tour was a watershed. The players rebelled and four – Berbizier, Serge Blanco, Philippe Sella and Laurent Rodriguez – went in deputation to Fouroux demanding more emphasis on skill and less on brute force. He did not like what he heard and four months later took his revenge.

After France had lost the first Test 32–15 to Australia in November, he dropped Blanco, Rodriguez and even Berbizier. Ferrasse, true to form, rallied to his protégé's aid. 'I have absolute confidence in Jacques Fouroux, he said.'

Ferrasse marched into the dressing-room and demanded that all fifteen be dropped. 'Even I could have done better,' the 72-year-old president fulminated. After that, Fouroux let the players off lightly by making only nine changes, and France won the second Test to save his reputation. They did not save his job because it was never at risk.

The relationship with Berbizier will never be the same again but the scrum-half was still restored as captain for the Welsh game a fortnight ago. His omission against Australia had been a not-so-gentle reminder that 'Napoleon' still had the absolute power on the field that Ferrasse had off it.

So we should take this comment from Robert Paparemborde, another of his exalted team-mates from '77, with a heavy pinch of sel de mer: 'Fouroux is not the autocratic general he is made out to be. Rugby players, certainly not French ones, don't wag their tail every time the coach orders. You'd better believe it.' The trouble is, Papa, no one else does.

From *The Independent*

Next, two studies in dedication: Ian Kirkpatrick of New Zealand, the inarticulate epitome of manly modesty, and Bob Hiller, probably the most meticulous of place-kickers in the game.

Black is In for All Black Skippers

Norman Harris

The captain of the All Blacks had been invited back to a Piccadilly pub, the other night, following a team reception. The atmosphere at the bar was cosy and intimate, the company admiring, and also good-looking. Within half-an-hour, Ian Kirkpatrick and a couple of his mates seemed well-ensconced.

Then, suddenly, the captain of the All Blacks got to his feet, quietly and courteously said good night to his companion, nodded to another Black blazer at the bar, and in the batting of an eye, the New Zealanders had gone.

Captain Kirkpatrick says he could have gone sooner. It was no hard decision. In fact, he brushes the thought aside. 'Well, you're here for a job,' he explains earnestly, 'not to socialize all night.'

Kirkpatrick, a great flank forward, is a comparatively young captain. He is not impressively articulate, and not an ostentatious leader on the field. But there is a certain solidity in his face – seriousness, even gravity – which suggests responsibility, and age well beyond his 26 years.

As for 'socializing', Kirkie says that at home, if he wants to go out, there's a hotel a mile or so from his house (hotels are the only pubs in New Zealand, and only recently were the hours extended beyond 6 pm).

'But I just can't drink with a clear conscience if there's a game coming up – an important club game, say – I can't drink and relax. I go home. Or I don't go at all.'

Hardly the George Best of New Zealand rugby – and there are not many of those there. On the field, he may be seen as brilliant, a stick of dynamite on the side of the All Blacks scrum, but statements about his being the 'greatest flanker in the world' are a real embarrassment to him.

His most famous try, certainly for British viewers, is his break-away from half-way, in the Christchurch test against the last Lions. Mention it, and a smile comes to his face. Evidently, it is often mentioned. Kirkie says it was 'lucky' and 'it just happened'.

'He had nowhere else to go,' says a friend.

'You're dead right,' Kirkie reacts as to a revelation, 'you're dead right there.'

In that series, lost to the Lions, there was some criticism about the New Zealand forwards. Wherever the fault lay, Kirkpatrick agrees that the forward play had got too loose (the result of runaway wins against provincial sides in South Africa) and he concedes that it was not nice being pushed around by the Lions' pack – 'It was a shock all right. Pretty demoralizing.'

But now the All Black pack is bigger than ever, and especially it is stronger in the crucial front row. They still believe in their superior 'hardness', as Kirkpatrick sees it. And this is a team that left home knowing it has to redeem New Zealand's rugby reputation.

'It's only when you get away on tour like this,' says Kirkpatrick, 'that you realize so many people back home are pinning their hopes on us. And you're very lucky to get away – there's so many thousands of players that you're representing.'

The All Black captain was wearing, as he spoke, regulation touring kit. So was everyone else. It hasn't changed much in many, many tours – except that this time the New Zealand Council was persuaded to change the shirts from white to pin-striped.

The Australian cricket team might appear here dressed as for a fashion showing, and the off-duty attire of the victorious Lions may have made them appear, in one New Zealander's eyes, 'like refugees from the King's Road' – but the All Blacks, steadfastly and proudly, wear the same grey slacks and black blazers of all their honourable predecessors.

'I've never taken anything else on tour,' says Kirkpatrick. 'It's all you've got to wear. It's all you *want* to wear.'

What Ian Kirkpatrick will make of the captaincy of the 1972–73 All Blacks hardly seems worth debating. The importance of the job will mean that it is done well.

From *The Sunday Times*

The Fine Art of Bob Hiller

John Reason

Bob Hiller was in the middle of his usual meticulous preparations when the referee told him to hurry up. This naturally disconcerted Hiller, because he understood that the change in the laws affecting the time allowed for a kick at goal meant that, short of deliberate time-wasting, a goalkicker was allowed to take his kick in his own style and his own time. Certainly, this was the interpretation of the law in Europe.

It is true that Hiller has a deliberate style of kicking, but like golfers who are great putters, he goes through exactly the same routine each time and sets himself up for the kick so carefully that he gives himself a far better chance of kicking the goal than more slapdash mortals.

Hiller kicks the ball off a tee. This has to be kicked out of the ground with his heel and then constructed like a horseshoe. If the ground is fairly firm, obviously it takes him some time to disturb enough divots to build a tee which is high enough to meet his requirements. Having done that, he cleans the ball, just as a golfer would clean the ball and dry it most carefully before putting. Then he examines both ends of the ball and studies its four panels. He says that one end of the ball is always better than the other for kicking and that one panel is always truer than the others and therefore better for holding the ball on course through the air. Having selected the rounder of the two ends to kick and which panel to place uppermost, Hiller settles the ball into the tee with as much care as a hen thrush placing an egg in a nest. He clears his nasal passages by spitting a couple of times, too. Then he stands up, with the toe of his right boot behind the ball, and walks back six paces, shaking his right leg to loosen the muscles as he goes. He makes the minimal adjustment he feels necessary to his position to put him on exactly the line he wants to run up to the ball and cleans the toe and side of his kicking boot on his left sock. If it is very muddy, he also cleans his studs. That done, he squares his shoulders and takes three deep breaths. It is at this time that he builds up his concentration, and it is at this time that the unknowing louts in the crowd usually give him the worst of their ribaldry. Once Hiller is ready to kick, he moves into the ball slowly and hits it with a sharp stabbing action. He does not use a big hip swing and a big follow through. In his judgment, this makes for inaccuracy. His results seem to prove his point.

This, then, was the kicking technique which Mr McDavitt thought fit to harass on that day at Hamilton. He not only told Hiller to hurry up but also once did it as he was beginning his run-up to the ball. It was scarcely surprising that Hiller missed two kicks in succession and that John Dawes thought it better to give the subsequent goalkicking to Barry John. Dawes also wanted to discuss the matter with the referee, but Hiller asked him not to bother.

From *The Victorious Lions*

The Genius of Carwyn James

John Reason

We end this sequence of cameos with a short piece from John Reason on the almost paranormal skills of Carwyn James. It was my good fortune to be in Llanelli just before their historic win over the 1972 All Blacks, and I shall never forget his tactical talk to the Llanelli players. In their darkened club-house the whining cinema projector gave us a black-and-white re-enact-ment of that heart-stopping fourth Test that had given the Lions the series the year before. First Going, the New Zealand half-back, came into focus. The sound was turned down, and Carwyn drew a word picture of the man and how to deal with him. Then the All Blacks pack, averaging sixteen stone a man, was shown in action but not, in Carwyn's view, shoving their full weight. They were binding wrongly. Llanelli were half a stone a man lighter, but weight, in his view, was not everything. Then a line-out and a maul. Carwyn's comments were colourful, but must be censored. His sum-ming up: 'When they're going forwards, they're magnificent. When they're going backwards, they look quite ordinary.' That Tuesday, Carwyn's magic worked. 'Who beat the All Blacks,' as the Llanelli song now runs, 'but Good Old Sospan Fach?'

Here John Reason pays tribute to Carwyn's achievement as coach to the 1971 Lions.

The Lions won not because they were overwhelmingly the better team but because they made better use of their resources than the All Blacks, and the man who put them into that happy position was Carwyn James. It was an incredible stroke of good fortune for the Lions to turn up a man like him so early in the history of coaching in Britain.

No one could possibly have known in advance what a success he would make of the job. He had been involved in the day-to-day routine of coaching Llanelli, who are one of the busiest as well as one of the most successful Welsh clubs, but as yet, the opportunity for coaching at a higher level in Britain is restricted by the lack of provincial football. However, the sheer pressure of preparing teams to meet Llanelli's crow-ded and high class fixtures list was an excellent grounding for the work he did on the Lions' tour. He knew the way to work before he went to New Zealand so he did not have to waste any time finding out how to do his job. Coaching is so much in its infancy in Britain that this was a precious asset.

Carwyn James had done his homework, too, months and months of it. He had taken advice from many people who had experience of New Zealand football and he had used every ounce of their brains. He had a dossier on everything and everybody, from the North Auckland scissors plays to referees, from the free-for-all barging of a New Zealand line-out to an analysis of the needs and the characters of the various New Zealand

Rugby writers. Carwyn James added a section about television, too, and became so good at it and appeared so often that when he was called on to say a few words at the gathering after the last Test, John Taylor drew a huge grin from everyone when he adopted a broad American accent and called out, 'And it's the Carwyn James show.'

The Lions' coach was a great listener and a great evaluator of opinion. He searched for the truth with quick, accurate questions and if he disagreed, he did not waste his time on damaging arguments. He simply closed off that section of his mind and pushed on to more fruitful ground. He quickly discerned the acute intellects in the touring party and he always took soundings of their opinions. He had a marvellous capacity for learning as well as for teaching and the knowledge that he absorbed on the tour each day was processed overnight so that the next day it was available to his players as a lesson they could easily assimilate. He paid great attention to detail even to the extent of having the players weighed each week to make sure that there were none of the astronomical increases in poundage shown by some of the 1968 Lions in South Africa.

James had such a grand strategy for the tour that he picked his first seven teams before he left Eastbourne and yet he always coached his players as individuals, and he always maintained an extraordinary flexibility as to the needs of the moment. He coached by encouragement and not by denigration. He did not abuse his players. If the players did things wrong, he said so, and in the early part of the tour, he introduced the lap of dishonour to punish careless work, but one of the foundations of his coaching was that he preferred the carrot to the whip.

Carwyn James usually worked sixteen hours a day. If he was not coaching or holding special training clinics, he was having tactical discussions or attending team meetings, and if he was not doing that, he was giving interviews or going off to talk to schools and clubs and meetings of referees. He was the most available of men, and despite the inevitable strain, he was never anything other than courteous. The strain, of course, was considerable. He always found sleep difficult, particularly on the night before a match, and the only time he stopped smoking was when he was in a track suit on the field . . .

The status to which Carwyn James elevated the job of coach created a situation which was quite new in the experience of British rugby teams touring abroad, and it was a measure of the quality of Doug Smith, the Lions' manager, that he not only accepted that situation but even encouraged it. As a British Lion himself, and one who had toured New Zealand as a player, Doug Smith could have been forgiven if he had given way to the temptation of thinking that he knew more about it than Carwyn James, who had never been to New Zealand.

As a Scot, too, Doug Smith must have harboured some apprehensions about the principle of giving so much responsibility to a coach. Indeed, he confessed as much late in the tour. This was only natural. His countrymen in previous generations have always had reservations about coaching. It was all the more to his credit, therefore, that he was a big enough man to efface himself, even though it must have been a lonely business, and to work unsparingly to give his coach and his players the best possible conditions in which to do their jobs . . .

Doug Smith's treatment of his players was considered, too. He did not make any favourites and he led them like a benevolent sergeant-major. He was always approachable but they knew who was boss.

As a doctor and a Rotarian, Doug Smith also found time to visit local hospitals and to talk to local Rotary clubs. Never can two men have given more of their time on tour than he and Carwyn James, and they richly deserved the tribute which was paid to them at the end by Jack Sullivan, the chairman of the New Zealand Rugby Council: 'This has been the best managed tour that has come to New Zealand in my experience.'

From *The Victorious Lions*

9 – 3

Max Boyce

Needless to say, the remarkable 1972 victory at Llanelli was hymned by Max Boyce. I can confirm that the Llanelli pubs quite literally did run dry on that historic night.

And when I'm old and my hair turns grey
And they put me in a chair
I'll tell my great-grandchildren
That their *Datcu* was there.

It was on a dark and dismal day
In a week that had seen rain,
When all roads led to Stradey Park
With the All Blacks here again.
They poured down from the valleys,
They came from far and wide;
There were twenty-thousand in the ground
And me and Dai outside!

The shops were closed like Sunday,
And the streets were silent still.
And those who chose to stay away
Were either dead or ill.
But those who went to Stradey, boys,
Will remember till they die
How New Zealand were defeated,
And how the pubs ran dry.

Oh, the beer flowed at Stradey
(Piped down from Felinfoel),
And the hands that held the glasses high
Were strong from steel and coal.
And the air was filled with singing,
And I saw a grown man cry.
Not because we'd won
But because the pubs ran dry!

Then dawned the morning after
On empty factories.
But we were still at Stradey –
Bloodshot absentees.
But we all had doctors' papers
And they all said just the same:
That we all had 'Scarlet Fever',
And we caught it at the game!

Now all the little babies
In Llanelli from now on
Will be christened Ray or Carwyn,
Derek, Delme, Phil or John.
And in a hundred years again
They'll sing this song for me
Of when the scoreboard read 'Llanelli 9,
Seland Newydd 3'.

And when I'm old and my hair turns grey,
And they put me in a chair,
I'll tell my great-grandchildren
That their *Datcu* was there.
And they'll ask to hear the story
Of that damp October day,
When I went down to Stradey
And I saw the 'Scarlets' play.

In a Dark and Secret World

Mike Burton and Steve Jones

There are two Burtons in this book and neither was born with that name. Richard Burton, as we have seen, was born Jenkins; Mike Burton, the rugged and uncompromising Gloucester and England prop forward, was born Harrop, to a sixteen-year-old unmarried mother in 1945. He fought his way from a bleak, rough and deprived childhood to his present eminence as one of the most successful businessmen in sport. Here he gives us a unique insight into the arcane world of the front row forward.

Front row play is in a world of its own; a place for experience and sheer, iron strength; at the top level, it is vitally important. In many ways, propping can only be learned in the heat of the scrum: there are so many little tricks of binding, foot placement and sheer villainy. Like coal mining, it is so hard it gives rise to a certain wry humour, largely because there is so little to laugh about. A side on top in the scrummage through the superiority of its props gains a tremendous psychological boost as well as a practical one. It is satisfying to see the opposition struggling from the scrum where all the action starts, and, also, the side going forward finds it easier to keep up the momentum in the resulting play. The side being put under pressure in the scrum are back on their heels – the forwards have to run backwards to rejoin the game when they get up.

Quite naturally, international prop forwards are a different breed; they are even supposed to have their own trade union. Over the years I set myself on some collision courses, because while I was considered an aggressive prop there were plenty of others who fancied they were every bit as effective. This made for some bone-crunching confrontations, some nasty moments, and some genuinely funny situations. I also came to grips, literally, with some of the biggest, hardest and most single-minded men in any sport. Props are often the characters most loved by the supporters, and the most disliked by opposing supporters.

Very few people have any inkling of what is really happening after the two front rows have come thumping together, with the resulting swaying and bucking. In fact, the only people who can speak with real authority are the players involved. On countless occasions I have heard or read explanations of what has happened in the scrums in a particular match, what I was supposed to have done to their prop and what he was supposed to have done to me, and it seems as if a completely different match has been watched.

I was mainly noted as a scrummager, and I revelled in the battles both physical and psychological. What follows describes the realities of the scrums when our heads locked and the scrum-halves prepared to feed in the ball. It is also, I hope, an insight into front row play as a whole. If you didn't once see me in open play in any match, at least I may be able to convince you that I was up to something in my own little world.

The first of my tenets of front row play was always to keep the other front row guessing, which required a full repertoire of moves and tricks, some of which were allowed and some which were not. I always had to keep one step ahead of the other prop and switch the point of attack if he had developed counters to my last move. As tight head, I was packed down against the opposite loose head on the right of my hooker. On our own put-in, I had to stand as comfortably as possible and take the scrum to a good height so that my hooker would be comfortable too. That was basically defensive, because each team expects to win the ball on its own put-in and had to withstand the pressure from the opposition. I came into my own when it was the opposition's put-in, and we wanted to attack it.

For a couple of scrums, often I would attempt nothing at all. I would pack down with a straight back, standing still and square to my hooker. I would attempt none of my ploys. I might just exert a little pressure on the neck of the loose head, but that was all. He might be packing fairly high and be comfortable, but I would allow that. Then, after a few scrums of inactivity, I would throw out my foot and strike for the ball myself as it came in, just when the opposition were becoming confident and making a mental note that Burton wasn't too much of a handful after all. Of course, on the right of the scrum and nearer the opposition put-in, I was far nearer the ball than the opposition hooker. Often, I was able to hook the ball back through my own scrummage before the ball had got anywhere near their hooker. I'd be striking the instant it left the hands of their scrum-half.

The advantages of winning the ball against the head are numerous. Firstly, it is a blow to the pride of the opposition front row. (After all, there are numerous funny stories told about front rows coming off the field proclaiming victory by 2–0 or 3–1 or whatever; they mean that they won the scrums and omit to mention that their side actually lost the match 66–3!) There is also the obvious advantage that you have provided possession for your side, and your backs may even be given a yard start on the opposing back row, who are perhaps still searching in vain for the ball coming out on their own side as expected. Perhaps most important, it may unsettle the hooker and his props. They don't want to lose any more and may be tempted to press too hard, to infringe.

For example, if I had some success with my strike for the ball, the opposition hooker would often start flapping away with his leg like a Bluebell girl. He would be determined to get his strike in first, and be all too aware that I was having first bite of the cherry – and probably giving him some verbal opinions on how slow he had become. He would strike faster and faster and often be penalized for foot-up. All he had to do to counter me, in fact, was to get his loose head to take the scrum low. If the tight head is forced to scrummage low then his feet have to be placed further back out of the way of the ball as it comes down the tunnel. Once the scrum was low and the tight head's flailing feet were safely back down the scrum, a nice, slow put-in by the scrum-half would enable the hooker to make a clean strike. Yet my snap hooking was often fruitful; teams panicked, failed to use the counter, or were just not good enough to take the scrum down to a level at which I and my foot could not operate.

Mind you, if they did counter me, I had a counter-counter. With my feet right back, I was able to take the loose head even lower, just below a comfortable height for him. He should have been standing firm, steady and comfortable to set up his hooker, but by taking the scrum that little bit lower he would be under pressure and his hooker would be in a worse position as a consequence. As with all my moves in the scrum, I made them in the last few split-seconds before the ball came in. After all, there is no point in charging into the opposition, bucking and fighting like a sumo wrestler when the ball is still in the back row of the stand.

With my man a little uncomfortable, my next move would come when the scrum-half's feet appeared by the tunnel and he prepared to put the ball in. I would then increase the pressure on the loose head to take him down even lower so that he would then be in a very poor position – ideally with a bent back. The hooker would be calling desperately for him to take the scrum back up, and trying to see underneath for the put-in. Then, I would wait for the put-in itself. It is very easy to tell when the ball is coming even if you are low: you can see the scrum-half's knees bend, and you know he is making that final little stoop before he flicks the ball in.

As the ball was coming in I would then increase the pressure to the absolute maximum. The hooker would find his position worsening by the millisecond, and be forced to scrabble blindly for the ball, or be unable to strike for it at all, or kick it straight through our scrum. Most hookers use the 'tap' to indicate to the scrum-half when the ball should be put in. They tap their left hand on the loose head prop and that is the signal for the scrum-half to feed. The hooker does not tap unless he is in a good position: so either my late move would come after he had tapped and it was too late, the damage to his position already done; or he would feel the increased pressure and delay his tap so long that the scrum-half was penalized. If the opposition decided to feed as soon as the scrums came together so that I didn't have time to put on the pressure, I would be ready for that too.

If a front row can continually cause such disruption, the implications are numerous. I have already spoken of the effect on morale and the practical drawbacks of being under pressure in the scrum. But there are other effects too. The scrum-half could quite easily become engrossed in the scrum battle, trying desperately to follow the progress of his hooker's attempts to counter, waiting for the 'tap' and taking in the front row's instructions for a quick ball, a slow ball, anything to put them one jump ahead again. The scrum-half's mind is taken off his own game, and, vitally, off his service to and understanding with his fly-half.

Naturally, not all these moves worked for me all the time. There were front rows around who knew the tricks, and the counters, and had a few ideas of their own. Sometimes, the disruption my front row and I caused was minor. But often we managed to agitate, to irritate, to pressurize and to win the ball. I found that the Springboks in 1972 were susceptible, so it was not only at club level that things came off. I would come out with part of my repertoire and gain great satisfaction if the opposition were fooled. There was always the last variation, too – the eight-man shove. Everyone, the front row and even the hooker, would pack down in a powerful shoving position. We would concede the strike but, as it was made, unleash such a combined drive that we would either cause slow and erratic ball for the other side or even push them right off it and win it ourselves.

Some props, the best and strongest, would attack the opposition scrum by going low with a straight back: Ray McLoughlin, Fran Cotton and Phil Blakeway used that method. All the opposition prop could do was attempt to twist them, and then they would play their ace. When the ball came in, and with the pressure coming on from the colleagues behind, they would raise the scrum six inches. That was the opposite of my move, of trying to disrupt by lowering – but lifting could be equally effective. The opposition would find their position changing at the vital moment. Very, very few props were good enough to do that, though.

Yet things are changing. Until now, a top tight head has needed to have a full range of abilities. He has had to be tremendously strong and experienced, good with his feet, and a poacher of the ball. Ability with a bunch of fives has been useful though not essential. But now the skills of front row play are waning, mainly because they are no longer needed. The eight-man shove is no longer the last resort, nor even a cunning variation nor a frequent ploy: it is the standard operation on the opposition put-in. The tight head is rarely called upon to strike, or take his man up, down or anywhere. He merely has to take his feet back and push like the devil. The day of the skilful small hooker is also over. Today's hookers are big men and wide men – scrummagers first and hooking technicians second. In many ways, an ideal international pack for the modern scrum would con- sist of eight well-trained gorillas, who all bound tight and pushed as a unit. It may be effective but the skills needed are almost nil.

The recent new laws are a further blow for the tight head. He has to bind on the back of the loose head and is unable to make those small adjustments to the height of the scrummage which cause dismay and disruption. On the other hand, the loose head can bind wherever he wishes, and can even rest his hand on his outside knee if he feels tired. With the hooker allowed to use that 'tap' signal, things are stacked against the attacking tight head even more.

All this is good news, of course, for those who dismiss props and hookers as lunatics who prevent the game flowing freely by their insistence on having their own little game within a game. People bemoan the fact that the skills of thatchers, blacksmiths, master carpenters and the like are no longer needed – so why not tight head props too?

The other great factor in the decline of front row skills (and I am talking about front row *skills* rather than front row *effectiveness*: I'm not saying some of the modern ploys are not effective) is rank bad refereeing. Like those people I spoke of earlier who pontificate on front row play from the tenth row of the stand, referees often haven't a clue what is going on in the front row. Some of them can just about work out when a hooker has struck for the ball too early or when the scrum-half has rolled the ball in crooked, but when it comes to the other laws affecting the scrum – bind- ing, angle of packing, and so on – they are guessing. In one of the scrums at the start of every match, most referees will gravely tap hookers on the back and mumble something about binding. Then they will go away and everyone will go back to infringing their chosen law.

In my playing days, I would stand up and look at the referee with a serious expression, nodding and agreeing enthusiastically as he spoke. Then I would go down and make my move. John Pullin, far from binding over his loose head, had his hand in his loose head's shorts pockets for four seasons, which allowed him to creep to his right a lot nearer the tunnel entrance when going for a ball against the head. And to think I am castigating referees for not applying the laws properly! I must sound like a criminal dashing into a police station and complaining about the lawless state of the country.

Sadly, the rugby world is no longer full of clever tight heads. Ah well. I'll sit by my fireside and remember how front row play used to be.

From *Never Stay Down*

With What Result I Know Not

M. H. Bloxam

The origins of rugby football are so well known that they hardly need recounting here. For the record, however, here is the story of how it all started, as told in The Meteor, *Rugby school's magazine, in an article on 10 October 1876 quoting M. H. Bloxam. He went to Rugby in the same year as William Webb Ellis, the boy who first took the ball in his arms and ran with it. The trouble is that Bloxam did not record it till 53 years after the event and four years after Ellis died. Still, as the official history of the Rugby Football Union comments, something very like this must have happened. We know little about Ellis, except that he went up to Brasenose College, Oxford, took holy orders and ended up as Rector of St Clement Danes, later to be the church of the Royal Air Force. There is a tablet in the church to his memory. His death was a mystery until October 1959, when the late Ross McWhirter found his grave at Menton, where he was probably following the English custom of wintering on the Riviera. Since then, the French Rugby Union has tended the grave and fifteen red roses are placed on it annually.*

A boy of the name of Ellis – William Webb Ellis – a town boy and a foundationer, who at the age of nine entered the school after the mid-summer holidays in 1816, who in the second half-year of 1823, was, I believe, a praeposter, whilst playing Bigside at football in that half-year, caught the ball in his arms. This being so, according to the then rules, he ought to have retired back as far as he pleased, without parting with the ball, for the combatants on the opposite side could only advance to the spot where he had caught the ball, and were unable to rush forward until he had either punted it or placed it for someone else to kick, for it was by means of these placed kicks that most of the goals were in those days kicked, but the moment it touched the ground the opposite side might rush on. Ellis, for the first time, disregarded this rule, and on catching the ball, instead of retiring backwards, rushed forward with the ball in his hands towards the opposite goal, with what result as to the game I know not, neither do I know how this infringement of a well known rule was followed up, or when it became, as it is now, the standing rule.

Mr Ellis was high up in the school and as to scholarship of fair average abilities. He left school in the summer of 1825, being the second Rugby Exhibitioner of that year, and was entered at Brasenose College, Oxford. He subsequently took Holy Orders and at a later period became Incumbent of the church of St Clement Danes, Strand. He died on the Continent some years ago (January 24, 1872, a year after the founding of Rugby Union, of which, therefore, he probably knew nothing). When at school, though in a high form, Mr Ellis was not what we should call a 'swell', at least none of his compeers considered him as such; he had, however, plenty of assurance, and was ambitious of being thought something of. In fact, he did an act which if a fag had ventured to have done, he would probably have received more kicks than commendations. How oft it is that such small matters lead to such great results!

From *The Meteor*

Football Company v. Harlequins

Next we come to the historic game between the newly formed Football Company and Harlequins – the first played under the rules of the new Rugby Union in 1871. The abolition of hacking in the new rules obviously improved the game immensely. Two of the Football Company team that day were to play for England: J. E. Bentley, who had two games against Scotland as half-back; and Francis Luscombe, who won six caps, became a vice-president of the RFU, which he had helped to found, and was a noted race horse owner who won the Cambridgeshire twice.

The members of this company inaugurated their establishment on Saturday last by the above match on their ground at Peckham Rye. Play commenced at 3.30, and as all were eager to get to business, the game was very rapid for the first quarter of an hour, both teams being apparently pretty equal. The warm work, however, soon found out the untrained ones, and the Harlequins were slowly but surely forced towards their own goal. Thus, playing a defensive game, it was some time before they were compelled to rouge the ball. After about twenty minutes, the play, having been principally confined to the forward ranks, was transferred to the half-backs, the Harlequins' captain making some good attempts to get away, but the holding ground militated against quick running. E. P.

Vacher then by a very clever run scored a touch-down, which was neatly placed by A. H. Young, who thus kicked the first goal for the Company. After this event the Harlequins roused themselves, and drove their opponents back for a time, the forwards still having all the work, Berkeley, Hewitt, and Schooley bearing the brunt of it for them, while Luscombe, Riley, and Sclater were prominent in their exertions to prevent the former getting through. After the rouge the Harlequins were almost penned, and the leather was driven close to their goal and touch-line. Another try was obtained, and failed; the ball coming out of a scrimmage was cleverly taken by A. Tucker, who dropped a well-judged goal, and 'no side' was called at 5.15. The evident want of condition told very much against the Harlequins, and the lightness of their team; at times there was a great want of energy on the part of some of their forwards, who appeared to be new men, who had no knowledge of each other's play; while the Company's representatives immediately after starting went to work in the most business-like manner; the passing and playing together were remarkably good, seeing that they are quite a new team. Bentley (half-back) and Vacher played remarkably well, while in the forward ranks F. Luscombe was unexceptionably brilliant. The whole team, with one exception, were hard-working and in good training. This was the first match where the play was under the Rugby Union Rules, and they worked admirably, more especially having the ball down at once, and thus preventing the long and serious mauls so long complained of in the London–Rugby game, while hacking through was entirely dispensed with, to the evident improvement of the good feeling of all players.

From the newspaper collection of Mr E. P. Vacher of Gypsies Club now in the library of the Rugby Football Union at Twickenham.

Play the Game, You Cads

It is one of the principal delights of rugby that it has engendered a vast literature of anecdote and epigram. I give a few here which have always appealed to me. Taken in sequence, they demonstrate the dramatic change in attitude from the unthinking orthodoxy and unquestioning patriotism of a man like L. R. Tosswill who served with distinction in the First World War and was one of the earliest of broadcasters on rugby, all the way to the flip cynicism of modern players.

In conclusion I would like to refer to one of our dinners a few years ago at which I expressed the opinion that the three greatest civilizing influences since the Christian Era were to be found in the work of the Salvation Army, secondly in the institution of the Boy Scouts, and thirdly in the spread of outdoor games, particularly rugby football. My belief in the importance of rugby football in the formation both of individual and national character is increasingly profound. – C. C. HOYER MILLAR

. . . he [the rugby player] answered the call of his country as he would to the whistle – without question. – L. R. TOSSWILL

A game for gentlemen in all classes, but never for a bad sportsman in any class. – BISHOP CAREY

A bomb under the west stand on an international day at Twickenham would end fascism in England for a generation. – PHILIP TOYNBEE

An international at Twickenham is more than a mere spectacle. It is an immense family party. It is the gathering of the clan. – ALEC WAUGH

Twickenham is the last fortress of the Forsytes. – IVOR BROWN

A great sportsman, both on and off the field, it was Edgar Mobbs who punted a rugby ball into 'No Man's Land' in the 1914–18 war and fell at the head of his men, when leading them in a charge on the enemy trenches. – GERARD HOLMES

Training which would be too severe for the rapidly grown or anaemic boy is the best possible discipline for the flabby, lazy, greedy boy, or the boy who prefers sitting over the fire with a book to the free air of heaven. – DR ALMOND, Headmaster of Loretto

So far as kicking a man on the ball is concerned, always remember that, played cleanly, rugby football is quite dangerous enough for most people's liking, and that a man who kicks another man intentionally is a blackguard and a coward.

Recently a well-known international, in his book on rugby, said that a gentleman kicks another with his instep instead of with the toe of his boot. Personally I think that no gentleman ever kicks another. – I. B. M. STUART

It is because of the freedom of rugger and its consequent risks that it breeds hardiness, which in these days of cocktails and lounge-lizards is a quality to be encouraged. – W. W. WAKEFIELD

My mother was up there in the stand. She doesn't know a bugger about rugby, but she knows we won. – DELME THOMAS, Llanelli's captain, after the famous Llanelli 9, New Zealand 3, on 31.10.72

'What do you mean coming off the field smiling? You lost.' – LONDON WELSH OFFICIAL TO FIRST XV CAPTAIN.

Two Cambridge University players were called to Twickenham to take part in an England Trial. On their expenses claim after the game they included three pounds for rail fares.

The RFU treasurer of the day demurred. 'I happen to know that the fare is actually £2 19s 11d,' he objected, handing over three pound notes to each of the young men and demanding a penny change. They obliged with a bad grace.

Capped a month later the pair came again to Twickenham to represent England for the first time. Once more they met the treasurer afterwards to present expenses sheets.

This time, however, they had written: 'Train fare to and from Twickenham, £2 19s 11d. Toilet, one penny.'

BBC Wales television director Dewi Griffiths recalls playing for a suburban Cardiff club in his younger days.

The team kit was sent to a nearby convent for laundering. It always came back neatly listed, 'Fifteen jerseys @ 3d, 3s 9d; fifteen pairs of shorts @ 4d, 5s,' and so on.

One Saturday a player inadvertently left his jock-strap in the bundle of kit. The nuns dealt with it resourcefully.

At the bottom of the list was the item, 'One crash-helmet, 6d.'

The political tensions in Dublin during the early seventies prompted Scotland and Wales to pull out of fixtures scheduled for Lansdowne Road. England, however, honoured the engagement, only to lose 18–9.

According to Willie John McBride, however, it was England captain John Pullin who brought the house down at the post-match banquet.

'We may not be the best team in the world,' he told his audience. 'But at least we turn up.'

At Llanelli RFC's Centenary Banquet Lord Elwyn Jones recounted the story of the Welsh resistance leader Caradoc, who was taken prisoner in battle by the Romans, shipped back to Rome, and condemned to die back in the great arena there.

He was buried up to his neck in the sand, after which an enormous male rhinoceros was released from its cage. Spotting the Welshman's head, the beast launched itself upon a thunderous charge, intent on goring the target.

Its eyesight, however, was not up to the task, and it completely missed with its horn thrust, being carried over the top of Caradoc by sheer momentum. At which point the victim managed to lift his head far enough to bite savagely into the rhino's vitals. It ran away squealing with pain.

Then for the first time, according to Lord Elwyn Jones, was heard a cry from the bloodthirsty mob around the arena which has often since that time echoed around the Twickenham terraces: 'Play fair, you bloody Welshman!'

Since I was glad to see that a true story in which I myself figured had already crept into one rugby anthology, David Parry-Jones's admirable Out of the Ruck, *perhaps I should repeat it as I remember it here.*

I had been invited to speak at Llanelli, the little steel town in West Wales where rugby is a religion. I was led, like a lamb to the slaughter, into a seething cavern packed with curly-haired, black-eyed, barrel-chested, Welsh-speaking steelworkers and introduced by the Llanelli chairman as follows: 'Well, boys, tonight we are going to be addressed by Mr Godfrey Smith, who was educated at Oxford University, where as president of the Union he took over from Sir Robin Day and handed on to Mr Jeremy Thorpe.' Voice from the back: 'Reverse pass was it?' Collapse of audience. Collapse of speaker.

A View from the Land of the Forward Pass

Bob Donahue

Bob Donahue, who works for the International Herald Tribune *in Paris, is one of that small band of Americans who are masters both of rugby and of his native football code. His comparison between the two games is instructive; after all, they stem from the same root. Not too many of us this side of the water realize that the first college football game – in 1869, between Princeton and Rutgers – was played with a round ball and scoring through the goal. In 1873 soccer still prevailed as the college game; three years later rugby – as then understood – had superseded it. Harvard was dominant in the change-over, but it was a Yale man, the legendary half-back and later coach, Walter C. Camp, who dominated the divergence between the two sets of rules over the next half-century. A transatlantic C. B. Fry, he was a phenomenally gifted all-rounder and paradigm of the American Dream who rose – effortlessly as it seemed – to be chairman of the New Haven Clock company. It was he who introduced the eleven-man team, the unrestricted feed back from the scrimmage, the three – later four – downs that governed possession, and the characteristic grid pattern that was its natural corollary. American football is now on all our television screens, but rugby flourishes in the United States and the American Eagles will be competing at the World Cup in autumn 1991. Nor should we forget that America are the reigning Olympic rugby champions – having won the contest in the 1924 Games, when our kind of football was last included in them.*

The Five Nations rugby openers in Edinburgh and Dublin (Saturday) and the Super Bowl in Miami (Sunday) come this year on the same weekend. From the coincidence flows an opportunity for millions to make comparisons.

The American ball is smaller, the better to pitch it. Rugby's pitch, as the field is usually called, is wider – which is just as well, since a rugby team has 15 players compared to American football's 11.

Still, all those substitutions make a Super Bowl seem to have a cast of thousands, many of whom are officials. In order to get off a rugby pitch, you have to convince a doctor that you've broken something.

In Miami, they'll be scoring touchdowns without touching down. The misnomer is a genealogical pointer. In rugby you still have to touch the ball down. (And the solitary referee has to see you do it.) The four-point score thus obtained is called a try – because now you can try to convert it.

Kicking the ball was the main thing in the early days. Which is why all that running and passing in Miami is called football.

The most obvious similarity this weekend will be the physical contact. 'I think the very violence is one of the great things about the game,' Vince Lombardi once said, 'because a man has to learn control.'

There is death and injury. 'The danger has always been there in rugby,' Gerald Davies, a former Welsh star, conceded last year. 'But rugby has survived because of the grace of reasonable men, gentle men by and large, who have known where to draw the line.'

Survived, yes. The kids were playing it (more or less) at Rugby School in England in the 1820s. When they got to nearby Cambridge, they missed their old game. The rest of the story is much about wrangles to impose or change rules. 'Rugby rules' – now imperiously just 'The Laws' – conquered the world from placid Warwickshire.

In British clubs, soccer (association football) and rugger (rugby football) coalesced as forever-to-be-rival sports in the 1860s. A decade later, a Princeton undergraduate named Woodrow Wilson was the prime campaigner in turning American colleges away from soccer. 'Rugby has a great advantage over the association game,' Wilson said. 'All the croakers in our midst must be silenced!'

Scotland challenged England to the first international rugby match in 1871. Ireland joined the fray in 1875 – south and north united, as they remain in the Irish Rugby Football Union today. Wales played its first international match in 1881, South Africa in 1891, Australia in 1899, New Zealand in 1903, France in 1906.

That last year saw the first forward pass in American football. Woodrow Wilson, by now president of Princeton, had been involved in the collegiate rules change.

Scrimmage and *scrummage* are the same word. Rugby has eight forwards and seven backs. American football typically has seven linemen and four backs. The big men are up front, face to face. 'Matches are won in the forwards,' says the adage in rugby – where the offense has to start by winning the ball in combat.

Much streamlined over the years, the rugby scrum has three rows shoving on each side – in front, a hooker (No. 2) is supported by props (1 and 3); locks (4 and 5) are behind them; a third row, the so-called loose forwards, is composed of a No. 8 between flankers (6 and 7). The ball, flipped in by the scrumhalf (9), is 'hooked' back between the hooker's legs.

The same spirit of disengagement that gave us the forward pass separated American linemen into facing rows. The ball comes back between the legs of a center flanked by guards. Center is hooker, guards are props, tackles are locks, ends are flankers. The game has downs and turnovers – as does rugby league, an 1895 offshoot with 13-man teams.

American football is super-specialized. Rugby has no padding, and the match is over in about 90 minutes. Americans block for one runner. In rugby everybody carries, passes, tackles. Absurd pile-ups occur in both sports.

Backs hog the glory. American football typically aligns a quarterback, two halfbacks and a fullback. Rugby's unreformed arithmetic has a scrumhalf (9), a flyhalf (10), two centers (12 and 13), two wings (11 and 14) and a fullback (15). In most of the world, Nos. 9 and 10 are called halfbacks; the wings and centers are called threequarters. But New Zealanders call Nos. 10 and 12 the first and second five-eighth.

Anyhow, America's long pass is a glory. The technical equivalent in rugby, precision punting by the flyhalf, pales in comparison. In terms of thrill, rugby offers the chess suspense, crowd roaring in crescendo, of loose forwards and threequarters probing and sweeping toward a breakthrough – the try.

The big London crowd was pro-American at Twickenham, world rugby's shrine stadium, when the U.S. national team took on England in 1977. So was the Sydney crowd at the World Cup in 1987, when England beat the Yanks again. New Zealand beat France in the final.

Argentina, Romania, Japan, the United States, Canada, Fiji, the Soviet Union and Italy head world rugby's second tier. 'If we could just have a Super Bowl between Russia and the United States, instead of all those tanks and ballistic missiles,' Paul Brown of the Cleveland Browns once mused. The U.S.A. lost to the U.S.S.R., 31–16, in a rugby test in Moscow this past September that the American press didn't notice.

In London this week, Five Nations rugby competes with the Super Bowl for space on the sports pages. Rugby's dead ball zone is gridiron's end zone. Touch is the sideline. Ruck, maul, scrum, punt, hack, chip, pass, goal – most of rugby's one-syllable schoolboy words are Greek to American football fans.

From Maine comes an L. L. Bean catalogue plugging five choices of 'Striped American Rugby Shirt.' But really, the football tribes speak different languages. The Geological Survey has determined the geographic center of North America to be a place called Rugby, North Dakota, but in 1989 that's just another coincidence.

From *International Herald Tribune*

Goodbye to Glory

Terry McClean

Goodbye to Glory, the book Terry McClean wrote about the 1976 All Black tour of South Africa, has been called the finest account of a rugby tour ever written. The political situation in South Africa compounded the problems in the All Black camp and led them to disaster. Indeed, it is something of a shock to the average British rugby lover to realize that the Springboks have had much the better of their encounters with the All Blacks over all the years. This series, which was to have restored All Black pride, was in effect lost at the first Test, as McClean recounts. Confusingly, three Robertsons were on the field that day: Ian, the Springbok full-back; Duncan, the All Black full-back and Bruce, the All Black centre. The All Blacks won the second Test comfortably; South Africa the vital third – a game marked by gratuitous violence – and the Springboks tied up the contest with a hotly disputed 15–14 win in the fourth and final Test. The All Blacks flew home with their hearts in their boots.

South Africa 16, New Zealand 7

It is the quaint and pleasant custom at the King's Park in Durban for spectators of the Rugby matches on that magnificent field to go to their cars at the end of play, take out barbecue stands and while cooking steaks and chops and sausages to toss down their throats beer and spirits, copiously. Also they argue the events of the game. On such an evening as this when, long after the whistle for no-side, the temperature was still about 25°, the smoke from scores of fires lifted vertically in the tranquil air.

Taking with it, on this particular day, the dreams of the All Blacks. Dreams of the glory of an unbeaten Test series. Dreams of the feat of becoming the first touring team, in the whole history of encounters between the two countries, to win the First Test. Dreams of superiority, of refined skills, of quality play untarnished by avoidable errors.

For these three past years, these All Blacks had conditioned them-selves for this moment in their lives. In two tours in one year, they had played unbeaten through Australia and then to Ireland, Cardiff and London, yielding but two drawn games in 21 matches. In the next year, they had beaten Scotland in monsoon conditions by four goals to nil. Their wind-up to the tour of South Africa, defeat of Ireland only a fortnight before they set out for their opening game at East London, was not con-vincing. In fact the televised showing of this match heartened many thousands of South Africans into believing the chosen All Black team would not be superhuman. Nevertheless, three years of success were encouraging. They suggested that New Zealand had produced a team capable of playing a lively, imaginative game which by its pace would cause opponents to wilt and turn bedraggled in that last quarter hour when dreams turn into glories and greatness reaches out a beckoning hand.

> I'm forever blowing bubbles (says the old song),
>> Pretty bubbles in the air.
> They fly so high, nearly reach the sky.
>> Then like my dreams, they fade and die.

So with the All Blacks. Their defeat by a goal, a try, a penalty goal and a drop goal to a try and a penalty goal had many causes. One was a decision by Mr Ian Gourlay so unfortunate and so palpably wrong that he was not again invited to control a match on the tour. Because of it, the All Blacks were denied a drawn game and thus some fragments of glory. But this was not the most serious feature of their play, nor, indeed, the most serious feature of the day. The propensity to error of the New Zealanders was the theme which ran through the game.

Ken Stewart and Paul Bayvel gazed at a ball lying in the South African in-goal and which invited no more than a tap to become a try. Terror spurted through Bayvel more quickly than triumph through Stewart. The chance was lost. Duggie Bruce kicked far down the field and Bruce Robertson, swooping after it, had a try at command. But Mr Gourlay ruled Robertson had started from in front of the ball and a scrum was formed 40 metres up the field. Andy Leslie was shockingly unlucky when he dived at a ball on the very line, on one side of the South African upright, and found that it had popped the other side, out of his reach – but if he had fractionally hesitated, might he not have identified with the bounce? Ian Kirkpatrick plunged at the South African defensive wall and by prodigious wrenches and fends sought to break into the clear. But he neglected, in making these breaks, the consideration that team-mates might be better placed if they were given the ball.

In a strategical sense, the All Blacks continued to parade their blunders big and their blunders small which determined the loss of the match because they never tried for the consistent, rhythmical chain-passing movement to the wings which is fundamental to sound Rugby. Worst of all were the errors which let Gerrie Germishuys and Edrich Krantz score tries. Duncan Robertson had Germishuys side-on, the touchline not far away, as the admittedly brilliant winger slashed down the field. Robertson's tackle was made high, almost up to the shoulders. With a wiggle of his hips and a shrug of his shoulders, Germishuys escaped the clasp and sped on. Krantz scored by closely supporting Bayvel as the latter broke for 27 metres on the blindside. The break should not have happened. Kirkpatrick first and Leslie second should have nabbed Bayvel.

The last score of all, a drop goal by Ian Robertson from far out in the field, was also the consequence of blunder. Duncan Robertson, moving out of his goal area, kicked far up the field. He had no choice as to this. The situation had been desperate. But he did have a choice as to direction and it was in this that he failed. Ian Robertson was in splendid isolation, 10 metres clear of All Black or Springbok, when he struck at the ball.

'Springboks,' the 1949 South African captain, Felix du Plessis, had warned on Test match eve, 'do not make mistakes.' Many a year before, in 1937, the Springbok captain, Philip Nel, enunciated to a young sprog of the Rugby trail, Terry McLean, his theory as to test matches. These, said Nel, must always end in scoreless draws because 15 perfect players representing one country were opposed by 15 perfect players of the other and, naturally, perfect players did not make mistakes. But, said Nel, the factor common to all human effort was fallibility. The presence of this, the propensity toward error, was therefore constant; and the team which by taking suitable safeguards reduced its proportion of error, if possible to negligible amounts, must come out on top.

Case Study Number One: South Africa versus New Zealand. King's Park, Durban, 24 July 1976. The Springboks also made their errors. By an irony, the most diabolical was by their captain, Morné du Plessis, who happened to be the son of Felix, the man who inveighed against mistakes by Springboks. Immediately after half-time, Morne's intended pass to Peter Whipp was cut off by Grant Batty who, racing and dodging, reached almost the try-line before he was brought down. Going to ground, he flicked a pass to Stewart and the latter, brilliantly, flung a high pass to Lyn Jaffray, who scored in the corner. There were other South African errors, too. One, a serious error of judgment, was the apprehension that their leading line-out players, John Williams and Moaner van Heerden, would demolish Peter Whiting and Hamish Macdonald in the battle for the ball within the lines and that, at the line-out's end, du Plessis, 6 ft 6 in (1.98 m) tall, would make a mockery of his contest with Stewart or Leslie. In the event, the All Blacks won this encounter within the encounter by 19 clearcut possessions to 13. It was a remarkable achievement. But the sum of South Africa's blunders big and blunders small was much, much less than the sum of New Zealand's. Ergo, South Africa victorious. Quod erat demonstrandum.

Was the experiment of playing Duncan Robertson at full-back sensible? South Africans thought not. They were delighted. Far, far away, New Zealanders thought not, too. They were appalled. Volleys of criticism were launched at the All Blacks' coach, John Stewart, who was identified as selector-in-chief, if not sole selector, of all teams of the tour. Let it be said that the two blunders Robertson made in failing to tackle Germishuys and in offering Ian Robertson his comfortable drop goal were ghastly, they probably would not have been made by a full-back of the first class. Yet, what was Stewart to do? Laurie Mains had failed the goals and a tackle that turned the Western Province game. Kit Fawcett was still a boy who saw stars every time he looked in a mirror – and the surreptitious swim he took in the sea on the morning of the Test ('Don't tell anyone you saw me, will you?' he said to photographer Peter Bush), was not, perhaps, the act of a man sensitive to the responsibilities of Test match rugby.

Stewart consulted an inner group of senior All Blacks. He talked with Robertson himself. The former said, to a man, that neither Mains nor Fawcett had earned the place. The latter said he had played full-back a number of times for his Dunedin club, Zingari, and thought the position the best in the game. It may be said, incidentally, that if Terry Mitchell and Neil Purvis, the second-string wings, had been of international quality, Stewart would probably have played Bryan Williams at back. The choice of Robertson was a case of needs must where the devil drives.

Undoubtedly the biggest blunder of all was the decision of the New Zealand Rugby Union, made in secret in April, 1975, not to accept the South African Rugby Board's offer of neutral referees for the Tests of the tour. Mr Gourlay and the All Blacks were equal sufferers. In many eyes, not all of them New Zealand's, Mr Gourlay lost his reputation. The President of the South African Rugby Board, Dr Danie Craven, said there had been no infringement in the maul, the penalizing of which cost the All Blacks a drawn game. It was an unusual and condemnatory statement by an official of such importance.

The maul was formed about five minutes from the end of play when Leslie made a break and Kirkpatrick joined him. As Bruce took hold of the ball, he was enclasped by All Blacks and South Africans. The maul moved nearer and nearer the Springbok tryline. Bruce could see it a few centimetres ahead of him. In another second, he would somehow have dropped to ground, over the line, with the ball for a try; and even the All Blacks would surely have placed the goal, so close was the place to the goalposts. Ahead of Bruce, Leslie's head became visible. He was engulfed, he had no chance of escaping the clutches of the maul. A few metres ahead of him, standing in the in-goal area, Mr Gourlay inspected the situation. Of a sudden, he blew his whistle, penalizing Leslie, so he later said, for joining the maul illegally.

This was nonsense. Leslie had been there from the first. The All Blacks protested the decision. Mr Gourlay promptly declared his authority by ordering a double-penalty, marching 10 metres up the field. South African referees are good at this. They have the attitude of dominies, of unbending schoolmasters. It is a major, and chronic, weakness of South African Rugby.

Warwick Spicer, of New Zealand Newspapers, approached Mr Gourlay after the game. 'I do not recall the incident,' Mr Gourlay told him. John Stewart, not a man to be brushed off, asked Mr Gourlay to explain the decision. Leslie, Stewart was told, was offside.

'There is no way,' Stewart said to Mr Gourlay, 'that a player involved in a maul can be ruled offside. The only offences which can be committed at a maul concern men who join it on the wrong side or men, not attached to the mass, who move upfield in advance of the last line of feet.' Mr Gourlay responded: 'I'll look it (the law) up.'

It was not a reassuring remark by an international referee. Nor was it pleasant to hear All Blacks *screaming* – the word is not unjustified – about injustice. Tension was keen that night. It always is when, because of your own boneheadedness, you are compelled to say goodbye to glory.

Yet, with everything chucked in, it was a monstrously exciting game. The temperature was at least 30°. This was, if nothing else, 'The Shirtsleeves Test'. The field was perfect. At least 45,000 spectators were present, the bulk of them on the concrete terraces of King's Park, the remainder on auxiliary stands reaching high. The crowd snarled when two men who bore a South African flag to midfield before kick-off were abruptly hustled off by police – yet the Rugby Board had announced it wanted no provocative gestures.

The Springboks lost the toss. At the second line-out, they were given a penalty but Gerald Bosch was both short and wide with his kick at goal from 48 metres. As early as the fourth minute, the All Blacks lost the chance of a try when Stewart gazed at the ball and did not move to it in the in-goal. Batty and Bruce Robertson crisscrossed and dropped the pass, which was not helpful, but when Sid Going was late-tackled, Bryan Williams, kicking straight instead of around the corner, placed a 45-metre goal.

Leslie was robbed of his try by that cruelly unlucky bounce and only for want of another metre of speed did Going miss a try after a great breaking run. Williams sliced a 42-metre penalty attempt. A minute later, the All Blacks obstructed at the line out and from 34 metres Bosch placed the goal. Bruce tried a drop at goal, not with skill, and after there had been punching at a lineout Williams had a chance to goal from 31 metres. He kicked, also not with skill.

So it was 3-all going into the second half. Immediately, Jaffray had his try. The crowd warmly applauded, principally for Batty's darting run which set it up. But Williams hooked the goalkick. The Springboks dangerously responded when Johan Oosthuizen was held and let go – New Zealand's tackling was not of prize-winning quality – and Germishuys carried the ball dangerously far. Stewart was neglected when Batty and Kirkpatrick between them made a run. Not so Germishuys when Whipp, in a formal passing rush, cut out Oosthuizen and gave to Ian Robertson. Bryan Williams had been sucked in to look after Robertson and Duncan Robertson, for want of practice in the defensive arts, was out of position by three, four, perhaps five metres, as Germishuys began his run. Great stuff. Gerrie cut in and cut out. Duncan Robertson reached out despairingly and was shaken off. Bosch placed the goal to put South Africa ahead by 9 to 7.

What followed was exciting but academic. The All Blacks had muffed their chances. The Springboks took theirs – the try by Krantz (Bosch was dreadfully unlucky that his converting kick rebounded from an upright), the drop-kick by Ian Robertson. There was a sharp tussle when Whiting knocked John Williams to the ground and few understood that

Going, who was pulling Williams down at the time, was trying to end the scrap. There were sharp reactions within the All Blacks when Bosch went down and stayed down and was led from the field, certified too ill to continue play. His replacement, de Wet Ras, could have placed a penalty after a line-out. In fact, with a penalty advantage of 19 to 9, the Springboks might have done much more. But when Mr Gourlay made his unfortunate ruling against Leslie, the lights went out for New Zealand. In the big encounters they stayed dim, with one exception, for most of the rest of the tour. Goodbye to glory.

Fewer than 48 hours after Bezuidenhout's final whistle, a Qantas 707 bore away from Jan Smuts Airport that unhappy band of brothers who were the 1976 All Blacks.

South African newspapers surprisingly reported that Stewart had departed with tears streaming from his eyes and implied that others of the party had blubbed, too. Since the press had been evicted from the VIP room in which the All Blacks were briefly entertained before they left, this had to be reckoned as a pleasing fancy by one or more reporters. What was notable was that the press, which numbered about twenty or so, was by far the largest of the small groups of individuals who had journeyed from Johannesburg city to see the team depart. Three months before, there had been a crowd of many hundreds to welcome the All Blacks as they arrived. Now there were few. The team had served its purpose. It had played all over the country, under constant strain from travel, injuries, too great an indulgence in training sessions, altitude and, not least, especially in the last few weeks, blazing sunshine.

The record of six matches lost in 24 played was grim. New Zealand rugby, which had climbed many stairs from the cellar of the early 1970s, had been kicked down them again, clattering into a heap. Whether South African rugby had now climbed as many stairs from its own cellar of 1974 was arguable; but at least, by means good, bad or indifferent according to taste, it had sustained its age-long dominance over New Zealand. Now the question was, as the plane's nose-wheel lifted and the team was homeward bound, whether there would be more contests between the countries, on a regular basis, or whether, because of politics, refereeing, rough play, incompetent rugby or a combination of these things, all of the young men of the two countries would end up by going surfing.

On one point, there could be certainty. Unless South African rugby embraced the concept of nonracialism and offered adequate opportunity to all, no more Springbok teams would tour in New Zealand or All Blacks in South Africa. It would be, in the words of Jan Ellis, so many weeks before, Finish and Klaar.

From *Goodbye to Glory*

How They Gave Luck a Chance

Chris Greyvenstein

The South Africans saw it rather differently from the despondent All Blacks, as Chris Greyvenstein relates.

The Springboks won the series 3–1 but the All Blacks were distinctly unlucky in the final Test and instead of jubilation, South Africans were left with a vague feeling of unease. Not enough was accomplished, either against France the previous season or against New Zealand, to completely dispel the gloom caused by the appalling performances against the 1974 Lions.

The Tests were hard and merciless in the accepted tradition of clashes between these two implacable rivals but, with rare exceptions, there was no enterprise from behind the scrum.

Barry Glasspool, sports editor of the [Johannesburg] Sunday Times, summed it up well in *One in the Eye*, a book he wrote after the tour:

'Total commitment to the capabilities of a freakishly brilliant goalkicker (Gerald Bosch) whose form otherwise had slumped alarmingly, but who operated behind a screen of aggressive forward play, meant that the exciting talents of runners like Gerrie Germishuys, Peter Whipp and Johan Oosthuizen were largely unexploited.

'With the exception of that breathtaking first Test try by Germishuys which rounded off a back-line thrust of sheer uncomplicated artistry, the Springboks hardly put together another worthwhile back-line move for the rest of the series.'

Glasspool suggests that the coaching responsibility for all future Springbok teams be given back to the captain, and considering the success Du Plessis has had in this capacity in restoring the dented prestige of Western Province, it is certainly a move worth making.

The Springbok forwards did a sound enough job against the All Blacks. Moaner van Heerden, Jan (Boland) Coetzee, Kevin de Klerk and Morne du Plessis were always good and frequently outstanding, and the Transvaal frontranker Johan Strauss was of inestimable value in the crucial third Test at Newlands.

Three-quarters like Peter Whipp, who was dropped for the second Test for no apparent reason, Johan Oosthuizen, Gerrie Germishuys and Chris Pope were neglected, however, as either Paul Bayvel, at scrum-half, or Gerald Bosch, at fly-half, kicked away possession. Bayvel had an erratic season while Bosch lacked the delicate judgment required of an international fly-half.

Gerald Bosch is a courageous player with safe hands, the temperament for the big occasion, and he is indisputably the most successful place- and drop-kicker in South African rugby history, as a glance at the statistics will prove. His tactical kicking, particularly on a hard ground, is also excellent and it all adds up to a formidable array of qualities. Unfortunately, probably because he had been straitjacketed from the start by his phenomenal talent for kicking, Bosch seems constitutionally unable to play a balanced game.

If he had the ability to know when and how to employ his three-quarters with snap and decisiveness, Gerald Raymond Bosch would have ranked with the great fly-halves in history. But his mental make-up has been programmed for 10-man rugby only, and in an era where Springbok packs can no longer guarantee their backs the major portion of possession against international teams, it is an approach which fails as often as it succeeds. Hypothetically at least, Springbok backs like Whipp, Oosthuizen, Germishuys and Pope could perhaps have accomplished with tries what Bosch did with his boot had they been given enough opportunities against the All Blacks.

Looking at the records only, there is no doubt that Bosch was the deciding factor in the 1976 series, played between two teams who were otherwise so evenly matched. He scored 33 out of the Springboks' total of 55 points and the lack of a goal-kicker of his stature was the All Blacks' biggest weakness. With 89 points scored in only nine Tests, the important role this affable sports shop owner who also has his own race-horse – his colours are green and gold, of course – has played in Springbok rugby in the mid-70's cannot be minimized whatever criticism might be levelled at him.

Controversy over refereeing decisions cast a shadow over the tour, but the All Blacks had only themselves to blame. The South African Rugby Board had offered them the services of neutral referees, but their own authorities had declined, probably because acceptance would have created a precedent with future touring teams to New Zealand expecting the same privilege. To halt the perpetuation of 'feuds', the wait until-we-get-you-in-our-backyard attitude, it is high time that the use of neutral referees became compulsory.

The wrangle after the final Test left a particularly sour taste. Throughout the match the All Blacks showed their annoyance with Mr Gert Bezuidenhout, a referee whom they had praised after they had won the second Test, had criticized after they had lost the third, and were prepared to draw and quarter long before his whistle ended the last Test.

When Oosthuizen prevented Bruce Robertson from chasing a rolling ball he might well have reached in the in-goal area before the covering Gerald Bosch and Peter Whipp, the All Blacks expected a penalty try. Mr Bezuidenhout was not certain that Robertson would have got to the ball before the defence and, acting according to the rules, he gave New Zealand a penalty instead. It was the final straw as far as the All Blacks were concerned and Andy Leslie, who had proved to be a most tactful tour captain up till then, bluntly described the match as a 'hollow Springbok victory' in a television interview immediately after the game.

Their anger was understandable as many good judges had agreed that a penalty try should have been awarded but their general dismissal of their defeats as being mainly due to refereeing decisions can never be accepted. The All Blacks also received their share of penalties which could have been converted into points but both Sid Going and Bryan Williams were erratic and the tour management seemed to have no confidence in Laurie Mains, the only specialist kicker in their party.

The balding and pugnacious Sid Going, and the reliable Doug Bruce formed a most capable half-back combination while Peter ('Pole') Whiting was the best lock-forward on either side. Ian Kirkpatrick, was still an outstanding flanker in spite of his age and Joe Morgan, Duncan Robertson (who should never have been switched to full-back), and loose-forward Kevin Eveleigh were consistently competent. Bryan Williams, who was so brilliant in 1970, seemed to have lost his edge, however, and Gerrie Germishuys, if anything, looked more dangerous than his famous opponent. Grant Batty, a small and bustling wing, was severely handicapped by injury but he did enough to earn the respect of opponents and spectators alike. Generally speaking, it was a team, however, which could not bear comparison with any of their predecessors.

The Springbok backs gave their best performance of the series in the first Test in Durban when Gerrie Germishuys scored a try to remember after everyone, from Bayvel to Ian Robertson, who had slipped into the line from full-back, had done his job with passes as swift and precise as could be found outside the pages of a text book.

A slashing break by Bayvel initiated the Springboks' other try of the match, scored by Edrich Krantz after the young Free Stater who was making his international debut, had kept his head admirably as he snapped up a flicked-away ball on the try-line.

Ian Robertson, the versatile Rhodesian who substituted for the ailing Dawie Snyman at full-back, put over a dropped goal to crown a quite outstanding display and Bosch, who had been ill during the week preceding the Test, added a penalty and conversion to make the final score 16–7. The Springbok fly-half, in fact, had to be replaced by substitute De Wet Ras a few minutes before the end.

Lyn Jaffray scored New Zealand's sole try after a superbly individualistic effort from Grant Batty while Bryan Williams contributed a penalty to his team's total. Although the score indicates a convincing victory for the Springboks, there was actually little to choose between the two sides, with only tremendous work on the defence by Boland Coetzee, Moaner van Heerden, Morne du Plessis, Peter Whipp and Johan Oosthuizen halting powerful drives by the New Zealand forwards.

The Springbok selectors wielded the axe with abandon when they selected the side for the second Test in Bloemfontein. Peter Whipp, so brilliant in Durban, was dropped and Ian Robertson, a success at full-back, was pushed into his place at centre to allow the out-of-form Dawie Snyman to return to the team at full-back. Krantz, who had done well in his debut, was nevertheless dropped for the more experienced Chris Pope while Jan Ellis, who had obviously reached the end of the line, had to make way for Martinus Theunis Steyn Stofberg, a 21-year-old Free State forward of immense, if raw, potential. Ellis had played in 38 Tests and shares with Frik du Preez the distinction of being the most-capped Springbok ever.

The All Blacks never looked like losing the second Test. Sid Going was at his considerable best and apart from nursing his pack and his backs, he scored two penalty goals and a conversion and also harrassed the life out of his opposite number Paul Bayvel. Joe Morgan broke through for an excellent try and Doug Bruce, making good use of Going's impeccable service, dropped a goal. All the Springboks could produce were three penalty goals by Gerald Bosch.

It was an even more bruising, and far less enterprising, test than the first one, and the Springboks lost their best line-out forward, John Williams, with a gruesome injury to his nose in the second half. He was replaced by Kevin de Klerk and the big Transvaal lock made sure of his place for the rest of the series with a furious display. The Springboks were generally subdued, however, and too many key players faltered and fumbled for them to be a serious threat at any stage of the match.

South Africa won the vital third Test at Newlands because of a truly great performance by Morne du Plessis, who so inspired his team that they completely wiped out the bad memory of their groping incompetence at Bloemfontein. Play was rough to the point of being vicious, and Du Plessis afterwards looked as if he had fought a losing battle for the world heavyweight championship. But, then, hardly a player came out of this match without scars of some sort or other.

The Springbok front-row of Rampie Stander, veteran Piston van Wyk, and the barrel-chested Johannesburg carpenter Johan Strauss, as well as the second-row men, De Klerk and Van Heerden, were magnificent, while Boland Coetzee with typical courage, skill and sheer doggedness, gave a rampaging Du Plessis all the support he needed. Even the young Stofberg, in company as rough as he is ever likely to encounter, showed that he was not a boy trying to do a man's job.

Oosthuizen, with a try after a perfectly-timed interception followed by electrifying acceleration, Bosch with two penalties and a conversion and a drop goal, three minutes from the end, by Dawie Snyman gave the Springboks their 15 points. Bruce Robertson, with an opportunistic try after Germishuys had got himself in a tangle near his own line, and Bryan Williams, with two penalties, made the All Blacks' total of 10 points.

John Reason, of the London *Daily Telegraph*, summarized the fourth Test accurately when he wrote:

'The final test of this series was, sadly, a game which is all too typical of international rugby. It was a brutally hard, bludgeoning business, repeatedly interrupted by stoppages for deliberately inflicted injuries.

'It contained the minimum of movement and there were blood and bandages everywhere . . .'

Prolonged complaining over the referee and some of his decisions overshadowed the Springboks' 15–14 victory, and it was repeatedly claimed that the South Africans had been lucky to have won. It is true that the All Blacks scored two tries to one and that Bosch with two penalties, a drop goal and a conversion, had made all the difference. Going and Kirkpatrick scored tries for the All Blacks, while 'Klippies' Kritzinger went over for the Springboks' only try.

But Morne du Plessis put it in perspective when he said afterwards:

'Sure we were lucky, but I've also played in games where the opposition had been lucky. It's part of the game . . .'

But it is a pity that the 1976 series could not have ended on a more positive note.

After all, when the two teams disappeared into the tunnel under the huge grandstand at Ellis Park, the curtain closed on what will one day be known as only an era in our rugby history. An era which lasted for 85 years, leaving all South Africans a legacy of achievement in the rugby arenas of the world. It is a precious heritage and it is there for all of us to share and to build on so as to ensure that there will be more, much more, for the generations to come.

From *Springbok Saga*

Blood, Toil, Tears and Sweat

The annual contest between Oxford and Cambridge is celebrated because the result is always in doubt. Previous form is no guide. In 1985, for example, Cambridge, with five wins in a row under their belt, were easy favourites to win a sixth time and so create a new record for the event. The year before they had won a pulverizing game 32–6. It was fourteen years since Cambridge had been outscored in tries, and Oxford had just two tries to show for all their efforts in the last six Twickenham matches. Andy Ripley, the giant England forward who had captained teams against both university sides, rated Cambridge 4 to 1 on. Yet on the day Oxford were to win a marvellously exciting game 7–6. In 1990 there was to be a re-run of that upset.

The 1990 game had another haunting echo of the past when a palace revolution decided the Oxford Captain, Mark Egan, against playing his key Australian players: Brian Smith and Troy Coker. It seemed like a replay of two famous American revolts in the university boat race: the first in 1959, the second in 1987, both of which Oxford went on to win against what looked like impossible odds. This is how it looked, after the game, to John Mason and Michael Calvin of The Daily Telegraph *and Stephen Jones of* The Sunday Times.

Oxford University 21 pts, Cambridge University 12

Mark Egan, Oxford's captain, was chaired from the pitch by delighted team-mates, moments before receiving the Bowring Bowl at Twickenham yesterday. The compliment, better than any words, summed up Egan's mighty contribution to the Oxford cause.

Egan, a graduate student from Dublin and London Irish member, was being thanked not only for leading the Dark Blues to comforting victory over Cambridge, the pre-match firm favourites.

Here was the weighty seal of approval for having united Oxford rugby after a winter of discontent which, ultimately, meant that Egan went to Twickenham yesterday without four of last year's available Blues, including internationals Brian Smith – who was running the line – and Troy Coker.

Even in his heady moment of triumph – by two goals, a dropped goal and two penalty goals to a goal and two penalty goals – the modest Egan insisted that the honours belonged to the Oxford team, not an individual.

In essence, Egan was right. While his leadership qualities and personal example as a muscular, foraging No. 8 pointed the way from early on in this absorbing contest, it was a team effort that finally toppled unhappy Cambridge.

The Light Blues, though threatening to break out for long periods, were never allowed to settle. Possession was erratic and the scrum, having started capably, began to disintegrate.

Then, when they did get the ball, Cambridge were so anxious to impose themselves that they fretted and fumbled. Later, if there was a wrong option to be taken, the Cambridge midfield managed to find it so frequently that confidence seeped away.

Yet despite these handicaps, for an hour, perhaps longer, Cambridge were either a pass or a stride away from putting Egan's men in their place. It seemed the logic of judgments, based in part on match results in the build-up to the 109th University Match, would prevail.

The wheels on the Cambridge wagon began to wobble at about the time Norwitz, Oxford's hooker, took the first of two strikes against the head. Before that the scrum had twice not budged an inch as Oxford pitched camp in front of the Cambridge posts.

The second time, Moloney dropped for goal and Oxford, having been 6–9 down, were level again ten minutes before half-time. They did not falter thereafter. In the end Oxford's forwards could permit Egan to stand off various scrums. Their superiority was complete.

For once, the opening salvoes were curiously muted. Referee Owen Doyle required Taylor and Booth to shake hands after adrenalin had drowned common sense, and when an Oxford scrum collaped, Davies kicked a penalty goal to launch the Cambridge challenge.

At that stage everything was going according to the book. Davies drilled the ball deep to the south-east corner to set Oxford nerves on edge. The calming influence of Egan pulled them out of that mess.

Next, the ball bowled along the Cambridge line, going left. Parton came steaming in on cue and there was space for Underwood on the left. Plan A was on song . . . or was it?

Hein, who reached Oxford via UCLA and the American Eagles, swooped. For a moment the ball was not to be seen and Underwood continued towards the corner.

But Hein, who scored two tries last year, was streaming in the other direction, the ball joyously held. He finished close to the posts, unchallenged after a dash of 60 yards, and Haly's conversion took Oxford to 6–3.

Haly enjoyed that relatively easy kick to start his Twickenham career. Three more kicks sailed between the posts to cap another important contribution to Oxford's 47th win in the series.

Sheasby, Cambridge's No. 8, picked up at a scrum with 25 minutes gone and strode round the blind side for the try which Davies converted from the south-west touchline. Here was another period in which Cambridge were at ease, only to give best to competent Oxford who stuck to the basic principles of forward play. Rising Cambridge frustration allowed Haly a penalty goal four minutes from half-time and though Davies levelled the scores when Roberts came flying over the top, Oxford's control in the awkward moments was shaping towards victory.

Haly's second penalty goal with eight minutes remaining took Oxford ahead for the third time and when Underwood lost the ball in the tackle, Durand counter-attacked splendidly. The ball was kicked upfield and Moore sped away in pursuit along the touchline. He was not ruled offside, the bounce was accommodating and the scrum-half escaped the cover to reach the corner. From close to touch Haly converted amid a mighty roar.

From *The Daily Telegraph*

Five Oxford forwards, drawn from four different nations and distinct cultures, wept as they huddled together in the dressing-room before the most important match of their lives. The intense sense of unity was overwhelming.

'You're looking good boys, you're looking good,' proclaimed Mark Egan, through the tears that were to be translated into a performance which provided the ultimate vindication of his vision of university rugby.

Toshiyuki Hayashi, product of the social scrum that passes as a Tokyo suburb, positively howled in anticipation. His intensity of commitment was such he was to dismiss dislocation of his left knee-cap, after just five minutes, as little more than a minor inconvenience.

Andrew Everett, Oxford's other prop, embraced lock Charles Bonham-Carter, his fellow-South African. William Stileman, Bonham-Carter's second-row colleague whose future lies in the Church of England, was similarly stirred.

'It was just incredible,' recalled Egan, whose easy Irish manner disguises the strength of character essential to the success of his traumatic captaincy. 'I have never seen such emotion.

'We were crying our eyes out, but we were very calm. There was no banging of heads against the wall, no caveman antics. We just got around each other, and started thinking about the game plan.'

The cameo was revealing. It underlined that a student's nationality is irrelevant when the captain is sufficiently strong to suggest a star system will not be allowed to operate. The point did not appear to be lost on Brian Smith, who ran the line when he should, logically, have been playing.

The Brisbane-born fly-half, who may yet be Egan's Ireland team-mate in the forthcoming Five Nations Championship, sprinted from the field, without a backward glance, as the jubilant Oxford team began the joyous ritual of hauling Egan on to their shoulders.

Smith ignored the tradition that the outgoing captain changes with his university colleagues before acting as touch judge, and was nowhere to be seen when bellowed Christmas carols, from the dressing-room, signalled the start of celebrations.

Egan, understandably enough, did his best to deflect public scrutiny of the scars left by Australian Troy Coker's unsuccessful challenge to his captaincy earlier in the year. But the sense of self-justification was tangible.

'We had to do something to get back on the rails again,' he admitted. 'Spirits were low last year. We were losing sight of where we were going and what university rugby is all about.

'If a win vindicates us, that can speak for itself. The club is a happy place. It's about fifteen guys, playing for each other, playing for the other members of the club. It's about enjoying your football with good friends.'

Lynn Evans, the Welshman invited to return as director of coaching when the influence of Australia's Alan Jones began to wane in the face of Smith and Coker's refusal to acknowledge the new regime, sat beside him.

'Mark has pulled this side together better than any captain I have ever been associated with,' he said in quiet, measured tones. 'Maybe it's the Irish in him, but the feeling of everyone pulling towards him, and Oxford, is tremendous. His contribution tips it over when the pressure is on, when the bodies are flying in.'

Even without the internecine squabbling that has blighted Varsity sport in recent years, it is easy to underestimate the annual pressures on students who are expected to light a beacon of hope for their sport.

'I have thought about this match every day since I was appointed captain,' acknowledged Egan. 'It's the one day we are treated like internationals.

'You realize you are being watched by 57,000 people at Twickenham. When you're out there, in the middle of the pitch, the intensity is incredible. I just hope it was a good game. I can't remember a thing about it.'

He plans to refresh his memory today when, over several cold cans of beer, he watches a video recording of the match. However satisfying the viewing, he will need time to appreciate the enormity of what he has achieved.

From *The Daily Telegraph*

There are still two weeks of the year left and still time for someone to challenge Mark Egan as sportsman of the year. But it really would take a feat of sublime brilliance to catch him now. Certainly there is no one in sport who could have felt the same fulfilment – raging, galloping fulfilment – as did Egan, the young Irishman, when his joyful Oxford team-mates shouldered him from Twickenham after the varsity match. I wonder if he is doing panto this year?

The match was the last act in a long-running soap-like drama.

Last season, Egan was among many members of the Oxford club who felt that the club was derailed.

Oxford teams have always been exotic and have contained players whose sporting ability allowed them to enter the university through the side door. But last season was something else. Oxford fielded a highly controversial mix of strolling players. There was not so much a side door as a tradesmen's entrance.

'I haven't even heard of some of the courses they were supposed to be on,' one club member recalled last week.

The other bone of contention was the approach of the team's hierarchy. The captain last year was Brian Smith, the Australian who plays for Ireland. He set the club revolving around himself, and dispensed with the services of Lynn Evans, a loyal and able Oxford coach.

For fine-tuning, Smith drafted in his mentor, Alan Jones, the voluble Australian who, depending on which player you were talking to, is either one of the great coaches and motivators of all time or the most over-estimated.

Smith angrily dismissed allegations that the team betrayed the concepts of university rugby. None of this, he maintained, was exceeding his prerogative as Oxford captain.

Yet Oxford lost the 1989 varsity match with a poor and curiously passionless performance. The elections for Smith's successor pitted Troy Coker, an Australian of the Smith-Jones axis, against Egan and those who felt the old harmonies in the club had been lost. Coker was defeated in the vote and the two sides were never to make up.

Egan was determined to rediscover what he considered the lost heart of the club, and he felt that by their words and actions neither Coker nor Smith nor their allies were helping.

Courageously but precariously, Egan decided at the start of this season that his unglittering side would have to do without them. (The other 'rebels' were irrelevant in that Oxford had better players anyway.)

The whole business seemed a faithful re-run of the Boat Race mutiny of 1987, another clash between olde Oxford and brash colonials. Dan Topolski, the coach of that Oxford crew, wrote last week that the two disputes were different, that the rugby fuss was chiefly a personality clash.

Unquestionably there was an element of that, but insiders at the rugby club believe that Topolski is wrong, that it was indeed a carbon copy of the rowing dispute.

It was only as the varsity match approached with Oxford struggling that the full implications and the sharp irony of Egan's decision became clear. The two areas in which Oxford were sadly lacking were fly-half, where Smith plays, and the line-out, the domain of Coker.

There was the looming probability that in front of a packed Twickenham, a live TV audience and generations of old blues, Egan would lose because of problems in the very two positions in which he had rejected international players.

Yet Egan simply faced down every painful prospect. He inspired such loyalty and intensity in his men that some of them cried their eyes out in the dressing-room *before* the match. In concert with the calculating Lynn Evans, he boosted the confidence of Jay Durand, the fly-half who was to reveal such calmness and tactical awareness.

The outcome was an afternoon of the highest emotion. It was a match of movement and frequent psychological shifts. Oxford thoroughly deserved to win, aided by a 12-point try when Gary Hein, in a desperate intercepting lunge to cut out what would certainly have been a scoring pass to Tony Underwood of Cambridge, was able to make off and score at the other end.

Egan's own performance was one of the most heroic that even Twickenham has seen. He picked Oxford up in a double-handed grip. He had to take on all the Cambridge jumpers in the line-out and time and again jumped high above the line-out maelstrom. He made wonderful tackles – and missed one, garishly, when Chris Sheasby of Cambridge scored. Otherwise, he defended his line, and his destiny, wonderfully well.

In the press conference (after a gracious performance by Simon Holmes, the outstanding Cambridge captain), we gave Egan veiled but open invitations to gloat, to celebrate vindication by savaging the opposition at Oxford.

He replied with exactly the same dignity which characterized his long weeks of soul-searching and public explanation before the match. He felt, he said, that the Oxford University club was a happy place again. We felt, to a man, that we were in the company of a giant.

From *The Sunday Times*

For Ireland, Boys!

Frank Keating

If rugby has no Neville Cardus it does have Frank Keating, who will do nicely for the brave new world of the 1990s. Put Keating among the Irish, in the land of his fathers, sit well back, and enjoy the action.

It was good to be back in Dublin after long winters of cricketing, though the soft weather of centuries was more chill than I can remember as the biting north-easterly yapped in from an ice-cold Irish Sea.

But the grass was a bright green and the sky a crisp, glistening blue. 'Ah,' enquired my purple-faced, jug-eared taximan, 'for the match, I suppose?' For the match, I said. 'Ah,' mused he, 'I don't know about the rugger, sor, but it's sure a lovely day for ploughin'. There'll be a lot out ploughing tomorrow.' But he agreed that no one would be out ploughin' come tomorrow afternoon. 'Every man, woman and child is keyed up. It does the old country good, does the rugger. Livens it up. They should play these games more often.'

The city has changed radically since I was last here. They have closed off Grafton Street to cars and everything else 'up there' is one-way. The Royal Hibernian Hotel has gone for good. Nobody could park nearby it, you see – 'you never used to be able to park up there at all, but now you can't park at all, at all,' my man said. I went to make sure one of my favourite shopsigns was still there – 'Haircutting While-U-Wait'. The office-workers were taking brisk and animated constitutionals around Stephen's Green. The sacred smudge of ash from Wednesday was still on some foreheads, on the brow of solicitors and senators, and shining-faced secretaries with smiling Irish eyes and terrible Irish hang-ups. On their knees that morning, I fancy, more than a few candles were lit and prayers wafted up to Blessed Oliver Plunkett, the martyred seventeenth-century Bishop of Armagh, and patron saint of the Blessed Seamus Oliver Campbell, to whom many with their eyes on Lansdowne Road will be making their own individual prayers. Last winter Campbell's forty-six points ensured the Triple Crown for Ireland for the first time in twenty-five years. This season they are the only side who can win it again – indeed, a Grand Slam is within their grasp.

Last year in Paris the French stopped the Irish with – in the words of an editorial in a Dublin newspaper – 'head-bucking, gouging, boring, punching and similar skulduggery with the intent fully to send home the Irish forwards back across the sea in plastic bags.' So Saturday's match will be an occasion of terrible fury. But it's invariably tit-for-tat. As long ago as 1892 a J. J. McCarthy contributed thus an Irish chapter to the then definitive volume *The Rugby Game*:

'Football in Ireland may be said to consist of three parts – Rugbeian,

Associationist and Gaelic. The rule of play in these organizations had been defined as follows: in rugby, you kick the ball; in Association, you kick the man if you cannot kick the ball; and in Gaelic, you kick the ball if you cannot kick the man.' The rugger headquarters at Clonturk Park, McCarthy went on, was, 'conveniently situated between Glasnevin graveyard and the Mater Miserecordiae Hospital. A man has been known to pass from the football direct to the hospital, and from the hospital to the cemetery; another match being then got up to raise funds for the benefit of the next-of-kin, thus running the risk of killing a few more for the benefit of the deceased.'

In spirit at least, I reckon, things won't have changed much by tomorrow. The very thought of those first two or three scrums makes me wince. For the Irish are no angels, and their battle-scarred pack has been getting in first with the retaliation for a long time now. And when admonished – oh! the innocence of those open, guileless faces.

The stokers in the engine room this week have been working at more than just looking fierce, I can tell you. A stream of curses has been pouring forth as the eight-man juggernaut has clanked and clamped and charged itself up on the practice ground at Old Belvedere.

'Dad's Army' is led, of course, by that live regular Army captain, Ciaran Fitzgerald, squat and ferocious-looking with tree-trunk thighs, no neck and much charm. Fitzgerald was brought up on hurling and the aforesaid Gaelic stuff. He was born in Mayo in 1952 on 4 June. He was brought up in County Galway where his father owned a garage. At twelve he came to Dublin to win a schools' boxing title, so early on he learned to take a thump in the face. At fifteen he was sent to Ballinasloe, to St Joseph's College. He had never even seen a rugger match but at once took to it – so heartily that when he left to go to the military college at The Curragh his games master, Fr John Kirby, forecast he would one day captain Ireland. He was well on the way to fulfilling the prophecy after he led the provincial minnows of Connacht to a stirring win over Munster in 1979. That was like me knocking out Henry Cooper.

Now this operations officer in the Second Infantry Battalion says captaincy on the rugby field is not unlike his daily preparations for leadership on the battlefield. 'All the preparation has been done beforehand. Leadership is reacting to the unexpected, choosing your options. You must always have alternatives up your sleeve: you must know when to turn on the tap, when to close it; when to accelerate, when to consolidate.' Before Fitzgerald came, the other six in his platoon of eight must have thought they had won all the campaign medals they could. Their man inspired them to more.

From the deep green southern state where they also rear them to the tempests of Gaelic games come Moss Keane and Willie Duggan, thirty-five and thirty-three respectively. Slattery, the Blackrock boy who has laid waste more midfield men than just about anyone in the game, is thirty-four. The two cornerstones, Phil Orr, the four-square Dubliner, and Gerry

McLoughlin, flame-haired Limerick landlord of The Triple Crown bar, are both in their early thirties. The Stonyhurst public-schoolboy medic from Manchester, John O'Driscoll – a gentle fellow in civvies whom they call on the field 'O'Desperate' – has also seen the last of his twenties. One of the 'old' men's tasks tomorrow will be to defend the one youngster in their pack: if they do so he might well settle the thing, might Donal 'Loine-out' Lenihan, the twenty-three-year-old beanpole lock from Cork. They will hope to furnish Campbell with the wherewithal. Campbell is much more than a kicker, of course. He has a beautiful pair of hands and feet with a delicate, deceptive pit-a-pat stride. The scrum-half Robbie McGrath is by no means the quickest nor the most accurate passer with whom to be paired, yet he explained this week how last year they agreed on signals for an attempted drop goal. In the event, McGrath's pass squirted out at Campbell's bootlace – 'he was completely off balance and unready, yet he picked the thing off his toe, changed direction and intent in one stride, and took off on a mazy, bewildering run that presented a try to Moss Finn.'

Campbell is as shy as he is unaffected and friendly. He could pass, at a glance, for twenty: in fact he is thirty next year. To anyone else's knowledge he has no regular girlfriend. He works as salesman for the family's clothing firm. He still lives with Dad and Mam in the attractive Dublin suburb of Malahide. 'I'm spoiled, pampered, no doubt about it. I'm probably still tied to my mother's apron strings. If I come in late at night she'll always be up for me, just as if I was nine, not almost twenty-nine. No, she's never watched me play, since I was around fourteen. She won't even watch a recording of a match on television in case I'm murdered before her eyes!'

At Belvedere College old boys' ground on the Anglesea Road one can often find him alone at practice. Solitary. All weathers. Till the lights wink warm in the city yonder. Kick, kick, kick. Fetch and carry, fetch and carry. Kick, kick, kick. Short ones, long ones, wide ones, narrow ones. Fetch and carry, fetch and carry. Kick, kick, kick. Punting ones, torpedo ones, considered ones and hasty ones. He ends up with one from the half-way line, soccer's centre circle. He claws the mud from studs. With care he lines up his right instep against the ball, his left foot forward and alongside. He looks down at the ball, then up to gauge the distance. The goal-posts are far away in the murk. Then, neither hurried nor too cautious, one-two-three-four-five steps back; a little one-and-a-half chassé sideways and left. A glance at the ball, the posts, then back to the ball. Up on his tiptoes just once, then a rhythmic, slightly curving run, eyes down, and . . . woompf! The 'H' is perfectly bisected.

Campbell's kicking is so prodigious that people in high places are talking about changing the rules and the points system. It's not a fair game when Ollie's around. Although he had been a schoolboy fly-half since he was nine he never kicked at goal – 'not even a 25 drop-out' – till he was seventeen. 'After that I got the taste – so started practising.' He does bridle shyly at being thought of only as a kicker – 'I actually think I do passing best,' he says. 'Though you lot would never write that, would you?'

Ned van Esbeck, doyen of the *Irish Times*, once explained how the boy had never sought to bargain with his talent: 'Ollie's a humble man. If he were locked up in a room or stuck in a lift with four other men for twenty-four hours they'd all come out of that room none the wiser as to who he was. They wouldn't even know he *liked* rugby football. His modesty is such that he wouldn't have even mentioned it.'

Last year, not long after Ireland had won the Triple Crown, there was celebrated in St Patrick's Cathedral, Dublin, an annual ecumenical service for sports folk. One of the lessons was read by Ollie Campbell. He chose a passage from the first epistle of St Paul to the Corinthians. Softly, reverently, he read: 'You know, do ye not, that at the sports all the runners run the race, though only one wins the prize. Like them, run to win. But every athlete goes into strict training. They do it to win a fading wreath; we, a wreath that never fades. For my part, I run with a clear goal before me; I am like a boxer who does not merely beat the air; I discipline my own body, and make it know its master, lest that by any means, having preached to others, I myself should be a failure.'

At Belvedere, he was taught by the Jesuit priest, Fr Jim Moran, who now works in Chicago. They are still in regular touch on the telephone. 'Don't let others define your pinnacles for you: set them yourself,' says Fr Moran. He would, however, always tell Ollie throughout his schooldays, 'Just because you are a good sportsman, don't think that makes you a better *person*,' and Campbell reflects on that to this day. 'Sure, I'm enjoying the rugby, though I admit the practising did once make me very blinkered. And it's nice to do well at it sometimes. But I know it's all a very temporary, transitory thing: soon, I know, I'll just fade into the distance and be an ordinary Joe Soap again.'

On the eve of the very confrontation itself I found myself sinking the black in the snug atmosphere of Sean Lynch's bar opposite Dublin's Carmelite Convent. Sean was a Lion of a prop who helped to bring the spoils home from New Zealand for Carwyn in 1971. But it was not to Sean that I was listening: in a wet-elbowed huddle, hammering out the ifs and buts and coulds and shoulds of the morrow, I was with none other than the Irish national coach himself, the old grey fox with the button snout, Tommy Kiernan.

Perhaps it was my Benedictine boyhood. Or an Irish father. But from the winter's day in 1960 that my uncle, who was from Cork, took me to Twickenham and introduced me to the boys from home I have ever worn the green weed on my sleeve on international days. We stayed at the Knights of St Columba Club in Kensington on the eve of the game and I remember that after midnight everyone stopped bibbing the black and started ordering Green Chartreuse. Next day everyone managed to be up for Mass. They were particularly looking to luck on account of it being a young Cork lad's first international. The Chartreuse and the heartfelt

Credo worked wonders, for Tom Kiernan, from the Presentation College, had a wonderful game.

He had the kick of a Kinsale mule, the whooshing, deadly tackle of a midsummer Sligo scythe, and still a gentle open face as serene and warm as a turf fire in a cosy cottage. He went on to become the most capped full-back in international history. I worshipped him. Indeed, from that first day I was entranced by the way the Irish played the game. And they do it to this day: a hotchpotch of jigs and jinks and darts and delicate invention and wild make-do-and-mend and all the time maintaining the most furious gusto imaginable.

The Irish scrum-half for that first team I saw at Twickenham was a smart little sprite called Andy Mulligan, who combined a mischievous break with a deal of courage and a grand pass to his out-half. He later became a friend of mine (though I haven't seen him for ages: come back Mulligan, the fiver's forgotten) and once explained the philosophy behind the fizz of those Shamrock sides. Andy's first international was long before the days of squad systems, let alone men-of-the-match. He was understandably nervous before they left the dressing room. Two minutes to go and the captain finished doing up his laces and addressed them:

'Right, lads, let's decide how we're going to play this game. What do you think, Jack [Kyle]?'

'I think that a few wee punts at the line would be dandy, and maybe Mulligan here can try a few wee darts on his own.'

'What do you think, Tony [O'Reilly]?'

'Jasus, the programme here says I'm playing against a midget. Just let me have a run with the ball.'

'What about youse, Cecil [Pedlow]?'

'I think a subtle little mix of runnin and kickin' and breakin' would be dandy.'

The captain summed up: 'So it's decided, lads – Jack's puntin', Andy's dartin', Tony's runnin' and Cecil's doing all three.'

The whole philosophy was precisely presented back in the 1950s by the North of Ireland centre three-quarter, Noel Henderson, who was doubtless lacing up his boots during that very exchange that afternoon. Said Noel: 'The state of English and Welsh rugger is sometimes serious but never hopeless; the state of Irish rugby is usually hopeless but never serious.'

The enchanting amateur feel of Irish rugby was further summed up for me when Tony Ward showed me a long-ago letter written by the late Mai Purcell to an Irish fly-half of the fifties, Mick English, on the occasion of Mick's first international match. They worked together on the *Limerick Leader*. The memo went: 'Mickie – I should like to impress on you that I'm spending me whole week's wages, *viz* £3 .00, on the trip to Dublin just to see you play, and I beseech you not to make an eejit of yourself on this occasion. I furthermore request that on this auspicious afternoon, mindful of your duties and responsibilities, not only to your club and the people of

Limerick, but to our country as a whole, that you keep y'bloody eye on the ball. Good luck, sir, and God Bless – Mai.'

The uncommitted will feel much the same as Mai these next two March Saturdays. Bejasus, what a hooley there'd be if they made it! It's high time they did. The Triple Crown is one glorious thing, the Grand Slam quite another – and how a Grand Slam for them would do the others good. They've won one this century – at Ravenhill, Belfast on 13 March 1948. Their winning try against Wales that day – a fly hack, an exuberant charge and a thudding bellyflop to a din that bounced all round the Mountains of Mourne – was scored by a cumbersome prop-forward called Jack Daly. At the final whistle the green shirt was torn from his back and, as he was shouldered off in triumph, the socks peeled from his feet. And still, they will tell you, little square relics of fading green cloth are in existence, to be sure, framed in passepartout on mantelpiece shelves all over the little land, right next to the nightlight in front of the Sacred Heart and alongside the fluorescent statues of Our Lady brought back with the duty free from Lourdes or Lisieux. Y'man Daly, mind you, didn't need the shirt again – his name made, he at once caught a boat to Liverpool and cashed in with the rugby league.

Unless it's because their chroniclers appreciate adjectival colour more, Irish sides over the years seem to be packed with far more pungent personalities. As a character and raconteur, they say even Tony O'Reilly, auburn-haired fifties high flyer and another Belvedere old boy – 'We at Belvedere are tops at everything, including humility' – would be awarded the bronze medal behind two from the 1920s, the hunchy full-back Ernie Crawford and the roustabout, exuberant flanker, Jammie Clinch.

Crawford, whose rasping Belfast accent never left him in spite of a long Dublin domicile, invented the word 'alickadoo', that marvellous collective rugby noun covering all the game's hangers-on, administrators, selectors or bucket men for the Extra B . . . all those involved with the game who never play it.

The term originated on a train trip to London when Ernie failed to entice some other player to join the ritual game of poker. His colleague preferred to read a book which was about some oriental potentate. Ernie growled his displeasure: 'You and your bloody Ali Khadu!' After that, anyone who strayed from Ernie's conception of the proper order of affairs became an 'Alikadoo'.

In 1924 Jammie Clinch toured South Africa with the Lions. His mentor was a *pukka* Englishman from Blackheath, A. F. 'Blakey' Blakiston. One time Jammie laid low a particularly troublesome Springbok forward – but a tough Afrikaaner who was quick to recover and get back on his feet. 'That's no good, old boy,' said Blakey to Jammie – 'jab your fingers in his eye when he's goin' down and he won't get up so readily.' The following season, England v Ireland at Twickenham, the two pirates were in opposition. Late in the match a group of white-jerseyed English players stood around the fallen Blakey when Jammie pushed his way in, presumably to discover the extent of his friendly rival's injuries. Jammie gazed down at the recumbent warrior and inquired innocently: 'Did I do it right that time, Blakey?'

In a nation of funny men, of bawdy bards and genius journalists, even one of the greatest of them all, Myles na Gopaleen, was partial to his rugger. Here he is meeting Jammie Clinch in a bar in 1959, and, naturally, discussing tactics:

'Ever hear of "the Box"? (I didn't say the 'Boks.) That crowd decided that, after a scrum, there was no future in passing the ball to a string of centres and wings, but to get it to the blind side of the scrum and get it to "the box", an area practically devoid of defence. The result of this conspiracy was a plethorium of scoretown. Ah, but shure I might as well be talking to the wall. Mick, two more pints!'

'Clinch. They call me "Jammie" Clinch.'

'Ah. So? Then you must know my pupils Farrell, Sugden, Davy, Pike, Stephenson? Promising lads, one and all. I, too, have played of course.'

'Rugby? For Ireland? Well . . . by gob!'

'Ah yes. I turned out in the first game against France in 1909. Odd, isn't it, that the 1959 match will be the fiftieth encounter. France had some very clever men in those days, Jauréguy for instance, or Cassayet. Glad to see you are turning out yourself. I suppose you know what a rugby ball is?'

'A what? It's an oval affair.'

'No. Oval connotes a plane configuration; you could never pick anything oval up, or kick it. You might, perhaps, do something with an ovoid. In fact, a rugby ball is a prolate spheroid.'

'I never knew that was what I scored with.'

It was an early morning to remember. Omens were good for the morrow and my only worry was whether I would be too bleary to savour the day. I was, as it happened, up early enough in Buswell's . . . but, alas, one pilgrimage is off the list, with the going of the Royal Hibernian, and so to sniff the congenial flavours there can now be no more morning promenade in the footsteps of another great Campbell – the late Paddy – who once so gloriously chronicled the days of the 1930s when the boys in green were due to kick off at 2.15. It would begin in the basement of the Hibernian outside the door of the Buttery – 'almost always as early as 10.25, to be in good time for the throwing-open of the portals at 10.30'. Once they were inside, service would be delayed by George and Jack behind the bar in discussion with the older members about 'What would be good for it?' 'It', of course, was the accumulated result of the two days and nights of conjecture about the possible result of the coming match: not a matter to be lightly dismissed.

This morning in 1983, I at least doffed my cap and white-frothed my top lip with 'just the one' as genuflection at Davy Byrne's to Campbell and his pilgrims from half a century ago. For them, by around eleven, a number would decide it was high time to see what was going on in Davy Byrne's just around the corner, followed – about 11.45 – by an investigation into Bailey's Hotel, almost opposite, a smooth flow that led them into Jammett's back bar as early as 12.30. Seeing that at that chilly hour it was much too soon for lunch the more socially-minded of them nipped around the corner of Nassau Street and back into the Buttery, where to many it seemed they had only been a minute or two before. And so they would repeat the route.

But as Campbell said, 'All this wasn't simply a vulgar drunken rout. It was much more the marvellous excitement at feeling the whole city *en fête*, that hundreds of thousands of people had abandoned care, work, wives and other encumbrances and were making devotedly, if circuitously, for the ultimate Mecca of Lansdowne Road.'

And after that, with a breakfast on the way at the Shelbourne with my friends, Lander of the *Mirror*, Todd of the *Sun* and Edwards of ITN, we proceeded down past Doheny & Nesbitt's and Gratton's, where we took another oncer and some warming stew with a bright-eyed friend of mine from years gone by who used to work for Aer Lingus, who is called Jeannie and without a word of a lie has got light brown hair . . .

At last, to Lansdowne Road. The crowds cram in. There were rumours that six thousand counterfeit tickets had been printed – and were being used. The An Garda Siochana band tinkled and blew, and did the occasional soft-shoe shuffle in unison – almost, you felt, in their sleep. Then the Fintan Lalor Pipe Band had a whistle. The gulls sailed and squealed over the misty distance that shrouded cranes, spires and, away to my left, a rusty, circled cluster of gasometers; an ancient anachronism, an industrial Stonehenge. The Garda ended with 'The Saints Go Marching In'. For a moment, silence; then a roar as the gladiators take to the amphitheatre. No anthems now in Dublin – too evocatively dangerous – no Soldier's Song. No *Queen* even for the two Ulstermen of the XV, Irwin and Ringland. Not a *Marseillaise* for Rives. Just on with the mayhem and motley, as, in Roy McFadden's 'Garryowen' poem, 'In forced tumescent waves the faceless crowd/Washes the field with sublimating sound;/Implores, deplores, ejaculates aloud./On, up and under, forwards. Charge the line.'

France made a hash of their start. Within a minute Campbell had missed a thirty-five-yard sighting pot at goal – but then within three minutes he had landed an even closer one after another over-tense charge by Paparemborde. Nine minutes later he put over another – and the whole congregation, convulsed and delirious, knew that their kicker had overtaken Kiernan's points record for Ireland. In fifty-four matches Kiernan scored 158 points. In just eighteen matches Campbell had overtaken it. That is why men want to change the rules for Campbell. It is dotty, to be sure, if kickers are to dominate a handling game.

Blanco retrieved three of those points before Campbell made it 9–3 – and then the fly-half's up and under into 'the box' had France in palpitations on their twenty-five. The Irish won the ball, spun it left and, with MacNeill haring into the line, Finn had room to dart over. The conversion made France's second half task a daunting one, and at 15–3 there seemed good reason for 'Sweet Molly Malone' to waft up, serenely, into the mists. The gulls glided, or squawked, to the lilt.

But the French were to rally with stupendous vim. Or rather, Blanco did. First he bazookered a penalty from the halfway line: 15–6. Then he swept into the line, going left. Esteve was boxed in, Blanco chipped through – low and delicate and as precise as Trevino into the wind. He galloped on to touch down and, converting the thing himself from half-way out, made it 15–12 – a very different affair. Dry throats turned from 'Molly Malone'. Fitzgerald was limping now, and indeed the whole Irish pack looked whacked – the more so when Esteve, looping into the centre, kicked ahead, found the bounce with him and scored another try: 15–16, and the French seemingly unstoppable. Just quarter of an hour remained. France came again: Blanco, Blanco all the way; Belascain fumbled; MacNeill, desperate, hacked at the bobbing ball . . . suddenly it was deep and dangerous inside French territory. Blanco and all France had to turn. MacNeill hacked on; the nippy Sella raced back, fell on the ball barely ten yards from his line; MacNeill was on him, the Irish pack fast behind. They won it, the movement went left and Finn was over in the corner – to tumult. Campbell missed the conversion, but sealed an historic victory with a penalty just before the end. Begob and glory be! 22–16.

Then we heard that Wales had beaten Scotland at Murrayfield by 19–15 – apparently a deserved result after a workmanlike performance: Holmes, as ever, a host unto himself. But their afternoon was illuminated by a try, sponsored on the left by Clive Rees and finished on the right by his namesake, Elgan. Between the two of them the ball had been handled in turn by Dacey, Butler, Ackerman, Richards and Wyatt.

And so when Ireland play Wales in Cardiff in a fortnight the thing was set for another truly tempestuous occasion. Yet in this last quarter of an hour the venerable Irish pack played themselves to such a standstill that I seriously suggest they might not have recovered by the time they travel to the rejuvenated Welsh.

In the set scrums and line-outs France had licked the Irish hollow. By midway through the second half victory for the Irish could only be won by guts and fervour and madcap mayhem. Through the final ferocious passages one could hear the fervent exhortation: 'C'mon boys, c'mon. Not long left, boys. Y'doing grand. For Ireland, boys!' Looking more like a nightclub bouncer or boxer who'd lost his licence, Ciaran Fitzgerald would shake his fist at his man, or walk down the line-out before throwing-in with a slap of encouragement on each of seven bottoms. 'C'mon, let's give it one more go, boys!'

Much later, showered and blazered, his Wolfhounds tie proving that there is a neck in there somewhere, he was swigging his bottle of Smeth-wicks and rejoicing in the afternoon's play. 'By Jove, they have a terribly strong set scrum. 'Twas a magnificent physical contest all through, a most rewarding experience to be part of.' Wasn't it a touch dirty in that front-row? 'Not at all; no messing about at all.' He could have fooled me. What about his own injury? ''Twas nothing. Me knee just twisted out of its socket for a moment or two.' He called for another Smethwicks – just as he had done deep into the night before at Sean Lynch's bar. Fitzgerald indeed is in the Lynch tradition.

His rival captain, Rives, sat dejected, disappointed but chivalrous. 'A good victory. They deserve. I think they play in the Irish tradition. It was difficult; Ireland's tradition is to play as near as it is possible to the ball. If the ball is over the line they are first . . .' And he gave a little shrug, and a little giggle. *Eh, voilà!*

In the *Irish Press* that very morning Cormac MacConnell had implored Rives and his Frenchmen to lose on purpose: 'We the Irish, never lower in spirit or morale, are totally dependent for our social and economic future upon Ciaran Fitzgerald's team to raise and heal our broken hearts and minds.' It was only half in jest. Consider the facts, he wrote. They were bankrupt. They were politically and geographically divided. They were disgraced internationally by a whole range of issues ranging from tapping and bugging to the kidnapping of harmless stallions. Fianna Fail lay in splinters, the Northern Assembly in ruins, while the Coalition Government was rapidly falling asunder on a matter of life and death. They were overtaxed, over-wrought, overstressed, and only in the matter of murdering each other, robbing banks and plotting against their leaders had they recently shown true Gaelic style.

'Every time Fitzgerald wins a strike against the head a score of different strikes in the industrial world are forgotten and 10,000 heads lift with pride, North and South. And every time the props heave powerfully the props of our entire national structures are made less vulnerable. And every time Ollie Campbell lands a penalty all of us tend to forget, however briefly, many of the daily penalties of living in this troubled land, lately so close to every wooden spoon on offer. I would, therefore, appeal to our French visitors, who do everything with great flair and style, to somehow contrive today to lose this game narrowly, gallantly and with style. It is quite within their compass and it would be marvellous altogether if they could manage to build up a first half lead, then fail to subdue the Irish fight-back over the last ten minutes.'

And so – more or less – it came to pass.

From Up and Under

A Great Day for the Irish

David Walsh

The average English aficionado perforce knows by a process of osmosis a good deal about the lore of Welsh rugby and something of the game in Scotland; but few Brits would claim to know much about Irish rugby. It is often perceived even over there as an elitist game, and there is an old Irish

joke that no fifteen ever takes the field without its quota of doctors to tend
the injured and lawyers to bend the laws. Yet there is a strong working-
class element in their rugby too, as David Walsh reveals in this enchanting
insight into a celebrated Irish rugby rivalry. Still, in this as in all else Irish,
the laughter is never far away.

At five o'clock on Wednesday evening five men sat on high stools in The
Mall. All nursed pints of stout. The Mall is a small pub in the parish of St
Mary's, less than a ten-minute walk from the centre of Limerick city.
Known in the parish as Angela's, the folk of Shannon RFC meet, drink and
talk rugby in this pub.

It is four days before The Match (the All Ireland League tie between
Shannon and their great rivals Garryowen) and conversation amongst the
Shannon men rages against the four pounds they will be charged at Door-
adoyle. One man claims it is against the Irish Rugby Football Union's
guidelines to charge more than three, and Elsie Cowhey, the barwoman
who chairs the discussion, approves of every condemnation.

In Limerick admission prices at rugby matches matter. And, for
Shannon, it is also a stick with which to beat Garryowen. The accusation is
serious – Garryowen charge four pounds because they don't care about
the ordinary man. A stranger had no difficulty sensing the mood. The
ordinary men of Shannon would pay their money and have their day.

One of those at the counter was John Barry, a member of the fine
Shannon side of the late seventies. He was there when Shannon, unfash-
ionable underdogs, turned over Garryowen in the Munster Cup finals of
1977 and '78. John played wing forward, open side, and had a relationship
of sorts with Garryowen's fly-half Tony Ward.

'Ward knew him alright,' says one of those at the counter.
'Intimately,' add another. John Barry smiles, appreciating the compliment.
An old gunslinger reminded of the days when he was fast and dangerous.

Backwards and forwards, the talk drifts. From old Shannon
triumphs to this afternoon's game with Garryowen. Elsie Cowhey stands
apart from the Shannon reflections, seeking and then taking the opportunity to explain her situation to the stranger:

'I married a Shannon captain,' she said. 'My sister married a Shannon captain. My two sons played for Shannon, now my two grandsons
play for Shannon. But, in my heart, I have always been and will always be
a Young Munster woman.'

One woman's allegiance to a rugby club? Much more than that. The
love for club is the life's blood of the game in Limerick. Young Munster,
Shannon and Garryowen have been the three best supported teams in the
All Ireland League. This afternoon's match will be watched by the biggest
League crowd of the season. Rugby in this town counts.

In the new league it is the Limerick clubs who have set the competitive tone and have forced others to roll up their sleeves and fight. Garryowen won their first four, Shannon won their first three AIL games

because they, more than any teams in the League, were prepared for the raising of the stakes. Wanderers and Lansdowne, the aristocrats of Leinster, suffered and learned.

Rugby in Limerick is different principally because the game has never been the preserve of the middle-class. Young Munster and Shannon are working-class clubs and so, too, the proud junior clubs Thomond, St Mary's and Richmond. Bohemians, Old Crescent and Garryowen may be closer to the middle-class nature of the Irish game, but they are mindful of their natural hinterland:

'Garryowen,' says Shannon man Bob Keane, 'are a middle-class club who always wanted about seven or eight working men in their team. In the old days they came to the parish (St Mary's) looking for them and they generally wanted them to be forwards.'

Even if perceived as middle-class, Garryowen has held its ground in the struggle for rugby supremacy. Part of the Garryowen strategy has been to recognize the irrelevance of social distinction in the Limerick game: 'Docker against doctor, it is the strength of Limerick rugby,' says Paddy Reid, a member of Ireland's Grand Slam team of 1949 and the current Garryowen president.

Reid tells a story about an international who came from Dolphin in Cork to Limerick. He was a bank manager. One afternoon he was taking his wife and dog for a walk through the centre of town when a voice from a lane called out 'Hello Charlie.' Further on there was a coal lorry and the driver's assistant knew the doctor. 'Hello Charlie,' the man shouted. Another road, there was another labourer and another greeting. Always, the banker returned the pleasantry. His wife was bemused:

'How,' she asked her husband, 'do you know these people?'

'My love,' the banker replied, 'if you play rugby against these men, you never forget them.'

Philip Danaher grew up in Abbeyfeale, on the Kerry side of the county boundary. Gaelic football was his game until he went as a boarding student to St Munchin's College in Limerick. At Munchin's, it was rugby. He was one of the best of his generation, could kick like a mule and was as brave as a lion. Danaher played for the Munster and Irish Schools and, later in his career, would play at the highest level for his province and country.

One year ahead of Danaher at Munchin's was Pat Murray. A Limerick boy, Murray, too, could play the oval ball and did so for the Munster and Irish Schools. Danaher was fly-half, Murray full-back. Together they played on the Munchin's side which won the Munster Schools Cup in 1982. Danaher says he can still see Tommy Leahy jumping on top of David Dineen after Dineen had scored Munchin's clinching try in the final defeat of Presentation College, Cork.

In that campaign of 1982 Munchin's played 24 games, losing just one friendly match and winning the Cup. Friendships and memories for life.

Together, Murray and Danaher are as comfortable now as they were then. Even if Murray is now captain of Shannon and Danaher skipper of Garryowen. As schoolboys they never imagined they would oppose each other, but the enormity of today's match cannot change all that has gone before.

They agreed to meet in the new bar at the Royal George Hotel on O'Connell Street. Danaher, warm and gregarious; Murray, as warm but in a quieter way. They have come from backgrounds outside of Limerick's rugby heartland and they are, in a sense, unworried by the weight of old traditions. Murray, especially, reflects the changing face of rugby in the city.

Many of the old St Mary's families have grown up and moved away from the parish, forcing Shannon to broaden its recruitment policy. Murray was plucked from the city's middle-class suburbs. He and Danaher can enjoy the build-up to one of the great sporting occasions in the city:

'This is the biggest game in Garryowen's history,' says Danaher.

'It is greater than a Cup Final,' says Murray. 'And it isn't just about the two League points. Pride in Limerick is a big thing and this is what this game is about. If you lose a Cup Final, at least the season is over and you can disappear. Lose this match and there is still half a season to play. If we lose I'll be looking for a job transfer to Galway.'

'It'll be the Aran Islands for me,' says Danaher.

What will the captains be saying to their teams in the moments before confrontation?:

'This is one game,' says Murray, 'when there won't be any need for talk. Anyway, any player who is still listening fifteen minutes before kick-off is lost.'

'I'll be listening,' says Danaher, 'trying to hear what Ger Mac (Ger McMahon, the Shannon coach) is saying about me in the other dressing-room.'

Danaher played for a few years with the Dublin club, Lansdowne. Playing in the capital and with a good side was fun but it didn't have the passion or homeliness of Limerick: 'In Dublin you played your game and, never mind seeing one of the fellows you played against, you were unlikely to see any member of your own team until you met at training three days later. Down here you bump into everybody all the time.'

Danaher says goodnight to Murray, telling his friend he will 'see him on Sunday, if not before.' As the Garryowen captain walks towards his car on O'Connell Street, a man passes. He is walking his dog, even if the dog moves four paces in front of his master and without a leash. 'G'night,' says the man to Danaher.

'Hope you're all set for Sunday,' replies Danaher. 'Sure am,' says the man without breaking stride.

'That's Frank O'Flynn,' says Danaher. 'A Shannon man. If they beat us on Sunday, Frank will lead the singing of their song "There Is an Isle". He does it for every big Shannon win.'

Ah, *the* Frank O'Flynn. He who played on the first Shannon team to win the Munster Senior Cup. That was 1960. Player then, supporter/singer ever since. There is a story told about O'Flynn, the singer. It concerns a Shannon woman, exiled in Manchester, and how she first heard about the famous Cup victory over Garryowen in 1977.

It was a Saturday afternoon and as the lady worked in her Manchester kitchen she listened to Radio Eireann. They were taking intermittent reports from Thomond Park and, as the reception of RTE in Manchester was also intermittent, the lady was not totally sure how the game was going. She described her epiphany thus:

'I had a feeling that the game was near the end and that Shannon were just in front. I couldn't bear to listen, went out of the kitchen for a minute and when I returned, what did I hear but my neighbour Frank O'Flynn, loud and clear on the radio, singing "There Is an Isle".'

Seventy-seven might have been Shannon's greatest triumph, but every victory over Garryowen is cherished. For the clubs go back a long, long way. They were both formed in the same year, 1884. Garryowen became a senior club and Shannon a junior club. The link between them was strong.

Shannon drew their players from the parish of St Mary's, which was then teeming with large, hardy families. The best players from the parish served an apprenticeship with Shannon and, if good enough, went on to play senior with Garryowen. If Garryowen attracted players from outside who were not good enough to play senior, it was suggested by the club that those players join Shannon. At the time, Garryowen did not have junior or under age sides.

Bob Keane is one of a battalion who grew up with dual citizenship: 'My family was a Shannon family, but most of us played senior with Garryowen. My uncles played with Shannon and then Garryowen in the late 1890s. My uncle Jack Burke, a Shannon man, who played senior with Garryowen, left for Australia in 1908. He was presented with his Garryowen cap at the railway station in Limerick before departure.

'He settled in Melbourne and called his house "Garryowen". His son grew up, got his own home in Australia and he too called it "Garryowen".'

Garryowen and Shannon grew up together. Their triumphs were shared and, like members of the same family, they often fell out. But that was within the family: to the outside world they were successful clubs who worked together for their mutual benefit. That was until Shannon decided it was time to move off the safe ledge of junior rugby and plunge into the unknown territory of their betters.

At the meeting of the Munster Branch to consider Shannon's request to join the senior ranks, it was Garryowen who proposed that their neighbours be accepted. That was 1954. Those Garryowen players who had originally been Shannon men returned to their ancestral home and the lines were drawn. Shannon and Garryowen were now rivals and their old alliance sharpened the rivalry, gave it an edge that would distinguish it from all other rivalries in Irish rugby.

Shannon's formative years in senior football were difficult. Through the first four seasons a handful of matches were won, a bagful lost. Garryowen remained amongst the elite of Irish rugby. Six years after the transition, Shannon found their feet and won their first Munster Cup. That was 1960, a time when the parish was still the well from which Shannon drew its players:

'If I am remembering correctly,' says Bob Keane, 'ten members of that Cup winning side had been together as young lads in the St Mary's Second Troop Boys Scouts.'

The first encounter of the one-time sister clubs in a Cup Final occurred in 1971. Garryowen delivered a cruel lesson, 29–0. According to the folklore of Limerick rugby, the president of Garryowen at the time walked into his team's dressing-room after the match and said 'Lads, t'was only a joke.' A Shannon official heard the comment and passed it on to his clubmates.

Four times through the seventies and eighties Garryowen and Shannon would meet in the final of the Cup. Each time Frank O'Flynn sang 'There Is an Isle' and Shannon left Thomond Park with the Cup. One Shannon official maintains that the 'joke of 1960' rebounded on Garryowen. As Pat Murray says, there will be no need for talk in the dressing-room before today's game.

And if Limerick's fascination with this afternoon's match could be encapsulated in one story, there is the tale of the celebrating Shannon supporter. His team had won the Cup and he began drinking immediately afterwards. For four days and four nights, his wife never laid eyes on him. In the early hours of Thursday morning, he returned to his home, stole a few hours' sleep, rose early, washed, shaved, changed his shirt, put back on his Shannon tie and was about to leave the house when his wife asked where he was going.

'Down to Angela's to celebrate Shannon's win with a drink,' he said.

'But you've been doin' that since Saturday,' she said.

'I am going again,' he replied.

'I understand,' she cried, 'You love Shannon more than you love me.'

'What,' he said, 'I love Garryowen more than I love you.'

From *The Sunday Tribune*

Why Was He Born So Beautiful?

No aspect of rugby life is more idiosyncratic than the singing after the game. Not all the songs have their origin in the clubhouse; some were born in the distant watches of the imperial night at the height of the British Raj. Comic and coarse, subversive and cynical, they now make up a huge sub-

terranean folklore that has spread wherever rugby is played. Such an institution have they become that they are typed and bound so that players can take them abroad on that other great staple of rugby life, the Easter tour. The songs that follow are nearly all from just such a book prepared by Cirencester RFC. I thought the tips for young players abroad which preface the songs so sensible that I am printing them too.

Yes, but what actually happens when the final whistle blows? Let me quote my godson, Rayne McKnight, who has just won his 316th cap for Old Alleynians, where he plays at centre three-quarter – thus beating by two the previous record for a back and ensuring that his cheery mug will be framed and hung in the clubhouse for good. Players, Rayne tells me, turn up a little before 1.15 and chat about the week's events until their skipper arrives and, if it's an important game, gives them a pep-talk. Then the game, and by 4.15 or 4.30 they are in their whopping communal bath with a few songs already if they've won, then a high tea of pies, beans and mash. The visiting team's grub is paid for by their hosts. Now the real sing-song begins; they will sink 8 to 10 pints of Shepheard Neame bitter each, or, for those with new-fangled tastes, of Steinbock lager. Now is the time for singing all the old good ones appended here. At about 9 pm they all adjourn for curry. Cabs are summoned after that these breathalysed days – quite rightly – and next morning they walk back to the ground to pick up their cars. So, in essence, it has gone on as far back as memory goes; long may it continue to do so.

1. Be courteous to your hosts.

2. *Be on time* for all appointments.

3. Be considerate.

4. Be particularly careful regarding personal cleanliness.

5. Dress smartly for matches, but during leisure time casual wear is perfectly acceptable.

6. Make own arrangements with your hosts regarding personal clothes washing.

7. At all times make sure your documents, cash and belongings are secure.

8. Do not enter into discussions or arguments regarding politics, race etc.

9. If you feel so inclined buy a small gift or present for your host.

10. During leisure time in cities avoid being alone and also avoid clip joints.

11. Please be conscious of the fact that the police in America are far more rigid than our own police.

Why was he born so beautiful?

Why was he born so beautiful?
Why was he born at all?
He's no bloody use to anyone
He's no bloody use at all.

Be kind to your web-footed friends

Be kind to your web-footed friends
For a duck may be somebody's mother
Be kind to your friends in the swamp
Where the weather is cool and damp
Now you may think that this is the end
Well it is . . .

Who killed Cock Robin

Who killed Cock Robin – I said the
Sparrow with my bow and arrow.

> All the birds of the air
> Fell a sighing and a sobbing when
> They heard of the death of poor
> Cock Robin, when they heard of the
> Death of poor Cock Robin.

Who saw him die – I said the fly with
My little eye.

Who caught his blood – I said the fish
With my little dish.

Who'll dig his grave – I said the owl with
My little trowel.

Who'll toll the bell – I said the bull
Because I can pull.

Who'll make his shroud – I said the beetle
With my thread and needle.

Down by the river side

Go-int lay down my rugby kit, down
By the river side, down by the river
Side, down by the river side,

Go-int lay down my rugby kit, down by
The river side, aint goin't study war
No more.

Go-int lay down my burden,

Go-int lay down my sword and shield,

Go-int try on my long white robe,

Go-int take up my old pint pot.

Gentlemen should please refrain

Gentlemen should please refrain
From flushing toilets while the train
Is standing in the station for a while.
We encourage contemplation
While the train is in the station,
Cross your legs and grit your teeth and smile.

If you wish to pass some water
You should sing out for a porter
Who will place a basin in the bog;
Tramps and hoboes underneath
Get it in the eye and teeth,
But that's what comes from being underdog.

Pissing while the train is moving
Is another way of proving,
That control of eye and hand is sure;
We like our clients to be neat,
So please don't wet upon the seat,
Or, even worse, don't splash upon the floor.

If the Ladies' Room be taken,
do not feel the least forsaken,
Never show the sign of sad defeat,
Try the Gents across the hall,
and if some man has felt the call
He'll courteously relinquish you his seat.

If these efforts are in vain,
then simply break the window pane,
This novel method's used by very few,

We go strolling through the park,
a-goosing statues in the dark,
If Peter Pan can take it, why can't you?

If I were the marrying kind

If I were the marrying kind,
Which thank the Lord I'm not, sir,
The kind of man that I would wed
Would be a rugby full-back.

And he'd find touch and I'd find touch,
We'd both find touch together,
We'd be all right in the middle of the night
Finding touch together.

If I were the marrying kind,
Which thank the Lord I'm not, sir,
The kind of man that I would wed
Would be a wing three-quarter.

And he'd go hard and I'd go hard,
We'd both go hard together,
We'd be all right in the middle of the night
Going hard together.

If I were the marrying kind,
Which thank the Lord I'm not, sir,
The kind of man that I would wed
Would be a centre three-quarter.

And he'd pass it out and I'd pass it out,
We'd both pass it out together,
We'd be all right in the middle of the night
Passing it out together.

If I were the marrying kind,
Which thank the Lord I'm not, sir,
The kind of man that I would wed
Would be a rugby fly-half.

And he'd whip it out and I'd whip it out,
We'd both whip it out together,
We'd be all right in the middle of the night
Whipping it out together.

If I were the marrying kind,
Which thank the Lord I'm not, sir,
The kind of man that I would wed
Would be a rugby scrum-half.

And he'd put it in and I'd put it in,
We'd both put it in together,
We'd be all right in the middle of the night
Putting it in together.

If I were the marrying kind,
Which thank the Lord I'm not, sir,
The kind of man that I would wed
Would be a rugby hooker.

And he'd strike hard and I'd strike hard,
We'd both strike hard together,
We'd be all right in the middle of the night
Striking hard together.

If I were the marrying kind,
Which thank the Lord I'm not, sir,
The kind of man that I would wed
Would be a big prop-forward.

And he'd bind tight and I'd bind tight,
We'd both bind tight together,
We'd be all right in the middle of the night
Binding tight together.

If I were the marrying kind,
Which thank the Lord I'm not, sir,
The kind of man that I would wed
Would be a referee.

And he would blow and I would blow
We'd both blow together;
We'd be all right in the middle of the night
Blowing hard together.

Seven old ladies

Oh, dear, what can the matter be,
Seven old ladies locked in the lavatory,
They were there from Sunday to Saturday,
Nobody knew they were there.

They said they were going to
have tea with the Vicar,
They went in together,
they thought it was quicker,
But the lavatory door was a bit of a sticker,
And the Vicar had tea all alone.

The first was the wife of a deacon in Dover,
And though she was known
as a bit of a rover,
She liked it so much
she thought she'd stay over,
And nobody knew she was there.

The next old lady was old Mrs Bickle,
She found herself in a desperate pickle,
Shut in a pay booth, she hadn't a nickel,
And nobody knew she was there.

The next was the
Bishop of Chichester's daughter,
Who went in to pass some superfluous water,
She pulled on the chain
and the rising tide caught her,
And nobody knew she was there.

The next old lady was Abigail Humphrey,
Who settled inside to make herself comfy,
And then she found out
she could not get her bum free
And nobody knew she was there.

The next old lady was Elizabeth Spender,
Who was doing all right
till a vagrant suspender
Got all twisted up in her feminine gender,
And nobody knew she was there.

The last was a lady named Jennifer Trim,
She only sat down on a personal whim
But she somehow got pinched
twixt the cup and the brim,
And nobody knew she was there.

But another old lady was Mrs McBligh,
Went in with a bottle to booze on the sly,

She jumped on the seat
and fell in with a cry,
And nobody knew she was there.

Small boys

Little boys are cheap today
Cheaper than yesterday.
Small ones are half a crown,
Standing up or lying down.
Big ones are four and six
'Cause they've got bigger dicks,
Little boys are cheap, cheaper today.

When Lady Jane became a tart

It fairly broke the family's heart
When Lady Jane became a tart
But blood is blood and race is race
And so to save the family face
They bought her an expensive flat
With 'Welcome' written on the mat.

It was not long ere Lady Jane
Brought her patrician charms to fame
A clientele of sahibs pukka
Who regularly came to fuck 'er,
And it was whispered without malice
She had a client from the palace.

No one could nestle in her charms
Unless he wore ancestral arms
No one to her could gain an entry,
Unless he were of the landed gentry,
And so before her sun had set
She'd worked her way through Debrett.

When Lady Anne became a whore
It grieved the family even more,
But they felt they couldn't do the same
As they had done for Lady Jane,
So they bought her an exclusive beat,
On the shady side of Jermyn Street.

When Lord St Clancy became a nancy
It did not please the family fancy

And so in order to protect him
They did inscribe upon his rectum,
'All commoners must now drive steerage,
This arse hole is reserved for peerage.'

Good night ladies

Good night ladies, good night ladies, good
Night ladies, we're going to leave you
Now.

> Merrily we roll along, roll along, roll
> Along, merrily we roll along, O'er the
> Deep blue sea.

Farewell ladies.

Sweet dreams ladies.

The Art of Coarse Rugby

Michael Green

One of the funniest writers now with us is Michael Green, author of that perennial best-seller, The Art of Coarse Rugby. *Since then he has written a whole generation of books in the coarse genre, two novels, three plays, and four other books, broadcast regularly on radio and television. He also does a brilliant one-man show based on coarse acting. He was brought up in Leicester, as he tells us in his engrossing autobiography* The Boy Who Shot Down an Airship, *where rugby is the ruling passion. When he was six Michael was taken by his parents to see the Leicester Tigers; and this was the beginning of a lifelong love affair with the game. When he asked his father why Leicester didn't play London clubs he replied that they weren't good enough: 'They are all chinless wonders and medical students down there.' Certainly the Leicester game was and is resolutely down to earth; and the revolting outside urinal, Michael says, is still there, the concrete stained green with fungus and the drain blocked by leaves. The fabled Russian Prince Obolensky turned out on the wing for Leicester, and in 1932 the combined Leicestershire and East Midlands team beat the Springboks. No matter; coarse rugby was the heart of the matter and no one knows more about it than Michael.*

'That we may wander o'er this bloody field . . .'

Shakespeare (Henry V).

It is a wet, drizzling, bitterly cold Saturday afternoon in February. A group of dismal figures in motley rugby kit are shambling along a rough cinder path between a refuse dump and a field of thistles. Behind them a coach driver who unwisely tried to drive down the path is endeavouring to extricate his vehicle from the ditch.

A player at the back of the group speaks. He is a tall lanky man in his late thirties with receding hair and a pronounced stoop. We shall call him Thinny, and he is the Old Rottinghamians Extra B stand-off. He furtively adjusts his surgical underwear as he speaks.

THINNY: Gosh it's cold. Why the hell does the Extra B pitch have to be so far from the pavilion? I don't know why we play the stupid game. You wouldn't think it was February would you? More like December.

Nobody replies. They trudge moodily along in silence. Thinny tries again.

THINNY (*blowing into cupped hands*): I said I thought it was too cold to play.

This at last rouses some response in his companion, a gross, waddling creature of about thirty-nine, wearing a tattered scrum cap and a faded, patched jersey. We shall call him Fatty.

FATTY: All right. We heard you. You aren't the only one. My mind may not be the delicate mechanism that yours is, but I can get just as cold as you can. To hear you go on, anyone'd think you were the only person in the world who ever got cold. It's all right for you. You don't have to keep going down in the mud like I do.

Thinny does not reply. He is too busy lighting a cigarette from the butt of another. Fatty pursues his theme.

FATTY: I don't know why we go through this stupid torture week after week. My wife and kids think I'm nuts. Why don't we sit at home and watch the telly? That's what I like about watching an international – seeing all those stupid fools running around injuring themselves and getting all uncomfortable in the rain and I'm sitting in the warm, drinking whisky and smoking myself sick.

The pair are joined by a third player, whom we shall call Gloomy. He is a lanky youth of about nineteen who has outgrown his strength and his mental powers.

GLOOMY: It'll be murder in this mud. You know the boiler's furred up and there won't be any water after the first team have had their bath?

Neither of his companions reply. Fatty lights up a butt end.

GLOOMY: Cor, don't the other side look huge? See that big bloke – I bet he's the wing forward. I bet when he tackles you he absolutely flattens you. You'd better watch out, Thinny.

Fatty and Thinny purse their lips and plod on in silence.

GLOOMY (*warming to his theme*): They say that bloke who broke his leg last week may have to have it off. . . .

This produces an instantaneous reaction on Fatty and Thinny, who blench and groan.

THINNY: Shut up, will ya?

GLOOMY: Must be rotten to have your leg off. Did you hear the crack when the bone snapped? I bet he wishes he never played last week. . . .

FATTY: Will you shut up if I give you a fag?

GLOOMY: Ta, very much. I knew a boy at school who died after smoking a fag just before a game. It affected his heart.

THINNY: I'll affect your heart in a minute. It's bad enough having to turn out on a foul afternoon like this without you making it worse.

GLOOMY: You ought to give up if you feel like that. You're old enough . . . you must be about forty-five.

THINNY: That's just it – you give up now and you admit old age. Once you stop at my age you never start again. It's like a woman putting on her first corset. It's an admission you're old.

GLOOMY: They say it's dangerous to play after thirty-five. The valves of the heart won't work properly. . . .

He is interrupted by a clod of wet earth on the back of the neck. The little group trudge on in silence. It is a quarter of an hour before they reach the pitch, which is a sodden, lumpy meadow, bearing strong evidence of having been recently occupied by a herd of cows with loose bowels. They are greeted by their captain, a harassed man of about thirty, who is probably the slowest centre threequarter in Europe.

CAPTAIN: Come on, where do you think you've all been? I wanted you. We've got to rearrange the forwards somehow.

FATTY: How many men have we got?

CAPTAIN: Eleven, not counting Knocker.

FATTY: He's not coming. I saw him in the Royal Oak and he said to tell you he was ill.

CAPTAIN (*bitterly*): The swine! And I think the others have got thirteen. That means we're two down.

THINNY (*instantly*): Cancel it. Say the ground's unfit. Look at it, it *is* unfit. I'm sinking in up to my ankles. (*Becoming feverish and hysterical*) I tell you it's unfit to play, I tell you we can't play on this. . . . I tell you it's absurd . . . aaaaaaaaaaahhhhh . . . (*he breaks off in a paroxysm of coughing as his cigarette smoke goes the wrong way*).

GLOOMY: I reckon he'll burst a lung before half-time.

The referee approaches. He is an earnest man, in late middle-age, kind-hearted and slow-witted. He can never understand why he is always allocated Extra B games.

REFEREE: Come along, Old Rottinghamians. It'll be dark soon. We're nearly an hour late already.

CAPTAIN: Coming, sir. O.K. you chaps, let's get sorted out. Jack, you'll have to be a sort of wing-three and full-back in one, and Fred, you float around generally between the pack and the backs. Use your discretion. We'll pack three-two-zero.

THINNY: Who'll go centre now Knocker's ratted on us?

CAPTAIN (*desperately*): Oh, George'll have to play centre.

GEORGE (*protesting*): But I'm a hooker.

CAPTAIN: Well, you're a centre now. Come on, stop this arguing and get stuck into them, Old Rottinghamians.

He says this without much conviction, and privately whispers to those around him, 'Don't hurry too much lads, let the bastards wait.' This is because the longer the start is delayed, the less time there will be for play, which is to the Old Rottinghamians' advantage in their weakened state. In any case, play is delayed because the match ball has landed in a heap of cow dirt, and no one will wipe it clean. Eventually the unpleasant task is performed by the captain of the opposing side, who realizes that as far as the Old Rottinghamians are concerned, it can stay there for ever.

Finally the opposition kick off in gathering gloom and at an hour when most first-class matches are just finishing. The ball is caught by Thinny who drops it. An opposing forward picks it up, knocks on four times and passes forward to a colleague, who puts one foot into touch and then dives over by the corner flag, dropping the ball as he does so.

The referee, who has not moved from the centre line, promptly awards a try.

OLD ROTTINGHAMIANS (*all together*): Hey ref, he went into touch! Hey, ref, what about the knock-on? Hey, ref, what about the forward pass? Hey, ref, what about the obstruction?

Fatty even goes so far as to stand ostentatiously waiting for the line-out, but the referee is adamant.

CAPTAIN (*self-righteously*): Stop moaning, Old Rottinghamians. Never mind if the ref's a short-sighted old sheep who doesn't know the rules, it doesn't help moaning.

He realizes he is standing about three feet from the referee and moves hurriedly away. Fortunately, the referee is deaf as well as short-sighted, and in any case he is used to a torrent of abuse from both sides. Meanwhile about four of the Old Rottinghamians have gathered under the crossbar. Fatty, Thinny and one or two others have flung themselves on the ground panting and grumbling.

The opposition kicker is now placing the ball with infinite pains. He has so far taken four minutes over this. Eventually he carefully marches backwards for about thirty paces and stands rigidly at attention before moving forward into an immense run. This is carried out to an accompaniment of continuous sotto voce jeering, blasphemy, insults and obscenity from the Old Rottinghamians, none of whom, however, can raise the energy to charge.

When the kicker reaches the ball, he aims a terrific lunge and digs his toe deep into the ground about two feet in front of it, leaving it quite undisturbed. With a look of intense agony he sinks slowly to the ground, clutching his shattered leg. Quick to seize this advantage, the Old Rottinghamian skipper leads his men in a belated charge. Ignoring the ball and the objections of the referee they trample all over the prostrate kicker, who recovers with alarming suddenness and fights his way clear, protesting.

Order is at last restored and another kick taken. This time the ball goes bowling along the ground and hits the corner flag. The kicker returns to the jeers of his own team and the Old Rottinghamians prepare to reduce the arrears.

It is now half-time. As the referee blows his whistle Fatty and Thinny collapse in their tracks.

FATTY (*coughing as if his lungs would burst, turning red in the face and retching*): Uuuuuuuurrrrggggghhhhh. Aaaahhh. Brrouge. Faaaaaaghh. Ooooyer . . . ooooyer . . . ooyer . . . splurge . . . bless me (*only he doesn't say 'bless'*). Gimme a cigarette someone.

Thinny feels in the pocket of his shorts and brings out a filthy, bent object which might at one time have been a cigarette. Fatty produces a book of matches from his shorts and lights it. Then he immediately doubles up in another paroxysm of coughing.

THINNY (*sitting down in a deep puddle as if it was a feather bed*): You're in a bad way, mate.

FATTY: You're telling me. Why the hell do we go through this ghastly torture week in, week out? Saturday after Saturday the agony goes on . . . retching . . . vomiting . . . panting for breath . . . in continual pain. . . .

THINNY (*looking round hopefully*): It's getting pretty dark. With luck the ref may have to abandon it.

The captain approaches. He is a worried man. Having forgotten the lemons for the last two home games, he tied a knot in his handkerchief and remembered them. Instead, he forgot a knife and a plate, and all he can offer the two teams is two whole lemons each.

CAPTAIN: Anyone want a bit of lemon? I forgot the knife, so you'll have to try and tear a bit off.

Between them Fatty and Thinny savage the lemons into an unrecognizable pulp which is rejected contemptuously by everyone else. The other side throw their lemons over the hedge. The referee blows an optimistic chirp on his whistle. There is a faint stir among the players but no one moves. He blows again and this time one or two of the younger ones line up in some sort of order.

CAPTAIN (*making a feeble attempt to rouse his men*): Now come along, Old Rottinghamians, let's get stuck into it this half. Thirty-six-nil isn't hopeless. If they can score it, so can we. Let's get some punch and life and go . . . go . . . go. . . .

He smacks his fist into his palm with such venom that it is paralyzed for the rest of the afternoon. Someone throws a bit of mud at him. Fatty discovers he has lined up with the other team and painfully crosses back to the right side.

Thinny, who is stand-off, places the ball upright for the kick-off. It falls over. With mathematical precision he carefully replaces it and stands back with the air of a master. The ball topples over again. A restive muttering grows among the forwards, who give him advice what to do with the ball. It falls over five times altogether.

Eventually Thinny lays it down sideways on the ground and takes a wild boot at it. It spins like a top and travels two feet. The second half has begun. . . .

The Old Rottinghamians' captain is hoarse with urging his men on – a job which is quite futile. But he sticks to it. 'Come on, Old Rotts,' he shouts, leading an untidy and half-hearted foot rush down the field. 'Now we've got them on the YURRRRP. . . .' This exclamation is forced from him as an opponent fly-kicks the ball with unerring accuracy straight into his navel (point first). He collapses. When he recovers the referee awards a penalty against him.

Now the score is 45-nil against the Old Rottinghamians. Holding on to a post as they line up for a conversion, the captain tries to flog some life into them. 'Old Rottinghamians,' he bleats, 'you mustn't let them come through like that. You must mark your men. Thinny, you must tackle.'

A violent bickering ensues. Everyone turns on Gloomy, who, like a sick sheep, is forced out of the flock and retreats to the corner flag. The skipper appeals for peace.

CAPTAIN: Stop this bickering, Old Rottinghamians. We can still do it. Let's try and get just one before the end.

Nobody pays any attention to him. They are still arguing when the kick is taken. From now on their morale goes to pieces and they are solely concerned with venting their irritation somehow. The climax of this comes when Thinny, having been fairly tackled, kicks his opponent as he gets up.

OPPONENT: You rat, I'll get you for that.

THINNY: Just you make a dirty tackle like that again, and I'll fix you proper.

OPPONENT: Oh yeah?

THINNY: Yeah.

OPPONENT: Yeah?

THINNY: Yeah.

OPPONENT: Yeah?

THINNY (*snarling*): Yeah.

OPPONENT: You and who else?

THINNY: Just me.

OPPONENT: You wouldn't dare, mate.

THINNY: Wouldn't I?

OPPONENT: No.

THINNY: No?

OPPONENT: No.

Suddenly, without warning, Thinny aims a wild and amateurish swipe at his opponent which catches him harmlessly on the shoulder. He lets out a shout of rage and they rush at each other, pummelling with all their not very considerable strength.

FATTY: Go on, Thinny, show the dirty so-and-so where he gets off!

Nobody shows any signs of stopping the fight. In fact each side encourage their own man. The referee comes puffing up, blowing his whistle wildly and in vain.

REFEREE: Now then you two, come along now and stop this nonsense. This isn't how rugby men should behave.

Neither fighter pays the slightest attention. Eventually they are separated by their captains who drag them apart and hold them while they continue to wave their fists and shout at each other.

THINNY: Let me go, Fred, just let me get at that filthy hog. He's not fit to play rugby with decent people. . . .

OPPONENT: I ask you . . . was it or was it not a fair tackle? He kicked me . . . and he bit me. Look at them bite marks. I'll murder him if I get him again.

This rouses Thinny to fury and he thrashes so violently that he breaks free. This is awkward, because he doesn't really want to fight, so he pretends to be restrained with difficulty.

REFEREE: Come along you two . . . shake hands and forget it.

After a moment's hesitation the two players advance and take each other's hands, each of them trying to grip the other in such a way as to hurt him. The result is that they look like a couple of Masons engaged in some remote ritual. Having failed to hurt each other they retire muttering and the match goes on. But not for long. It is now nearly pitch dark and lights can be seen twinkling in nearby suburbs. The referee looks at his watch. The first half lasted thirty-one minutes and the second has now lasted twenty-five minutes. It is good enough for Coarse Rugby. He blows a long blast.

CAPTAIN: Old Rottinghamians, three cheers for Bagford Vipers . . . hip . . . hip . . . hooray!

He is answered by a feeble moaning sound, so faint that it merges with the wind which is now beginning to whistle coldly over the pitch.

OPPOSING CAPTAIN (*quietly*): Don't cheer them, lads. They're the dirtiest crowd we've ever played.

THINNY (*approaching the man he fought with a let's-be-friends smile*): Jolly well played. Sorry we had that little fight.

All the time he is thinking: 'Filthy swine.'

From *The Art of Coarse Rugby*

The Unacceptable Face of Rugby

John Reason

It is one of the cardinal attributes of rugby that it teaches how violence should be treated; how it should be tamed and used. And we have already noted that, whatever fury is expended on the field of play, violence has never yet broken loose in the stands. Still, the trend is worrying. This sickening account by John Reason of what happened to Sandy Carmichael in New Zealand in 1971 is given simply as a stark reminder of what happens to the game when winning becomes the only objective; and perhaps what will happen more and more if money is allowed to motivate the game in the future.

The sight of Sandy Carmichael's face as he lay collapsed on the masseur's table in the Lions' dressing-room after the match against Canterbury will stay in the memory of all who saw it for as long as they live.

His left eye was closed and a huge blue swelling of agonised flesh hung out from the cheekbone like a grotesque plum. His right eye was a slit between the puffed skin above and below it. His right eyelid was gashed and straggling with blood. Another gash snagged away from the corner of his eye. He was quivering with emotion and frustration. His hands shook as they tried to hold the ice packed on the swellings.

I had seen Carwyn James, the Lions' coach, outside the dressing-room after the match. I had asked him how Carmichael was. 'Come and see for yourself,' he said. 'Our dressing-room is like a casualty clearing station.' I had never seen Carwyn so upset.

Rugby footballers are used to violence and ugly injuries. Theirs is a physical contact sport and injuries are inevitable, but even the Lions were horrified by the sight of Carmichael. They hung back, shaking their heads and talking in hushed tones of sheer disbelief, as people do who are unwilling witnesses of some appalling road accident. They sensed Carmichael's anguish, both physical and spiritual, and they showered and dressed and combed their hair and stood back and left him alone.

The scene was like the loser's dressing-room after a gory heavyweight fight. It had been a fight all right. It had been a heavyweight fight. The difference was that it was the winner's dressing-room at a rugby ground, and if a boxing referee had allowed the punishment which Carmichael had absorbed in the previous hour and a half, he would have been prosecuted.

Canterbury did not go out to play rugby football against the Lions. They were the Ranfurly Shield holders and as such were considered to be New Zealand's leading provincial side. In some twisted way, they seemed to think that their national honour was at stake and that their best hope of ending the Lions' unbeaten run in New Zealand was to punch and kick them off the field.

So many people seemed to know that it would happen. 'Don't follow the ball after the scrums and the line-outs,' I was told. 'Watch the front rows. Watch Hopkinson. Watch Wyllie.'

Even in the first ten minutes, the presence of the ball seemed a complete irrelevance. The fact that the Lions had switched the kick-off and were in one position on the field or another did not matter, either. The rugby was incidental to the punches which were being thrown by the Canterbury forwards. Hopkinson and Wyllie were not the only players involved. They were the principal combatants, it is true, but there were others almost as busy.

Hopkinson's chief target was Carmichael. In the first twelve minutes of the match, he had already done so much damage that Carmichael had to leave the field for treatment. The pity of it was that Carmichael went back. The Lions would have done better to move Bill McBride up to tight head and to bring on Derek Quinnell or Gordon Brown. Hopkinson would have thought twice about punching McBride and Quinnell was positively writhing in his seat in the stand in his anxiety to get on to the pitch.

Carmichael did go back, though. His headband was askew and as the match went on the flesh round his eyes puffed and blackened until he could scarcely see where he was going. The punching went on, too. John Pullin, the Lions hooker, could hear the blows going in, and he thought it was only a question of time before they came for him.

The line-out, too, was just another set position from which the Canterbury forwards threw punches. Fergus Slattery, the Lions wing-forward, stopped one in the mouth from Hopkinson which knocked two of his front teeth sideways. The Lions had won the ball at a line-out and Slattery was just turning to see what Mike Gibson was going to do with it when Hopkinson came round the back and swung at him. Slattery not only had his teeth loosened but was also so badly concussed that all he could remember at the end of the game was that he was in a foreign country. He had bought a mouthguard when he arrived in New Zealand but he forgot to take it to the match. Dentists and other specialists told him subsequently that if he had worn the guard it would have saved his teeth and also reduced the concussion.

Nothing much would have saved John Pullin, though. He did not see the punch coming which felled him after a line-out and neither did Gareth Edwards when Wyllie knocked him down with a rabbit punch in the back of the neck when the ball was 30 yards away. Wyllie also jumped on a ruck in front of the Lions post in the first half and stamped up the back of it as if he was running up a sand dune. That did incur a penalty kick.

By the most supreme of ironies, none of this cost Canterbury a single point, but when the Lions retaliated, it cost them a penalty goal. Ray McLoughlin lashed out when he was being blinded by a hand in his eyes. The referee, Dr Humphrey Rainey, awarded a penalty kick and McCormick, the Canterbury full-back, kicked the goal. He did it while Carmichael was off the field. I wonder what Dr Rainey would have thought if he had known that Carmichael was suffering from a multiple fracture of the cheekbone because he had been punched.

From *The Victorious Lions*

The Referee Everyone Wants

Steve Bale

We must not forget the referee, who in the end must orchestrate what happens on the field of play. Here are three sharply contrasting accounts of his role, beginning in real life with the majestic arbitration of Clive Norling.

It began when, as a 17-year-old schoolboy, he refereed Metal Box against

Penygroes Seconds in front of a few dozen people in his home town, Neath. It will reach 1,000 matches before 51,000 – the University match's first Twickenham sell-out – when Oxford play Cambridge a week today.

At a youthful 39, Clive Norling is at the summit of his authority, assailed from all sides not by the brickbats usually tossed at long-suffering referees but by bouquets. The Swansea college lecturer is the referee everyone wants but too few actually get.

His most recent admirer was Wayne Shelford, whose parting shot after his All Blacks had played the Barbarians was to the effect that the rugby world would be a better place if only all referees were like Norling. Shelford is in a long line.

Last January there was the remarkable admission by Geoff Cooke, the England manager, that his choice of referee for a Wales-England game in Cardiff would always be Norling. 'I'd love him to referee *every* England game,' Cooke added. 'He has this marvellous feel for what the players are trying to do.'

And here we have the secret of Clive Norling. 'At the end of the day it comes down to man-management,' he said. 'It's far better to have a knowledge of the game than a knowledge of the laws, because if you know what players are trying to do, you can make a positive contribution. If you don't know, it's a recipe for confusion.

'Becoming a qualified coach in 1975 certainly helped me. I had a player's background and knowledge but you need much more than that. How, for instance, can you rule on a collapsed scrummage if you don't know the ins and outs of scrummaging?'

After 997 games (it's not all glamour: the 997th was last Saturday's West Wales match between Waunarlwydd and Ammanford; the 998th will be Christ College Brecon v Stonyhurst College tomorrow and the 999th Ystradgynlais v Dunvant on Saturday), Norling's pre-eminence is secure. For one thing, he is the only referee who can so easily get away with a mistake. But then he makes so few.

Above all he has an unrivalled instinct for the advantage law which lends continuity to games under his control, not least last year's between Oxford and Cambridge, and therefore makes them entertaining for players and spectators alike. Blues of whichever shade clearly think so; next week's will be his fifth University match.

'Like everything else, advantage comes back to the players, and my philosophy is simple,' he said. '*They* dictate my style; if both sides decide early on to play 15-man rugby, I can hold my whistle back. But if they want to play 10-man rugby, the advantage gets shorter. You have to be aware of the difference.'

It has been said that Norling entered refereeing through the accident of a back injury when he was in school, but this is not the complete case. By the time the promising lock's playing career was terminally injured while he was being illegally lifted in a line-out, he had already joined the

Neath and District Referees' Society. It was they who allocated his first match.

'I used to referee in the afternoon after playing for Neath Grammar School in the morning. The injury happened against Millfield School; a disc came out and my back has nagged me ever since. Although I was already refereeing, it did make up my mind.'

Thereafter Norling's rise was spectacular. During five years at Portsmouth Polytechnic he reached the Rugby Football Union's top ten, high enough to handle important English Cup ties. He was only 23 when he dismissed Eddie Meredith, a Metropolitan Policeman, against Bristol in the 1973 RFU quarter-final.

It was one incident among several which established Norling's reputation as a disciplinarian. Another came after he had returned to Wales when he sent off Ian Eidman of Cardiff and Bridgend's Ian Stephens, both international props, for persistently collapsing.

But Norling is better known for his uncompromising attitude to foul play. He had the temerity to dismiss Jean-Pierre Garuet, the prop, in front of 55,000 baying Frenchmen in Paris – one of 49 players on whom he has imposed the ultimate sanction in his 22 years of refereeing.

'As time has gone by I've had to send off fewer players, because they are fully aware that if they want to step out of line I'll come down on them as heavily as I can. I don't hold reputations in any esteem; I've sent off at international level and all the way down the scale.' Last season there were only two; in the three months of this season, none.

Norling's refereeing has by its quality provoked a fierce debate over the way Test matches are allocated. The Buggins's turn by which appointments are shared out meant that he was excluded from last season's Five Nations' Championship apart from running the Ireland v. England line.

Through the old invitational system – the best referees in charge of the best players in the best games – Gwynne Walters (the last man to be invited annually by Oxbridge) and Kevin Kelleher reached their joint record, 23 Tests. Had he had the same advantage, Norling might by now have reached his half-century, and would also in all probability have taken the inaugural World Cup final in 1987.

Instead, his services were dispensed with after he had refereed two of the first-round group matches. 'I wasn't in the least surprised,' Norling said. 'I'd looked at the composition of the referees' committee – chaired by an Australian, sitting with two others from the southern hemisphere, a Scot and a Frenchman.

'The numbers were always against me. I'm delighted that for the next World Cup they're going outside International Board committee men and have active refereeing assessors. This is a great advance and should do a lot to ensure the best man gets the job.

'I'm always ambitious and for a referee there couldn't be a higher ambition than that match. But first of all I have to be re-elected to the Welsh international referees' panel and be selected as a Welsh referee at the World Cup. I've never taken anything for granted and I'm not going to start now.' The rest of us, though, have been taking Norling for granted for a long time.

From The Independent

Lesser Breeds Without the Law

Michael Green

Now we turn to fiction and the tribulations of the referee from the Bagford-shire Society whose misfortune it is to have to try to bring order to the Vipers in Michael Green's magnificent comedy.

The Secretary,
Bagfordshire Society of Rugby Union Referees.

Dear Sir,

Please do not send us any more of your referees.

I must admit it was partly our own fault in asking your society to provide one. Normally, of course, our games are taken by a club member, but on this occasion he was ill. I may say he has refereed our games very well for fifteen years, moving with incredible swiftness for a man with one leg, and we shall be happy to stick to him in future, as he seems to understand our type of rugby better than your representative.

The team complain that your man upset them even before the game began by inspecting their boots, dress and persons. He not only declared that no fewer than five of our thirteen men had illegal studs in their boots, with the result they had to play in plimsolls, but he ordered our popular hooker, Paddy Flynn, to remove a signet ring from his finger. Mr Flynn is descended from a long line of Irish kings and the ring is a family heirloom. Perhaps I should have stated before that tradition says anyone causing the ring to be removed will die horribly.

Your referee complains that when the time for kick-off arrived only ten players were on the ground, and his efforts to hurry up the rest were met with abuse. This may be so, but may I point out that he further delayed things by discovering that the ball was not inflated to a pressure of ten pounds per square inch at sea level, as I gather is required. There was further delay when he alleged the pitch was not marked out in accordance with the laws of the Rugby Union. I must admit that one end is distinctly narrower than the other, but this is compensated for by a bend in the half-way line. Anyway, we regard the interesting tapering shape of the pitch as a deterrent against indiscriminate touch-kicking.

The referee's action in playing forty minutes each way caused severe distress to several of our older players who are used to half an hour each half. But what disgusted our people most of all was his dastardly action in sending off Mr Flynn for persistently offending the laws. Mr Flynn assured me afterwards that he never knew standing on an opponent's foot in the line-out is classed as obstruction. I may also say it is our custom if a player is sent off to let him return if he apologizes properly. Mr Flynn proffered his normal apology at half-time and was rudely told to leave the field again.

When I interceded on Mr Flynn's behalf I was insulted to my face. Obviously your referee does not know that I had a county trial in 1956. Under the circumstances I do not blame Mr Flynn for hiding your referee's clothes, although I am sorry they were returned later in such a filthy condition.

Finally, there was absolutely no need to abandon the game just because the posts at one end sank into the waterlogged ground and eventually collapsed. Our normal procedure when this happens is to take all the kicks at one end and this has worked well enough for many years.

In future if our own referee is not available we shall do what we have done in the past, and that is to let the captain of each team referee one half of the game. Apart from a slight tendency to cause drawn matches, this always works perfectly well.

> I remain,
> Yours faithfully,
> F. Fogg (Hon Secretary, Bagford Vipers)

PS At the conclusion of the game the referee had the audacity to demand £8 expenses from me. I was too dumbfounded to refuse, but my committee have now decided to ask for the money back, especially as we made a loss on the annual dinner again.

From *Even Coarser Rugby*

I Am an Entertainer

Max Boyce

The last word on referees comes from Max Boyce. It was written after the Welsh defeat at Twickenham in 1974, when the referee, Mr John West, an Irishman, disallowed what every Welshman present thought a perfectly good try by J. J. Williams. Mr West was to tell Max later that it had given him a sort of immortality – though of a rather dubious kind. 'He was a lovely man,' Max relates, 'and he had taken the song in the spirit in which it was meant.'

I am an entertainer and I sing for charity;
For Oxfam and for Shelter, for those worse off than me.
Bangla Desh, Barnardo's Homes. And though I don't get paid,
It does one good to do some work for things like Christian Aid.

> But of all the concerts that I've done for the homeless overseas,
> The one I did that pleased me most was not for refugees,
> 'Twas for a home in Ireland that stands amongst the trees:
> The sunshine home in Dublin for blind Irish referees!

There was a sequel two years later when Max was having a quiet drink in the Glynneath Rugby Club on the eve of the Wales v. Ireland game. Four Irish referees with clenched fists burst in with cries of 'Where is he?' Even Max's staunchest friends shuffled away. 'Here I am,' said Max manfully. 'Ah,' they said, 'what will you drink?' They had come to ask him to speak at their annual dinner. The rest of the night was lost in a mixture of Welsh and Irish songs.

Altogether Now

Leo and Jilly Cooper

Leo Cooper has several claims to fame. He has managed to survive a quarter of a century as a military publisher; he turned out as scrum-half for the Honourable Artillery Company until he was fifty; and he is married to Jilly. Here they both are on two essential elements of rugby life we have not yet looked into: the plunge bath and the Easter tour.

The Plunge Bath

After the bar, these are the most important places in the clubhouse. There is a great mystique among women about what men do in the bath after the match. One suspects that they are simply fascinated by the fact that it is one of very few places where you might find thirty-one male organs simultaneously exposed. There is not, in fact, much mystique about having a bath.

Old style bathing arrangements used to consist of a bucket full of warm water hanging from the rafters – which turned into an instant, rather brief, shower when you pulled a string. Or sometimes there was an old bath which was filled with electric kettles – a less instant system, taking approximately three hours to set up. In some cases there were no baths at all, and you went to the pub encased in mud.

Really magnificent plunge baths can accommodate both sides and the referee all in one go. Although the water these days tends to be shallower and cooler than in the extravagant past, this is still a good place to begin the post-game rehabilitation and bonhomie.

The groundsman usually starts running the hot water at half-time. In clubs where several games may be played in an afternoon it is well worth inspecting the bathroom before you go out to play. You can then estimate how fast you will have to run at the end of the game to get the benefit of any hot water.

In clubs with only showers, your two chief interests will be, first, to get under the only sprinkler that works and, second, to identify, through the steam, which players have brought soap or shampoo that you can borrow. It is surprising how many men now take the trouble to wash their hair and soap themselves after a game – niceties which would once have been thought very excessive. Australian rugby players have even been known to use deodorant. Although, as far as we know, it is still only soccer players who have resorted to blow driers.

The advent of ladies in the clubhouse has certainly had some influence on the bathing routines. Heavy drinkers and womanizers wash least, in order to be first at the bar for a drink and a chat-up. Vainer players linger in the bath, opting for a later, but sweeter smelling, appearance at the après-rugby.

Banks and large corporations have the best washing facilities, provincial clubs the worst. At the former you will find, at best, a plunge bath big enough to allow you to swim a few strokes and, at worst, a concrete trough with half an inch of mud in the bottom. Anyone trying to plunge into one of these would be knocked immediately unconscious. In theory, there is a cold end and a hot end. In practice, there is either a tepid end and a freezing cold end, or a hot end and a boiling hot end. Very few clubhouses have enough hooks for towels. Very few showers work. Very few players have towels, and at least three players on your own side will want to borrow yours. Almost no towels get washed mid-season.

In smart clubs, your laundry is done for you, your shirts are numbered and hung on your hook and your boots are polished. This is quite out of keeping with the normal rugby playing attitude towards cleanliness. Washing, after all, is not one of the main activities of the day. And allergy to mud is certainly not one of the main qualities of the rugby player.

The Easter Tour

Most clubs have a tour. The Lions go to places like Australia and New Zealand. Lesser clubs set off on a drunken foray from Hull to Cornwall over Easter. More often than not they leave in their wake irate hotel managers, badly bruised young ladies of the town, unmemorable displays of the art of rugby football and, on frequent occasions, their own players.

A side on tour in France was once treated to an impressively indulgent pre-match dinner the evening before, plus a *vin d'honneur* immediately before the match. The captain of the side was sent off the field by his own vice-captain for being in an unfit state to play. Most of the rest of the team were in the same state. The French opposition, of course, proved to be a totally different set of players from those who had acted host to the visitors during the pre-match festivities. The English side lost 76–0. However they did beat the French on their return visit 35–0, having employed the same tactics in retaliation.

On one tour the captain of the visiting side agreed with the manager of their hotel that the cost of any damage done would be divided among the players' bills. During one evening a sofa was badly wrecked. The next morning the players were given their bills, and promptly afterwards they started to load the remains of the sofa on to a Land Rover. The hotel manager demanded furiously what they thought they were doing. They pointed out that, by their calculations, they had paid between them such a vast sum towards the sofa that they now regarded it as their property. The hotelier relented.

One of the perils of a rugby tour is the danger of being roped in for sightseeing by your hosts. The only sightseeing trips worth going on are those to vineyards and bottling plants. You must always take on tour an older (more sober) member, although the two are seldom synonymous. His job is to count people on to the coach and lend people money.

He is also the chap who knows how to dispose of unwanted oysters down a bidet.

Tours are useful opportunities to loot new road signs and the like to decorate your clubhouse on your return. They are also very often opportunities for rugby players to make friends and broaden their minds. You can certainly learn much about the French people by staying with the players' families when on tour. What they learn about us on the reciprocal visits is probably just as mind-broadening. After one such visit, a slightly exasperated home team wife was heard musing quietly as to how on earth anyone could be sick on the ceiling.

From Leo and Jilly Cooper on Rugby

Tom's First Game

Thomas Hughes

Thomas Hughes wanted to explain to his eight-year-old son what life at Rugby would be like. So he sat down and wrote Tom Brown's Schooldays, *first published in 1857 and an instant smash hit. The description of Tom's first game early on in the book is not only of unequalled historical interest; it is also one of the most vivid accounts of rugby football ever penned. Monstrously rough and primally chaotic though the game described is, we can already see in it most of the lineaments of the sophisticated game we now enjoy. It is no game for cowards or shirkers, but a capital game for those prepared to pitch in.*

There is a weird resonance in the casting of old Brooke as captain of School-house; it was another fifty years before William Parker Brooke went there as a housemaster and a further ten before his son Rupert, the poet, entered the school. Rupert played as a reliable centre three-quarter in the first XV. He was, said the school magazine, 'though not brilliant, usually in his place and makes good openings but' – and how many of us have heard similar words – 'tackles too high'. However, although Dr Arnold, the great

Rugby headmaster, appears as himself in the book, the Brooke who was
Tom Brown's skipper sixty years before seems to have had no connection
with the real one. His words about Tom at the end of the chapter resound
down the years: 'He is a plucky youngster, and will make a player.'

And now that the two sides have fairly sundered, and each occupies its
own ground, and we get a good look at them, what absurdity is this? You
don't mean to say that those fifty or sixty boys in white trousers, many of
them quite small, are going to play that huge mass opposite? Indeed I do,
gentlemen; they're going to try at any rate, and won't make such a bad
fight of it either, mark my word; for hasn't old Brooke won the toss, with
his lucky halfpenny, and got choice of goals and kick-off? The new ball you
may see lie there quite by itself, in the middle, pointing towards the school
or island goal; in another minute it will be well on its way there. Use that
minute in remarking how the School-house side is drilled. You will see in
the first place, that the sixth-form boy, who has the charge of goal, has
spread his force (the goal-keepers) so as to occupy the whole space behind
the goal-posts, at distances of about five yards apart; a safe and well kept
goal is the foundation of all good play. Old Brooke is talking to the captain
of quarters; and now he moves away; see how that youngster spreads his
men (the light brigade) carefully over the ground, half-way between their
own goal and the body of their own players-up (the heavy brigade). These
again play in several bodies; there is young Brooke and the bull-dogs –
mark them well – they are 'the fighting brigade', the 'die-hards', larking
about at leap-frog to keep themselves warm, and playing tricks on one
another. And on each side of old Brooke, who is now standing in the
middle of the ground and just going to kick-off, you see a separate wing of
players-up, each with a boy of acknowledged prowess to look to – here
Warner, and there Hedge; but over all is old Brooke, absolute as he of
Russia, but wisely and bravely ruling over willing and worshipping subjects, a true football king. His face is earnest and careful as he glances a
last time over his array, but full of pluck and hope, the sort of look I hope to
see in my general when I go out to fight.

The School side is not organized in the same way. The goal-keepers
are all in lumps, any-how and no-how; you can't distinguish between the
players-up and the boys in quarters, and there is divided leadership, but
with such odds in strength and weight it must take more than that to
hinder them from winning, and so their leaders seem to think, for they let
the players-up manage themselves.

But now look, there is a slight move forward of the School-house
wings; a shout of 'Are you ready?' and loud affirmative reply. Old Brooke
takes half-a-dozen quick steps, and away goes the ball spinning towards
the School goal; seventy yards before it touches ground and at no point
above twelve or fifteen feet high, a model kick-off; and the School-house
cheer and rush on; the ball is returned, and they meet it and drive it back
amongst the masses of the School already in motion. Then the two sides

close, and you can see nothing for minutes but a swaying crowd of boys, at one point violently agitated. That is where the ball is, and there are the keen players to be met, and the glory and the hard knocks to be got: you hear the dull thud thud of the ball, and the shouts of 'Off your side', 'Down with him', 'Put him over', 'Bravo'. This is what we call a scrummage, gentlemen, and the first scrummage in a School-house match is no joke in the consulship of Plancus.

But see! it has broken, the ball is driven out on the School-house side, and the rush of the School carries it past the School-house players-up. 'Look out in quarters,' Brooke's and twenty other voices ring out; no need to call tho', the School-house captain of quarters has caught it on the bound, dodges the foremost Schoolboys, who are heading the rush, and sends it back with a good drop-kick well into the enemies' country. And then follows rush upon rush, and scrummage upon scrummage, the ball now driven through into the School-house quarters, and now into the School goal; for the School-house have not lost the advantage which the kick-off and a slight wind gave them at the outset, and are slightly 'pen-ning' their adversaries. You say, you don't see much in it all; nothing but a struggling mass of boys, and a leather ball, which seems to excite them all to great fury, as a red rag does a bull. My dear sir, a battle would look much the same to you, except that the boys would be men, and the balls iron; but a battle would be worth your looking at for all that, and so is a football match. You can't be expected to appreciate the delicate strokes of play, the turns by which a game is lost and won – it takes an old player to do that, but the broad philosophy of football you can understand if you will. Come along with me a little nearer, and let us consider it together.

The ball has just fallen again where the two sides are thickest, and they close rapidly around it in a scrummage; it must be driven through now by force or skill, till it flies out on one side or the other. Look how differently the boys face it. Here come two of the bull-dogs, bursting through the outsiders; in they go, straight to the heart of the scrummage, bent on driving that ball out on the opposite side. That is what they mean to do. My sons, my sons! you are too hot; you have gone past the ball, and must struggle now right through the scrummage, and get round and back again to your own side, before you can be of any further use. Here comes young Brooke; he goes in as straight as you, but keeps his head, and backs and bends, holding himself still behind the ball, and driving it furiously when he gets the chance. Take a leaf out of his book, you young chargers. Here comes Speedicut, and Flashman the School-house bully, with shouts and great action. Won't you two come up to young Brooke, after locking-up, by the School-house fire, with 'Old fellow, wasn't that just a splendid scrummage by the three trees!' But he knows you, and so do we. You don't really want to drive that ball through that scrummage, chancing all hurt for the glory of the School-house – but to make us think that's what you want – a vastly different thing; and fellows of your kidney will never go through more than the skirts of a scrummage, where it's all push and no kicking. We respect boys who keep out of it, and don't sham going in; but you – we had rather not say what we think of you.

Then the boys who are bending and watching on the outside, mark them – they are most useful players, the dodgers; who seize on the ball the moment it rolls out from amongst the chargers, and away with it across to the opposite goal; they seldom go into the scrummage, but must have more coolness than the chargers: as endless as are boys' characters, so are their ways of facing or not facing a scrummage at football.

Three-quarters of an hour are gone; first winds are failing, and weight and numbers beginning to tell. Yard by yard the School-house have been driven back, contesting every inch of ground. The bull-dogs are the colour of mother earth from shoulder to ankle, except young Brooke, who has a marvellous knack of keeping his legs. The School-house are being penned in their turn, and now the ball is behind their goal, under the Doctor's wall. The Doctor and some of his family are there looking on, and seem as anxious as any boy for the success of the School-house. We get a minute's breathing time before old Brooke kicks out, and he gives the word to play strongly for touch, by the three trees. Away goes the ball, and the bull-dogs after it, and in another minute there is a shout of 'In touch', 'Our ball'. Now's your time, old Brooke, while your men are still fresh. He stands with the ball in his hand, while the two sides form in deep lines opposite one another: he must strike it straight out between them. The lines are thickest close to him, but young Brooke and two or three of his men are shifting up further, where the opposite line is weak. Old Brooke strikes it out straight and strong, and it falls opposite his brother. Hurra! that rush has taken it right through the School line, and away past the three trees, far into their quarters, and young Brooke and the bull-dogs are close upon it. The School leaders rush back shouting 'Look out in goal,' and strain every nerve to catch him, but they are after the fleetest foot in Rugby. There they go straight for the School goal-posts, quarters scattering before them. One after another the bull-dogs go down, but young Brooke holds on. 'He is down.' No! a long stagger, but the danger is past; that was the shock of Crew, the most dangerous of dodgers. And now he is close to the School goal, the ball not three yards before him. There is a hurried rush of the School fags to the spot, but no one throws himself on the ball, the only chance, and young Brooke has touched it right under the School goal-posts.

The School leaders come up furious, and administer toco to the wretched fags nearest at hand; they may well be angry, for it is all Lombard-street to a china orange that the School-house kick a goal with the ball touched in such a good place. Old Brooke of course will kick it out, but who shall catch and place it? Call Crab Jones. Here he comes, sauntering along with a straw in his mouth, the queerest, coolest fish in Rugby: if he were tumbled into the moon this minute, he would just pick himself up without taking his hands out of his pockets or turning a hair. But it is a moment when the boldest charger's heart beats quick. Old Brooke stands with the ball under his arm motioning the School back; he will not kick-out till they are all in goal, behind the posts; they are all edging forwards, inch by inch, to get nearer for the rush at Crab Jones, who stands there in front of old Brooke to catch the ball. If they can reach and destroy him before he catches, the danger is over; and with one and same rush they will carry it right away to the School-house goal. Fond hope! It is kicked out and caught beautifully. Crab strikes his heel into the ground, to mark the spot where the ball was caught, beyond which the School line may not advance; but there they stand, five deep, ready to rush the moment the ball touches the ground. Take plenty of room! don't give the rush a chance of reaching you! place it true and steady! Trust Crab Jones – he has made a small hole with his heel for the ball to lie on, by which he is resting on one knee, with his eye on old Brooke. 'Now!' Crab places the ball at the word, old Brooke kicks, and it rises slowly and truly as the School rush forward.

Then a moment's pause, while both sides look up at the spinning ball. There it flies, straight between the two posts, some five feet above the cross-bar, an unquestioned goal; and a shout of real genuine joy rings out from the School-house players-up, and a faint echo of it comes over the close from the goal-keepers under the Doctor's wall. A goal in the first hour – such a thing hasn't been done in the School-house match this five years.

'Over!' is the cry: the two sides change goals, and the School-house goal-keepers come threading their way across through the masses of the School; the most openly triumphant of them, amongst whom is Tom, a School-house boy of two hours' standing, getting their ears boxed in the transit. Tom indeed is excited beyond measure, and it is all the sixth-form boy, kindest and safest of goal-keepers, has been able to do, to keep him from rushing out whenever the ball has been near their goal. So he holds him by his side, and instructs him in the science of touching.

At this moment Griffith, the itinerant vendor of oranges from Hill Morton, enters the close with his heavy baskets; there is a rush of small boys upon the little pale-faced man, the two sides mingling together subdued by the great Goddess Thirst, like the English and French by the streams in the Pyrenees. The leaders are past oranges and apples, but some of them visit their coats, and apply innocent-looking ginger-beer bottles to their mouths. It is no ginger-beer though I fear, and will do you no good. One short mad rush, and then a stitch in the side, and no more honest play; that's what comes of those bottles.

But now Griffith's baskets are empty, the ball is placed again midway, and the School are going to kick off. Their leaders have sent their lumber into goal, and rated the rest soundly, and one hundred and twenty picked players-up are there, bent on retrieving the game. They are to keep the ball in front of the School-house goal, and then to drive it in by sheer strength and weight. They mean heavy play and no mistake, and so old Brooke sees; and places Crab Jones in quarters just before the goal, with four or five picked players, who are to keep the ball away to the sides, where a try at goal, if obtained, will be less dangerous than in front. He himself, and Warner and Hedge, who have saved themselves till now, will lead the charges.

'Are you ready?' 'Yes.' And away comes the ball kicked high in the air, to give the School time to rush on and catch it as it falls. And here they are amongst us. Meet them like Englishmen, you School-house boys, and charge them home. Now is the time to shew what mettle is in you – and there shall be a warm seat by the hall fire, and honour, and lots of bottled beer to-night, for him who does his duty in the next half-hour. And they are well met. Again and again the cloud of their players-up gathers before our goal, and comes threatening on, and Warner or Hedge, with young Brooke and the relics of the bull-dogs, break through and carry the ball back; and old Brooke ranges the field like Job's war-horse, the thickest scrummage parts asunder before his rush, like the waves before a clipper's bows; his cheery voice rings over the field, and his eye is everywhere. And if these miss the ball, and it rolls dangerously in front of our goal, Crab Jones and his men have seized it and sent it away towards the sides with the unerring drop-kick. This is worth living for; the whole sum of schoolboy existence gathered up into one straining, struggling half-hour, a half-hour worth a year of common life.

The quarter to five has struck, and the play slackens for a minute before goal; but there is Crew, the artful dodger, driving the ball in behind our goal, on the island side, where our quarters are weakest. Is there no one to meet him? Yes! look at little East! the ball is just at equal distances between the two, and they rush together, the young man of seventeen and the boy of twelve, and kick it at the same moment. Crew passes on without a stagger; East is hurled forward by the shock, and plunges on his shoulder, as if he would bury himself in the ground; but the ball rises straight into the air, and falls behind Crew's back, while the 'bravos' of the School-house attest the pluckiest charge of all that hard-fought day. Warner picks East up lame and half stunned, and he hobbles back into goal, conscious of having played the man.

And now the last minutes are come, and the School gather for their last rush every boy of the hundred and twenty who has a run left in him. Reckless of the defence of their own goal, on they come across the level big-side ground, the ball well down amongst them, straight for our goal, like the column of the old guard up the slope at Waterloo. All former charges have been child's play to this. Warner and Hedge have met them, but still on they come. The bull-dogs rush in for the last time; they are hurled over or carried back, striving hand, foot, and eyelids. Old Brooke comes sweeping round the skirts of the play, and turning short round, picks out the very heart of the scrummage, and plunges in. It wavers for a moment – he has the ball! No, it has passed him, and his voice rings out clear over the advancing tide, 'Look out in goal.' Crab Jones catches it for a moment; but before he can kick, the rush is upon him and passes over him; and he picks himself up behind them with his straw in his mouth, a little dirtier, but as cool as ever.

The ball rolls slowly in behind the School-house goal, not three yards in front of a dozen of the biggest School players-up.

There stand the School-house praepostor, safest of goal-keepers, and Tom Brown by his side, who has learned his trade by this time. Now is your time, Tom. The blood of all the Browns is up, and the two rush in together, and throw themselves on the ball, under the very feet of the advancing column; the praepostor on his hands and knees arching his back, and Tom all along on his face. Over them topple the leaders of the rush, shooting over the back of the praepostor, but falling flat on Tom, and knocking all the wind out of his small carcase. 'Our ball,' says the praepostor, rising with his prize, 'but get up there, there's a little fellow under you.' They are hauled and roll off him, and Tom is discovered a motionless body.

Old Brooke picks him up. 'Stand up, give him air,' he says; and then feeling his limbs, adds, 'No bones broken. How do you feel, young 'un?'

'Hah-hah,' gasps Tom as his wind comes back, 'pretty well, thank you – all right.'

'Who is he?' says Brooke. 'Oh, it's Brown, he's a new boy; I know him,' says East, coming up.

'Well, he is a plucky youngster, and will make a player,' says Brooke.

And five o'clock strikes. 'No side' is called, and the first day of the School-house match is over.

From *Tom Brown's Schooldays*

Shout, Crowd, Shout

Richard Llewellyn

Richard Llewellyn was the pseudonym for the novelist and playwright Richard Dafydd Vivian Llewellyn Lloyd, the son of a Welsh hotelier. He worked as a dishwasher in Claridge's before enlisting in the army and serving in India and Hong Kong, then working as a film reporter, bit player, assistant director, production manager and script-writer. His play Poison Pen *had a successful London run in 1937, and this enabled him to take off the time to complete his first novel* How Green was my Valley. *It was published in October 1939 and brought him instant celebrity. There were 21 translations, including Hindi, Japanese, Turkish and two into German. The setting was his paternal grandfather's village of Gilfach Goch, and the close, intimate, warm and vivid life of a Welsh mining village has seldom, if ever, been so faithfully portrayed.*

The story of the village rugby game has always appealed to me, not least because the village full-back, Cyfartha Lewis, is totally unconvinced by the opposing fly-half's dummy. The crowd actually laugh at the presumption for, as Llewellyn tells us, 'To sell a dummy to Cyfartha is to sell poison to a Borgia.' The try that follows is not one of your brilliant Welsh runs but one of those muddy, heaving, earthy forward tries in which the narrator's brother Davy, who seems to be playing at hooker, has a principal role. Whatever, it is an authentic piece of Welsh rugby lore.

I was glad to be by myself on the field for a little bit and I went to find a good place to see the match, up on a mound half-way between the goal posts. There I put the coats, and sat down with care again, and there is good to sit down with long trews and give the fronts a hitch so that the knees will be free of bag. It is almost a sign that you are a boy no longer, and then it is that you will think of a pipe and tobacco to round you off.

The other teams came in a brake with four good horses and changed behind the hedge, with a couple of boys to tell girls to keep clear. By that time our team were leaving their houses and there is pretty to see their jerseys coming down the street, and prettier still when the other team ran on to have some kicking practice. Now the field was filling, with crowds of people coming down the Hill, and dogcarts and traps and gigs coming along the mountain road every minute, until the square was full of wheels, and the fields up the mountain full of grazing horses, with some of the men looking after them to earn an extra pint.

Ivor went on to referee and spin the coin, and when we won the end with the wind a big cheer went up, for the wind always dropped low toward sunset, so what there was of it, we would have for the first half.

A healthy sound is the tamp of the leather ball on short green grass and pleasant, indeed, to watch it rise, turning itself lazily, as though it were enjoying every moment of the trip up there, against blue sky, and coming down against the green, in a low curve right into the ready hands of a back.

A whistle from Ivor, and the captain on the other side takes his run and kicks, and as you watch the ball climb you see the teams running into position to meet one another underneath it.

A forward has it, but before he can so much as feel it properly, he is flat on his back, and the two sides are packing over him. A whistle from Ivor, and the first scrum, and shouts for Davy as he lifts his arms to bind his front men. In goes the ball, and the tight, straining muscles are working, eight against eight, to hold one another and then to push each other the length of the field, but the ball comes free behind the pack, and their fly-half has it so fast that nobody knows till he is on his way toward our touch line with his three-quarters strung behind him and nothing but our full-back in his way. Shout, crowd, shout, with one voice that is long-drawn, deep, loud, and full of colour, rising now as the fly runs pell-mell and Cyfartha Lewis dances to meet him, and up on a rising note, for inches are between them, louder with the voice in an unwritten hymn to energy and bravery and strength among men.

But Cyfartha is like a fisherman's net. The fly has been too clever. He should have passed to his wing long ago, but he is greedy and wants the try himself, and on he goes, tries to sell a dummy, and how the crowd is laughing, now, for to sell a dummy to Cyfartha is to sell poison to a Borgia. The fly is down, and Cyfartha kicks the ball half-way down the field to our forwards, and has time to offer his hand to poor Mr Fly, who is bringing himself to think what happened after the mountain fell on him.

And my father is laughing so much that his glasses are having trouble to settle on his nose. Owen and Gwilym are shouting for all they are worth, for Davy has the ball and his forwards are all round him to push through the enemy. Shoulders and knees are hard at work, men are going down, men stumble on top of them, fall headlong and are pinned by treading, plunging boots. Red and green jerseys are mixed with yellow and white, and mud is plenty on both. On, on, an inch, two inches, bodies heave against bodies, hands grab, legs are twisted, fall and crawl, push and squirm, on, on, there are the white posts above you, but red and green jerseys hide the line and form a wall that never shows a gap. On, yellow and white, pack up behind and keep close, pull the ball into the belly and shield it with your arms, down with your head, more shoulder from the pack, keep closer at the sides, push now, push, push, push. A red and green down in front, another, who carries away a third. Another push now, and the ball is slipping from him. A hand has come from the press below and grasps with the strength of the drowning, but a wriggle to the side and a butt with the hip loosens it and on, on, half an inch more, with an ankle tight in the fist of red and green who lies beneath two yellow and white and only enough of sense and breath to hang on.

Down with the ball now, full flat, with eight or nine on top of you, and there is the whistle.

The ball rests an inch over the line.

Then see the hats and caps go into the air, and hear a shouting that brings all the women to the doors up and down the Hill, and some to lean from the back windows.

Again the whistle, and Maldwyn Pugh looks up at the posts, makes his lucky sign, and takes his run at the ball that rests in its heeled mark, and kept there by the hand of Willie Rees, who lies full length in the mud with his face turned away, not to be blinded by the slop that will come when the boot leaves his hand empty.

Empty it is, and the ball on its way, and the crowd quiet, with the quiet that is louder than noise, when all eyes are on the same spot and all voices are tuned for the same shout.

The ball travels high, drops in a curve, turns twice. The crowd is on its way to a groan, but now the wind takes it in his arms and gives it a gentle push over the bar, no need for it, but sometimes the wind is a friend, and there it is.

We are a try and a goal, five points, to the good.

From *How Green was my Valley*

Tuppy and the Red-Haired Bounder

P. G. Wodehouse

Although Bertie Wooster in the immortal oeuvre tells us he was not at a rugby school, his creator certainly was. P. G. Wodehouse was educated at Dulwich College and, as we shall see in the only poem included in this book, clearly knew what it was all about. It is, as usual among Bertie's friends and coevals, love that drives Tuppy Glossop to new peaks of endeavour on the rugby field. It is true that Jeeves, who knows about rugby as he knows about everything else, considers Mr Glossop ill-advised: 'I am informed by Mr Mulready, Sir Reginald's butler, Sir, that this contest differs in some respects from the ordinary football game. Owing to the fact that there has existed for many years considerable animus between the two villages, the struggle is conducted, it appears, on somewhat looser and more primitive lines than is usually the case when two teams meet in friendly rivalry. The primary object of the players, I am given to understand, is not so much to score points as to inflict violence . . . the opinion of the Servants' Hall is that it would be more judicious on Mr Glossop's part were he to refrain from mixing himself up in the affair.' However, Tuppy persists – with the consequences we now see.

You can always rely on Jeeves. Two-thirty I had said, and two-thirty it was. The telegram arrived almost on the minute. I was going to my room to change into something warmer at the moment, and I took it up with me. Then into the heavy tweeds and off in the car to the field of play. I got there just as the two teams were lining up, and half a minute later the whistle blew and the war was on.

What with one thing and another – having been at a school where they didn't play it and so forth – Rugby football is a game I can't claim absolutely to understand in all its niceties, if you know what I mean. I can follow the broad, general principles, of course. I mean to say, I know that the main scheme is to work the ball down the field somehow and deposit it over the line at the other end, and that, in order to squelch this programme, each side is allowed to put in a certain amount of assault and battery and do things to its fellow-man which, if done elsewhere, would result in fourteen days without the option, coupled with some strong remarks from the Bench. But there I stop. What you might call the science of the thing is to Bertram Wooster a sealed book. However, I am informed by experts that on this occasion there was not enough science for anyone to notice.

There had been a great deal of rain in the last few days, and the going appeared to be a bit sticky. In fact, I have seen swamps that were drier than this particular bit of ground. The red-haired bloke whom I had encountered in the pub paddled up and kicked off amidst cheers from the populace, and the ball went straight to where Tuppy was standing, a pretty colour-scheme in light blue and orange. Tuppy caught it neatly, and hoofed it back, and it was at this point that I understood that an Upper Bleaching versus Hockley-cum-Meston game had certain features not usually seen on the football-field.

For Tuppy, having done his bit, was just standing there, looking modest, when there was a thunder of large feet and the red-haired bird, galloping up, seized him by the neck, hurled him to earth, and fell on him. I had a glimpse of Tuppy's face, as it registered horror, dismay, and a general suggestion of stunned dissatisfaction with the scheme of things, and then he disappeared. By the time he had come to the surface, a sort of mob-warfare was going on at the other side of the field. Two assortments of sons of the soil had got their heads down and were shoving earnestly against each other, with the ball somewhere in the middle.

Tuppy wiped a fair portion of Hampshire out of his eye, peered round him in a dazed kind of way, saw the mass-meeting and ran towards it, arriving just in time for a couple of heavyweights to gather him in and give him the mud-treatment again. This placed him in an admirable position for a third heavyweight to kick him in the ribs with a boot like a violin-case. The red-haired man then fell on him. It was all good, brisk play, and looked fine from my side of the ropes.

I saw now where Tuppy had made his mistake. He was too dressy. On occasions such as this it is safest not to be conspicuous, and that blue and orange shirt rather caught the eye. A sober beige, blending with the colour of the ground, was what his best friends would have recommended. And, in addition to the fact that his costume attracted attention, I rather think that the men of Hockley-cum-Meston resented his being on the field at all. They felt that, as a non-local, he had butted in on a private fight and had no business there.

At any rate, it certainly appeared to me that they were giving him preferential treatment. After each of those shoving-bees to which I have alluded, when the edifice caved in and tons of humanity wallowed in a tangled mass in the juice, the last soul to be excavated always seemed to be Tuppy. And on the rare occasions when he actually managed to stand upright for a moment, somebody – generally the red-haired man – invariably sprang to the congenial task of spilling him again.

In fact, it was beginning to look as though that telegram would come too late to save a human life, when an interruption occurred. Play had worked round close to where I was standing, and there had been the customary collapse of all concerned, with Tuppy at the bottom of the basket as usual, but this time, when they got up and started to count the survivors, a sizeable cove in what had once been a white shirt remained on the ground. And a hearty cheer went up from a hundred patriotic throats as the news spread that Upper Bleaching had drawn first blood.

The victim was carried off by a couple of his old chums, and the rest of the players sat down and pulled their stockings up and thought of life for a bit. The moment had come, it seemed to me, to remove Tuppy from the *abattoir*, and I hopped over the ropes and toddled to where he sat scraping mud from his wishbone. His air was that of a man who has been passed through a wringer, and his eyes, what you could see of them, had a strange, smouldering gleam. He was so crusted with alluvial deposits that one realized how little a mere bath would ever be able to effect. To fit him to take his place once more in polite society, he would certainly have to be sent to the cleaner's. Indeed, it was a moot point whether it wouldn't be simpler just to throw him away.

'Tuppy, old man,' I said.

'Eh?' said Tuppy.

'A telegram for you.'

'Eh?'

'I've got a wire here that came after you left the house.'

'Eh?' said Tuppy.

I stirred him up a trifle with the ferrule of my stick, and he seemed to come to life.

'Be careful what you're doing, you silly ass,' he said, in part. 'I'm one solid bruise. What are you gibbering about?'

'A telegram has come for you. I think it may be important.'

He snorted in a bitter sort of way.

'Do you suppose I've time to read telegrams now?'

'But this one may be frightfully urgent,' I said. 'Here it is.'

But, if you understand me, it wasn't. How I had happened to do it, I don't know, but apparently, in changing the upholstery, I had left it in my other coat.

'Oh, my gosh,' I said, 'I've left it behind.'

'It doesn't matter.'

'But it does. It's probably something you ought to read at once. Immediately, if you know what I mean. If I were you, I'd just say a few words of farewell to the murder-squad and come back to the house right away.'

He raised his eyebrows. At least, I think he must have done, because the mud on his forehead stirred a little, as if something was going on underneath it.

'Do you imagine,' he said, 'that I would slink away under her very eyes? Good God! Besides,' he went on, in a quiet, meditative voice, 'there is no power on earth that could get me off this field until I've thoroughly disembowelled that red-haired bounder. Have you noticed how he keeps tackling me when I haven't got the ball?'

'Isn't that right?'

'Of course it's not right. Never mind! A bitter retribution awaits that bird. I've had enough of it. From now on I assert my personality.'

'I'm a bit foggy as to the rules of this pastime,' I said. 'Are you allowed to bite him?'

'I'll try, and see what happens,' said Tuppy, struck with the idea and brightening a little.

At this point, the pall-bearers returned, and fighting became general again all along the Front.

There's nothing like a bit of rest and what you might call folding of the hands for freshening up the shop-soiled athlete. The dirty work, resumed after this brief breather, started off with an added vim which it did one good to see. And the life and soul of the party was young Tuppy.

You know, only meeting a fellow at lunch or at the races or loafing round country-houses and so forth, you don't get on to his hidden depths, if you know what I mean. Until this moment, if asked, I would have said that Tuppy Glossop was, on the whole, essentially a pacific sort of bloke, with little or nothing of the tiger of the jungle in him. Yet here he was, running to and fro with fire streaming from his nostrils, a positive danger to traffic.

Yes, absolutely. Encouraged by the fact that the referee was either filled with the spirit of Live and Let Live or else had got his whistle choked up with mud, the result being that he appeared to regard the game with a sort of calm detachment, Tuppy was putting in some very impressive work. Even to me, knowing nothing of the finesse of the thing, it was plain that if Hockley-cum-Meston wanted the happy ending they must eliminate young Tuppy at the earliest possible moment. And I will say for them that they did their best, the red-haired man being particularly assiduous. But Tuppy was made of durable material. Every time the opposition talent ground him into the mire and sat on his head, he rose on stepping-stones of his dead self, if you follow me, to higher things. And in the end it was the red-haired bloke who did the dust-biting.

I couldn't tell you exactly how it happened, for by this time the shades of night were drawing in a bit and there was a dollop of mist rising, but one moment the fellow was hareing along, apparently without a care in the world, and then suddenly Tuppy had appeared from nowhere and was sailing through the air at his neck. They connected with a crash and a slither, and a little later the red-haired bird was hopping off, supported by a brace of friends, something having gone wrong with his left ankle.

After that, there was nothing in it. Upper Bleaching, thoroughly bucked, became busier than ever. There was a lot of earnest work in a sort of inland sea down at the Hockley end of the field, and then a kind of tidal wave poured over the line, and when the bodies had been removed and the tumult and the shouting had died, there was young Tuppy lying on the ball. And that, with exception of a few spots of mayhem in the last five minutes, concluded the proceedings.

From *Very Good, Jeeves!*

Wee Jaikie Wins the Game

John Buchan

John Buchan, though best known for giving us the resolute Scottish gentle-
man adventurer Richard Hannay, created many other fine Scottish heroes,
not least the Glasgow grocer Dickson McCunn who finds romance and
adventure in such magical sagas as Huntingtower, Castle Gay *and* The
House of the Four Winds. *In the first of these he is aided by a group of*
ragamuffins called The Gorbals Die-Hards. Dickson adopts them en masse
and they all do him immense credit. One indeed, Wee Jaikie, is chosen in
Castle Gay *to play on the wing for Scotland against an only slightly fiction-*
alized team of Australians. He may be a mere 5′6″ and slim as a wagtail, but
this product of the Gorbals and Cambridge University, as we shall see, has
sterling work to do for his country this afternoon.

The historian must return upon his tracks in order to tell of the great event
thus baldly announced. That year the Antipodes had despatched to Britain
such a constellation of Rugby stars that the hearts of the home enthusiasts
became as water and their joints were loosened. For years they had
known and suffered from the quality of those tall young men from the
South, whom the sun had toughened and tautened – their superb
physique, their resourcefulness, their uncanny combination. Hitherto,
while the fame of one or two players had reached these shores, the teams
had been in the main a batch of dark horses, and there had been no exact
knowledge to set a bar to hope. But now Australia had gathered herself
together for a mighty effort, and had sent to the field a fifteen most of
whose members were known only too well. She had collected her sons
wherever they were to be found. Four had already played for British
Universities; three had won a formidable repute in international matches
in which their country of ultimate origin had entitled them to play. What
club, county, or nation could resist so well equipped an enemy? And, as
luck decided, it fell to Scotland, which had been having a series of dis-
astrous seasons, to take the first shock.

That ancient land seemed for the moment to have forgotten her
prowess. She could produce a strong, hard-working and effective pack,
but her great three-quarter line had gone, and she had lost the scrum-half
who the year before had been her chief support. Most of her fifteen were
new to an international game, and had never played together. The danger
lay in the enemy halves and three-quarters. The Kangaroos had two
halves possessed of miraculous hands and a perfect knowledge of the
game. They might be trusted to get the ball to their three-quarters, who
were reputed the most formidable combination that ever played on turf.
On the left wing was the mighty Charvill, an Oxford Blue and an English
International; on the right Martineau, who had won fame on the cinder-

track as well as on the football-field. The centres were two cunning brothers, Clauson by name, who played in a unison like Siamese twins. Against such a four Scotland could scrape up only a quartet of possibles, men of promise but not yet of performance. The hosts of Tuscany seemed strong out of all proportion to the puny defenders of Rome. And as the Scottish right-wing three-quarter, to frustrate the terrible Charvill, stood the tiny figure of J. Galt, Cambridge University, five foot six inches in height and slim as a wagtail.

To the crowd of sixty thousand and more that waited for the teams to enter the field there was vouchsafed one slender comfort. The weather, which at Blaweary was clear and sunny, was abominable in the Scottish midlands. It had rained all the preceding night, and it was hoped that the ground might be soft, inclining to mud – mud dear to the heart of our islanders but hateful to men accustomed to the firm soil of the South.

The game began in a light drizzle, and for Scotland it began disastrously. The first scrimmage was in the centre of the ground, and the ball came out to the Kangaroo scrum-half, who sent it to his stand-off. From him it went to Clauson, and then to Martineau, who ran round his opposing wing, dodged the Scottish full-back, and scored a try, which was converted. After five minutes the Kangaroos led by five points.

After that the Scottish forwards woke up, and there was a spell of stubborn defence. The Scottish full-back had a long shot at goal from a free kick, and missed, but for the rest most of the play was in the Scottish twenty-five. The Scottish pack strove their hardest, but they did no more than hold their opponents. Then once more came a quick heel out, which went to one of the Clausons, a smart cut-through, a try secured between the posts and easily converted. The score was now ten points to nil.

Depression settled upon the crowd as deep as the weather, which had stopped raining but had developed into a sour *haar*. Followed a period of constant kicking into touch, a dull game which the Kangaroos were supposed to eschew. Just before half-time there was a thin ray of comfort. The Scottish left-wing three-quarter, one Smail, a Borderer, intercepted a Kangaroo pass and reached the enemy twenty-five before he was brought down from behind by Martineau's marvellous sprinting. He had been within sight of success, and half-time came with a faint hope that there was still a chance of averting a runaway defeat.

The second half began with three points to Scotland, secured from a penalty kick. Also the Scottish forwards seemed to have got a new lease of life. They carried the game well into the enemy territory, dribbling irresistibly in their loose rushes, and hooking and heeling in the grand manner from the scrums. The white uniforms of the Kangaroos were now plentifully soiled, and the dark blue of the Scots made them look the less bedraggled side. All but J. Galt. His duty had been that of desperate defence conducted with a resolute ferocity, and he had suffered in it. His jersey was half torn off his back, and his shorts were in ribbons: he limped heavily, and his small face looked as if it had been ground into the mud of his native land. He felt dull and stupid, as if he had been slightly concussed. His gift had hitherto been for invisibility; his fame had been made as a will-o'-the-wisp; now he seemed to be cast for the part of that Arnold von Winkelreid who drew all the spears to his bosom.

The ball was now coming out to the Scottish halves, but they mishandled it. It seemed impossible to get their three-quarters going. The ball either went loose, or was intercepted, or the holder was promptly tackled, and whenever there seemed a chance of a run there was always either a forward pass or a knock-on. At this period of the game the Scottish forwards were carrying everything on their shoulders, and their backs seemed hopeless. Any moment, too, might see the deadly echelon of the Kangaroo three-quarters ripple down the field.

And then came one of those sudden gifts of fortune which make Rugby an image of life. The ball came out from a heel in a scrum not far from the Kangaroo twenty-five, and went to the Kangaroo stand-off half. He dropped it, and, before he could recover, it was gathered by the Scottish stand-off. He sent it to Smail, who passed back to the Scottish left-centre, one Morrison, an Academical from Oxford who had hitherto been pretty much of a passenger. Morrison had the good luck to have a clear avenue before him, and he had a gift of pace. Dodging the Kangaroo full-back with a neat swerve, he scored in the corner of the goal-line amid a pandemonium of cheers. The try was miraculously converted, and the score stood at ten points to eight, with fifteen minutes to play.

Now began an epic struggle, not the least dramatic in the history of the game since a century ago the Rugby schoolboy William Webb Ellis first 'took the ball in his arms and ran with it'. The Kangaroos had no mind to let victory slip from their grasp, and, working like one man, they set themselves to assure it. For a little their magnificent three-quarter line seemed to have dropped out of the picture, but now most theatrically it returned to it. From a scrimmage in the Kangaroo half of the field, the ball went to their stand-off and from him to Martineau. At the moment the Scottish players were badly placed, for their three-quarters were standing wide in order to overlap the faster enemy line. It was a perfect occasion for one of Martineau's deadly runs. He was, however, well tackled by Morrison and passed back to his scrum-half, who kicked ahead towards the left wing to Charvill. The latter gathered the ball at top-speed, and went racing down the touch-line with nothing before him but the Scottish right-wing three-quarter. It seemed a certain score, and there fell on the spectators a sudden hush. That small figure, not hitherto renowned for pace, could never match the Australian's long, loping, deadly stride.

Had Jaikie had six more inches of height he would have failed. But a resolute small man who tackles low is the hardest defence to get round. Jaikie hurled himself at Charvill, and was handed off by a mighty palm. But he staggered back in the direction of his own goal, and there was just one fraction of a second for him to make another attempt. This time he succeeded. Charvill's great figure seemed to dive forward on the top of his tiny assailant, and the ball rolled into touch. For a minute, while the heavens echoed with the shouting, Jaikie lay on the ground bruised and winded. Then he got up, shook himself, like a heroic, bedraggled sparrow, and hobbled back to his place.

There were still five minutes before the whistle, and these minutes were that electric testing time, when one side is intent to consolidate a victory and the other resolute to avert too crushing a defeat. Scotland had never hoped to win; she had already done far better than her expectations, and she gathered herself together for a mighty effort to hold what she had gained. Her hopes lay still in her forwards. Her backs had far surpassed their form, but they were now almost at their last gasp.

But in one of them there was a touch of that genius which can triumph over fatigue. Jaikie had never in his life played so gruelling a game. He was accustomed to being maltreated, but now he seemed to have been pounded and smothered and kicked and flung about till he doubted whether he had a single bone undamaged. His whole body was one huge ache. Only the brain under his thatch of hair was still working well. . . . The Kangaroo pack had gone down field with a mighty rush, and there was a scrum close to the Scottish twenty-five. The ball went out cleanly to one of the Clausons, but it was now very greasy, and the light was bad, and he missed his catch. More, he stumbled after it and fell, for he had had a punishing game. Jaikie on the wing suddenly saw his chance. He darted in and gathered the ball, dodging Clauson's weary tackle. There was no other man of his side at hand to take a pass, but there seemed just a slender chance for a cut-through. He himself of course would be downed by Charvill, but there was a fraction of a hope, if he could gain a dozen yards, that he might be able to pass to Smail, who was not so closely marked.

His first obstacle was the Kangaroo scrum-half, who had come across the field. To him he adroitly sold the dummy, and ran towards the right touch-line, since there was no sign of Smail. He had little hope of success, for it must be only a question of seconds before he was brought down. He did not hear the roar from the spectators as he appeared in the open, for he was thinking of Charvill waiting for his revenge, and he was conscious that his heart was behaving violently quite outside its proper place. But he was also conscious that in some mysterious way he had got a second wind and that his body seemed a trifle less leaden.

He was now past the half-way line, a little distance ahead of one of the Clausons, with no colleague near him, and with Charvill racing to intercept him. For one of Jaikie's inches there could be no hand-off, but he had learned in his extreme youth certain arts not commonly familiar to Rugby players. He was a most cunning dodger. To the yelling crowd he appeared to be aiming at a direct collision with the Kangaroo left-wing. But just as it looked as if a two-seater must meet a Rolls-Royce head-on at full speed, the two-seater swerved and Jaikie wriggled somehow below Charvill's arm. Then sixty thousand people stood on their seats, waving caps and umbrellas and shouting like lunatics, for Charvill was prone on the ground, and Jaikie was stolidly cantering on.

He was now at the twenty-five line, and the Kangaroo full-back awaited him. This was a small man, very little taller than Jaikie, but immensely broad and solid, and a superlative place-kick. A different physique would have easily stopped the runner, now at the very limits of his strength, but the Kangaroo was too slow in his tackle to meet Jaikie's swerve. He retained indeed in his massive fist a considerable part of Jaikie's jersey, but the half-naked wearer managed to stumble on just ahead of him, and secured a try in the extreme corner. There he lay with his nose in the mud, utterly breathless, but obscurely happy. He was still dazed and panting when a minute later the whistle blew, and a noise like the Last Trump told him that by a single point he had won the match for his country.

There was a long table below the Grand Stand, a table reserved for the Press. On it might have been observed a wild figure with red hair dancing a war dance of triumph. Presently the table collapsed under him, and the rending of timber and the recriminations of journalists were added to the apocalyptic din.

From *Castle Gay*

Bread, Cheese and Beer

A. G. Macdonell

The account of the cricket match in chapter seven of A. G. Macdonell's immortal novel England, Their England *is rightly cherished as one of the funniest ever written. Less well known, and from the same book, is the account of how the innocent young Scottish hero Donald finds himself swept along to the game between Oxford and Cambridge at Twickenham. Not least among the delights and discoveries of this chapter is the moment when Donald lunches off bread, cheese and beer, fare that would be simple indeed compared with today's lavish indulgences, as we have already noted. Although art has no doubt magnified the confusion, there is something about the account that has the ring of truth. It sounds as if Donald – or was it Macdonell himself? – was present at the university game in 1930. This was indeed a three-all draw, although it was not a try each but an Oxford penalty goal and a Cambridge try that brought about the result. Vivian Jenkins, later to be the great Welsh and British Lions full-back, was playing at centre three-quarter for Oxford on that day, the first of his three Oxford caps.*

Another interesting experience of this period was a visit to the Rugby Football Ground at Twickenham to see the Oxford and Cambridge Rugby Football Match. At about midday on a warm, misty, winter's day Donald went to Waterloo Station and secured a place with eleven other passengers in a third-class railway carriage, having bumped and struggled his way through mobs of young men all looking exactly like each other except that no two of them wore the same coloured scarves or ties.

After about three-quarters of an hour, he reached Twickenham and lunched at an inn upon beer and bread and cheese, and at 1.45 p.m. found his place in an enormous grand stand and stared down at the bright green turf so far below. The sun was making a last sickly attempt to pierce the gathering mists, and shed a kind of pallid benevolence upon the rapidly filling stands. But the game did not begin for another hour, and by the time that sixty-five thousand spectators, of whom about thirty thousand appeared to be young men, thirty thousand young women, and five thousand parsons, had packed themselves into their places, the sun had long ago given up the unequal struggle, the mists were massing darkly in the north and east, and a slight drizzle was coming down.

The players ran out to the accompaniment of frenzied cheers and counter-cheers, kicked a ball about smartly for a minute or two, sat down for the photographers, stood up for the Prince of Wales, and then set to work.

By half-time the rain was pouring steadily down, the lovely green of the ground was a dark quagmire, the players were indistinguishable from one another, and before the end of the game the gloom of winter twilight had so enveloped the ground that it was impossible for the spectators to see more than twenty or thirty yards.

After the match was over, the sixty-five thousand spectators formed themselves into a single mighty queue, and set off at a slow shuffle through the mud and rain in the direction of the station. Motor-cars, with headlights flaring, crept along with the pedestrians. At the entrance to the station a long delay took place while train after train drew up at the platform, and railway officials with megaphones informed the crowd, correctly, that the next train was a non-stop to Waterloo and, incorrectly, that there was more room in front. Donald at last got into a carriage with twenty-three others and had to stand for an hour and five minutes, including a halt of twenty minutes outside Waterloo. There were two schools of opinion in the carriage. One faction, consisting of eleven young men with bedraggled light-blue favours and one rather passionate urban dean, maintained warmly that Cambridge had won by two goals, two tries, and a penalty goal against two tries, or nineteen points to six. The rival group of partisans were handicapped by internal dissensions, for seven of them were positive that Cambridge had not scored at all, whereas they had definitely seen Oxford score three tries, convert one of them, and also score a dropped goal, thus winning by fifteen points to nil; while four of them knew for an incontrovertible fact that Oxford had scored, in addition, three penalty goals from penalties awarded, and rightly awarded, against Cambridge for dirty play in the scrums.

It was only because they were tightly wedged into the carriage and none of them could move hand or foot that prevented, so it seemed to

Donald, actual violence – certainly the urban dean's language was enough to justify manslaughter – and he was astonished when the controversy dissolved into hearty laughter and they all started chaffing the dean. The dean's powers of repartee were quite devastating.

But all doubts were settled when the train at last pulled in to Waterloo at 6.25, for the evening papers were being sold on the platforms with the authoritative statement that the match had been drawn – each side having scored one try, or three points each.

Two days later Donald went to the Chelsea ground at Stamford Bridge to see Oxford play Cambridge at Association Football. The game began in bright sunshine at 2 p.m. and was played throughout in bright sunshine. A brilliantly open and fast match, resulting in a draw of three goals each, was watched by four thousand silent spectators.

From *England, Their England*

You Young Cad, Corder

Talbot Baines Reed

Talbot Baines Reed never went to a boarding school, though you would never have guessed it from the stream of books which flowed from his prolific pen. He was educated at the City of London School as a day-boy. Nevertheless, he powerfully conveys the public school ethos in this account of how Corder allowed his passion for rugby to overcome his loyalty to the Moderns. Who wouldn't be a Fellsgarth chap after all?

Corder was one of those obtuse youths who can never take in more than one idea at a time. His present idea was football. He had come up this term with a consuming ambition to get into the fifteen, and had played hard and desperately to secure his end. Last week, when Brinkman was obliged to retire, he thought his chance was come, and great was his mortification when he found that his nomination was not accepted by the captain. Still he didn't despair. When he saw the vacancies caused in the team by the defection of the Moderns, his hopes rose again: but once more they were dashed by the captain's announcement of a fifteen made up wholly of Classics.

To-day he had not the heart to come out and see the coaches start, and was moping in his own room, when some one brought in word that Rollitt was not going to play after all, and that the team was setting out a man short.

Whereupon Corder dashed into his ulster, flung his flannels into his bag, and tore out of his house just in time to secure for himself the long-coveted honour, and find himself in the glorious position of 'playing for the School'.

How was such a fellow likely to trouble his head about strikes, and protests, and organized desertion?

Fortunately for the comfort of his journey, he had to pack himself away on the floor between the feet of Ridgway and another of the team, who, if they kicked him at all, only did it by accident or by way of encouragement, and not as Dangle or Brinkman might have done, in spite.

The rain was coming down pretty steadily by the time the party got to their destination, and the gloom on the brows of the four Modern prefects deepened as they looked up and speculated on the delights of standing for an hour on the wet grass, watching their rivals play.

'Dangle,' said Clapperton, 'we must stop that cad Corder's playing at all cost. It will upset everything. Come and talk to him.'

But Corder, perhaps with an inkling of what was in store for him, had entrenched himself behind a number of other players, and in close proximity to Ranger, who had evidently told himself off to see that the last recruit of the fifteen was not tampered with.

The signals of the two seniors were studiously not observed, and when Dangle, getting desperate, said:

'Corder, half a minute; Clapperton wants you,' Ranger interposed with:

'Come on, you fellows, it's time we got into our flannels,' and effectually checkmated the manœuvre.

'If he doesn't get paid out for this,' growled Clapperton, 'I'm precious mistaken.'

'Yes; and the other fellows must see that he is. If this sort of thing spreads, we may as well cave in at once.'

The Rendlesham fellows hovered about under shelter till the last moment, grumbling at the weather, the grass, and the clock. At length the Fellsgarth boys put in an appearance; sides were solemnly tossed for, and the order to 'spread out' was given.

'Hullo!' said one of the Rendlesham men as he passed Clapperton and Dangle, 'why aren't you playing? Afraid of the cold?'

'No, we scratched because——'

'Have you got that big man down who was so hot in the scrimmages? I forget his name. *He's* not one of the delicate ones, I fancy.'

'No more are we; we're not playing because——'

'Hullo! they're waiting,' said the player, and went off, leaving the explanation still unfinished.

One of the last to run out was Corder.

'You young cad,' growled Clapperton as he passed; 'take my advice and don't play, unless——'

'Come on, Corder – waiting,' shouted Yorke.

Corder obeyed like lightning.

The match began disastrously for Fellsgarth. Within five minutes of the kick-off, a run up by one of the Rendlesham quarter-backs carried the ball right into the School lines, and a touch-down resulted. On a fine day like last Saturday a goal would have been certain, but on the wet grass the try did not come off. But five minutes later the Rendlesham captain secured a magnificent try and converted it for the home team.

Clapperton sneered.

'What I expected,' said he. 'They'll be lucky if they don't lose a dozen.'

Yorke, on the contrary, was cheering up. Bad as these opening ten minutes had been, he fancied his team was not going to do so badly after all. The new players were working like mad in the scrimmage. Ranger was as quick on his feet in the wet as in the dry; and Corder at half-back had been surprisingly steady.

Before kicking off again he made one or two changes. He moved Ridgway, who was a heavy weight, up into the forwards. Corder, greatly to his delight, was moved to full back, and Fisher I moved up to half-back. The forwards were ordered on no account to break loose, but if necessary to keep the ball among them till time was called.

Then, with his well-known 'On you go!' he kicked off.

The ball was almost immediately locked up in a tight, fierce scrimmage. The boys took the captain's advice with a vengeance, and held the ball among their feet doggedly, neither letting it through on their side nor forcing it out on the side of the enemy.

At length, however, it could be seen filtering out sideways, just where the captain was hovering outside the scrimmage.

'Let it come!' he whispered. 'Look out, Ranger!'

Next moment the ball was under his arm, and before any one realized that the scrimmage was up, he was off with it and among the enemy's half-backs. The half-backs knew Yorke of old, and closed upon him before he could double or get round them.

'Pass!' shouted Ranger.

It was beautifully done, while Yorke was falling and Ranger brushing past. The enemy's half-backs were not in it with the fleet Fellsgarth runner, nor was their back; and to their own utter amazement, three minutes later the School placed to their credit an easy goal.

Then did Clapperton and Dangle and Brinkman gnash their teeth till they ached, and Fullerton, standing near, had his gibe.

'It was worth coming here in the rain to see that, wasn't it?'

The match was not yet over. The Rendlesham men, startled into attention by this unexpected rebuff, took care that such a misadventure should not happen again, and making all the use they could of their superior weight, bore down the scrimmages and forced the ball into the open. Once they carried it through with a splendid rush, and their captain, picking it up under the very feet of the boys, ran it forward a few yards, and took a drop-kick which missed by only a few inches.

A little later came Corder's chance. He had lived all the term for this moment. If he was taken back to Fellsgarth on a shutter he would not care, so long as he did himself credit now.

He had a clear field to start with, and was well out of touch before the advance guard of the enemy bore down on him. Then it was a sight to see him wriggle and dodge, and twist and turn in and out among them, threading them like a needle through a string of beads, and slipping through their hands like an eel.

'Well played indeed, Corder!' cried Yorke.

Oh, what music was in the sound! What would he not dare now!

On he went, now diving under an arm, now staggering round a leg; now jumping like a kangaroo against an opponent. The very sight of his evolutions seemed to demoralize the Rendlesham men. They floundered and slid on the slippery grass, and made wild grabs without ever reaching him. It was really too ridiculous to be eluded by a raw hand like this – and yet he eluded them.

Half-way down the field he ran with a roar of applause at his back, and only a handful of the enemy left ahead. How splendid if he could only pass them, and make his record with a run from one goal to the other!

Alas! a swoop from behind greeted the proud thought; two hands clawed at his shoulders, and from his shoulders slipped to his waist, and from his waist slid down to his ankles, where for a moment they held, and sent the runner tripping over on his nose in the mud, with the ball spinning away a yard ahead.

It was all up. No! Fisher was on the spot, and at Fisher's heels Ridgway. The Rendlesham backs flung themselves in the way, but only to divert, not to stop their career. When Corder picked himself up and rubbed the mud out of his eyes, the first thing he saw was Ridgway sitting behind the enemy's line with the ball comfortably resting on his knee! It was another for the School – perhaps a goal.

Alas! on that ground the long side-kick was too much even for Yorke. It shot wide, and Rendlesham breathed again.

But the long and short of it was that the match was a tie; a goal and a try to each side; and that to Corder belonged the credit of a big hand in the lesser point.

'Awfully well run, Corder,' said the captain, as, time having been called, the two walked off the field together. 'You must play for us again.'

After that, who should say life was not worth living?

The very weather seemed to change for Corder. The sun came out, flowers sprang up at his feet, birds started singing in the trees overhead. What a letter he would have to write home to-morrow! The captain's pat on the back sent a glow all through him. Who wouldn't be a Fellsgarth chap after all?

From *The Cock House at Fellsgarth*

A Game for Gods

Eric Linklater

Eric Linklater made his name with his third novel, Juan in America, published in 1931. This was followed by a number of other entertaining middlebrow novels, none of which, however, punched quite so much weight. Yet his vivid pen is happily displayed in this account of a rugby international in Magnus Merriman, a novel published in 1934. The game he describes is a real one – that played between Scotland and England at Murrayfield on 21 March 1931, when the Scots won 28–19. J. A. Tallent was to become the 52nd president of the Rugby Football Union; Brian Black, a South African who gained his Blue at Oxford, was to die in active service while an RAF pilot officer in 1940. Ian Smith was part of the historic Oxford-Scotland three-quarter line who won a total of 82 international caps altogether: the others in it were A. C. Wallace, G. G. Aitken and G. P. S. Macpherson, but only Smith and Macpherson were playing on this day.

The bastard Faulconbridge, having discovered that the world was mad, came to a very sensible decision and declared:

> 'Well, whiles I am a beggar I will rail
> And say there is no sin but to be rich;
> And being rich, my virtue then shall be
> To say there is no vice but beggary.'

Without having precisely formulated such a code, Magnus was not insusceptible to this chameleon philosophy, and frequently found himself in happy agreement with his surroundings – though there were occasions when he yielded to an anti-chameleon ethic and, in the midst of white, proclaimed himself all black. It was rather in this latter mood that he went to the football ground at Murrayfield, for after Uncle Henry's port and his discussion with the Colonel he felt superior to, and impatient with people who had in their minds no thought but to be entertained by an idle game. Five minutes after the match started, however, he was at one with the vast throng about him, a very chameleon on that pounding field, coloured like eighty thousand others with the fierce hues of enthusiasm.

There is a kind of Rugby that is no more than dull squabbling in the mud, a drenched and witless wrangling punctuated by a fretful whistle. But, at its best, Rugby is a game that all the gods of Greece might crowd the northern skies to see, and, benched on our cold clouds, be not restrained either by frozen bottoms or the crowd's chill sceptic hearts from plunging to the aid of stronger Myrmidons, of plucking from the scrimmage some Hector trodden in the mire and nursing him to strength again. Well might the Thunderer send fleet Mercury, swooping from the heights, to pick from the empty air Achilles' mis-flung pass and with it race – dog-rose and buttercup fast springing in his track – to the eternal goal.

And that square Ajax – dirtier than his namesake and more brave – would Hera not guard his brow from flying boots as, dauntless, down he hurls himself to stop a forward rush? Is there in all that crowd a Helen not quick-breathing, tip-toed and ready to leave dull Menelaus in his office chair and flee with Paris there, who runs so lightning-swift on the left wing? – on the left wing only? Eagles would need two to fly so fast.

Rugby can be a game for gods to see and poets to describe, and such a match was this. *L'audace, encore l'audace, et toujours l'audace* was both sides' motto, and which was more gallant – England, taller and bulkier-seeming because clad in white: Scotland, running like stags and tackling like thunderbolts in blue – no one can truthfully say and none would care to know. If Tallent for England was magnificent, Simmers for Scotland was superb. Did Tallent run the whole length of the field and score? Then Simmers, leaping like a leopard, snatched from the air a high cross-kick of Macpherson's and scored from that. Did Black for England kick like a giant, long, true and hard? Then see what Logan at the scrum, Smith on the wing, did like giants for Scotland. And each side in turn, tireless and full of devil, came to the attack and ranged the field to score. Pace never slackened from start to finish, and every minute thrilled with excitement till, at the end, wisps of fog came down – perhaps the gods indeed, hiding their brightness in the mist – and in that haze the players still battled with unwearied zeal.

Judge, then, of the fervour of the crowd, poised as it were on the broad rim of a saucer, and as thick together as if the saucer had been smeared with treacle and black sand thrown on it. But they were more mobile than sand, and ever and again a movement would pass through them as when a wave of the wind goes through a cornfield. Ever and again, as when walls in an earthquake fall asunder, some twelve or fourteen thousand would shiver and drift away from their neighbouring twelve thousand and then, stability reasserted, fall slowly into place again. And now, like a monstrous and unheralded flowering of dark tulip-beds, the crowd would open to its heart and fling aloft, as countless petals, hats, sticks, and arms, and pretty handkerchieves, and threaten to burst the sky with cheers. Now they were wild as their poorer neighbours who, some mile or two away, were cheering their paid teams with coarser tongues. Now all Scotland was at one, united in its heat, and only the most sour of moralists would decry that heat because it had been lighted by a trivial game.

Magnus carried his excitement with him, through the voluminous outpouring of the crowd, all the way to Francis Meiklejohn's flat, and Frieda, walking beside him, was fervid as he, and willing even to admit that Rugby such as this transcended the staccato violence of American football. But Meiklejohn, who had not been to the match, was sceptical of its virtues and scoffed at their enthusiasm. Mrs Dolphin, who entered the room with them to hear the news, rejoiced to learn that Scotland had won, but was disinclined to believe that such a game was worthy to show off her country's virility.

'Was there any blood?' she asked, and on being told that injuries had been few, said, 'It's shinty they should have been playing.'

From *Magnus Merriman*

The Day that Someone Passed to Lowe

P. G. Wodehouse

P. G. Wodehouse, as we have seen, knew rather more about rugby than his magnificent hero Bertie Wooster. Indeed, he felt so strongly about it that he once penned a comic poem called The Great Day, *in which he sarcastically celebrated the occasion when someone at last passed to Lowe. He thus wittily etched the predicament of Group Captain Cyril Lowe, the England wing three-quarter, who won twenty-five successive caps just before and after the First World War (not to mention the nine German planes he shot down during it); by no means the first or last England wing to be starved of good ball. Lowe also captained Dulwich College, where Plum learned his three Rs, which no doubt explains his concern in the matter.*

The Great Day

'Lowe has yet to receive a pass in International football' The Press passim.

I can recollect it clearly,
Every detail pretty nearly,
    Though it happened many, many years ago.
Yes, my children, I, your grand-dad
A reserved seat in the stand had
On the afternoon when someone passed to Lowe.

There he stood, poor little chappie,
Looking lonely and unhappy,
    While the other players frolicked with the ball.
For he knew he could not mingle
In the fun with Coates and Dingle;
    He could simply go on tackling – that was all.
I had stopped to light my briar,
For the wind was getting higher,
    When a thousand voices screamed a startled 'Oh!'
I looked up. A try or something?
Then sat gaping like a dumb thing.
    My children, somebody had passed to Lowe!

I remember how he trembled
(For to him the thing resembled
    A miracle), then gave a little cry;
And spectators who were near him
Were too overcome to cheer him;
    There were sympathetic tears in every eye.
His astonishment was utter.
He was heard to gulp, and mutter,
    'What on earth has happened now, I'd like to know?'
And incredulous reporters
Shouted out to the three-quarters;
    'Do we dream? Or did you really pass to Lowe?'

There was sweat upon his forehead
And his stare was simply horrid:
    He stood and goggled feebly at the ball.
It was plain he suffered badly,
For the crowd, now cheering madly,
    Saw him shudder, start to run, then limply fall.
Then a doctor, who was handy,
Fanned his face and gave him brandy;
    And at last, though his recovery was slow,
He regained his health and reason
By the middle of next season;
    But the shock came very near to killing Lowe.

Crash Tackle

Danny Hearn

Rugby can be a dangerous game and the principal miracle is that more people do not get injured in what looks to the casual spectator like eighty minutes of sustained mayhem. Sometimes, though, a serious injury does happen. Danny Hearn had won six caps as an England centre three-quarter when he turned out for the Midland and Home Counties against the 1967 All Blacks. The venue was that same Leicester ground where, as we've just heard, Michael Green learned the game.

Hearn tells the story in his own words; we should add that his fight back from almost total paralysis to partial mobility has won great admiration. He is still a much-valued teacher at Haileybury where he is head of the politics department and takes a keen interest in all games. He recently made a trip to South Africa to talk about paraplegia in sport.

However unspectacular our lives may be, we can invariably recall an occasion or incident that will remain in our minds until the day we die. For me, the day I will never forget is 28 October 1967, for it was then that, in less than a moment, I bowed out of one world and into another. This involved me in a complete physical and social readjustment.

It was the day on which I broke my neck in a 'crash tackle' when playing for Midland and Home Counties against the 1967 New Zealand rugby tourists. The match was no ordinary game for me, or for the rest of the team. From my earliest days I had heard of the might of New Zealand rugby and I had nothing but the deepest respect for their game. More than anything else I wanted to be in the England team that was to face them at Twickenham before the Queen and Prime Minister Harold Wilson a week later. We had prepared for this international as no England side had ever prepared for a Test before. It was essential for me to have a good game at Leicester, since the England team that was to meet New Zealand was due to be selected after the match.

At the time I had just bought a second-hand car, and before leaving Haileybury on a foul and foggy Thursday morning I had had to push the car out of the school gates on to a slope from which I could get it started before setting off to Leicester to join the rest of the team. We had the usual rather feeble run-around at a club ground outside the town that afternoon – they call it a pre-match practice and it looks positive and workmanlike in the newspapers. These run-arounds were amateur in contrast to the All Blacks' professional approach. I don't think that there are many people in England who can run a training session effectively. The future England coach Don White, who was to mastermind England's first-ever victory against South Africa in 1969, handled our session on this particular occasion and everybody was asking everyone else, 'What do you think?'. In South Africa or New Zealand the coach would be the rugby equivalent of God and would leave the players in no uncertainty as to who was the master. The session tended to be something of a shambles because there was too much talking and backchat, in addition to the fact that players tend to restrain themselves from too much activity in the two days immediately before a big game.

The contrast supplied by the All Blacks is illustrated by the story of the 1953–4 New Zealanders training before one particular game in America. One would have thought that the opposition in that part of the world was hardly a match for the All Blacks, but to see the men in black training was quite a sight for the amazed Americans. When one of the tourists had to retire from the field with a broken leg, a spectator is reputed to have said: 'If that's what they do to themselves, Christ knows what they are going to do to us in the match!'

But don't run away with the idea that I think we should go completely the way of the New Zealanders. Their machine-like approach to the game would inevitably take away from British rugby its individual flair and remove the twinkling runners from our game. And the type of player who has made the British Lions so popular abroad might well disappear without trace.

On the Friday most of the team spent their time aimlessly walking round the town, playing cards and drinking coffee to pass the time. I had with me a number of school exercise books to mark up, but these were lost in the hurly burly following my accident and my pupils were never to see them again. That evening our time was spent at the cinema watching *Bonnie and Clyde* – quite the most depressing sort of film, and this pre-match depression never really left me. We got to bed at about half past ten. I was sharing a room with a young fly-half called Alan James, who had been with us on the Canadian tour. Although it sounds patronizing, I thought that I should make the move to make him feel at home and confident for the match the next day. (I remembered my own first game, or one of my first games, for England, when I shared a room with Britain's most capped back, Mike Weston. He is a great friend of mine, but on this occasion he never stopped telling me how he shouldn't be playing, how unfit he was, and how he was suffering from this and that injury! This hardly put me in the right frame of mind for the match and in the end I just said: 'For crying out loud, shut up, Mike.')

Before a big match I always got up as late as possible and satisfied the 'inner man' with brunch. This particular Saturday morning followed the familiar pattern and at the meal I suggested to the Irish referee Paddy D'Arcy that he should watch the All Blacks' notorious line-out work. He was a referee who had an indefinable flair for the game that was very similar to that of the little Welshman Gwynne Walters. The tourists were whistled up continually during the game for line-out infringements. This was not very much to their liking and, predictably, they did not call upon D'Arcy to referee another game on the tour.

On the other occasions when I had been on the Leicester Tigers' ground I had not played particularly well. Although it is the second largest rugby ground in England after Twickenham, I found it a drab place that always looked as if it needed a good coat of paint and a complete refurbishing, even though the pitch was always in immaculate order. The stadium as a whole lacked the atmosphere you find in so many of the other big grounds. I walked from the hotel to the ground for the game and met my mother by chance in the nearby park. As she walked to her seat, I said to her: 'I've never been so nervous in my life – I'll be glad when this game is over.' There was really no reason for this particular comment. I was twenty-six and had a wealth of rugby experience behind me, including six England caps. But basically I suffered from the inferiority complex that many Englishmen have when they face New Zealanders on the rugby field. I viewed them as Goliaths and was unprepared to accept that they are no different from us, except possibly physically, in that they are better-built – even their three-quarters seemed to be built like forwards. On the field the All Blacks have intense patriotism and pride for their homeland, so that when they play for New Zealand, they really do play for New Zealand. But in England the Test player is more often playing for himself first and his country last. The awe in which the giant forwards from New Zealand were held was best symbolized when a young schoolboy asked with great seriousness whether Colin Meads 'really ate barbed wire for breakfast' . . .

I did not believe that we could win this second match against the tourists. I was in charge of the backs and I was to play alongside Bob Lloyd, a school contemporary of mine. I knew that I would be marking the All Blacks' powerful second five-eighth Ian MacRae, who was renowned for running straight into his opposite number so as to create a ruck for his forwards to heel the ball back. I thought that I would spend most of the afternoon tackling the burly MacRae (he was 6ft 1in and weighed 13st 7lb), as the New Zealanders would win most of the ball. So I took the field determined to hit Ian with a crash tackle really early on; I would try and disrupt his game and show who was really the master.

My attitude was: 'If I hit MacRae really hard, he won't come at me again.' We kicked off and the New Zealand full-back Fergie McCormick dropped the ball near the posts. But they won the ball against the head and kicked to touch. From the line-out near the half-way line they again won the ball and it went along their back-line. I had plenty of time to hit MacRae and I really launched myself at him. I can only piece together what happened then with the help of others and with the aid of the film of the accident, for the impact of the crash tackle left me stunned on the ground. I always enjoyed tackling, as it was my greatest rugby skill, but this time I must have done something wrong, for the impact of my head on his hip left me, instead of him, on the turf. All he had to show afterwards was an enormous bruise. I wasn't knocked out, but apparently someone suggested that I should be stood up. This was the worst thing that could be done, but my defensive mechanism was apparently functioning enough for me to say, 'Don't touch me.' This probably saved my life, for if I had been moved my chances of survival would have been negligible. I was also very fortunate that a doctor came on to the pitch who realized the seriousness of the situation and saw to it that I was carefully placed upon a stretcher.

By then my father, who was a general practitioner, was by my side. I said to him: 'This is serious, isn't it?' without really comprehending what the word 'serious' meant, for I did not then know that I was paralysed. Again this was, I think, my defensive mechanism working; it would have been too hard to take in immediately the brutality of such a stroke of fate. At Stoke Mandeville they appreciated this fact and it was weeks, months even, before I understood to what extent I had been paralysed. Amazingly enough it was at least three years before the full implications of the accident finally registered. I was put in the isolation ward at the Royal Leicester Infirmary and I remember waking up – I had obviously been given drugs of some kind – about two in the morning and asking for scrambled eggs and chocolate because I was so hungry. And this they duly gave me! What would the medical men say about this, I wonder? When you fracture your neck, you lose all sensation from the point of break downwards, but, although I had been X-rayed, they were not certain whether I had severed my spinal cord completely.

I vaguely remember a doctor examining me and sticking pins into my body to test my sensation reaction; this was the standard test to determine the extent of damage to the spinal cord. The next morning I asked to see Micky Steele-Bodger and the *Sunday Times* rugby football critic, Vivian Jenkins, for whom I had always had great respect ever since he covered a Cheltenham v. Marlborough match way back in 1958. I asked Steele-Bodger the inevitable question: 'Would I have been selected for England next week?' I just wanted to know in my own mind whether I would have been chosen. 'Absolutely without question,' he told me, which was a comforting reply. Whether my state of ill-health influenced what he said I do not know.

I did not realize at the time that the crash tackle was being shown over and over again on the news on television. I suppose if you are going to break your neck, you cannot do it in a more noble way than by playing rugby against a foreign team. The fact that the game was seen by millions on BBC television provided a dramatic story for the world's press and television. What better story than that of a rugby international cut down in the prime of his career? How would he react against such adversity? Although I did not know it at the time, the film of the game provided doctors with one of the few live shots of a man breaking his neck. The medical staff at Stoke Mandeville acquired the film from the BBC, but found that my blow was relatively straightforward in medical terms. The film is of more use to would-be rugby tacklers as an example of where not to place their heads! Little did I know at the time of the impact how much the mass media can impose upon an individual. Only later did I realize the responsibility placed upon me by the fact that I was now a celebrity, and it was rather different from what I had at first imagined.

On the Sunday I learnt that I was to be transferred to Stoke Mandeville and at once resisted, for I knew what this implied. I was taken to Mandeville, and in my half-drugged state I remember part of the journey along the motorway (I am sorry to disillusion those who thought I was flown there!) because it seemed to me that the ambulance was travelling at breakneck speed, which perhaps it was. This, of course, was only natural, because when you are motionless all sensation of speed is greatly accentuated. I also recall my arrival at the hospital, because they were totally unprepared for yet another patient – and this hardly lessened my previous attitude towards the establishment. For instance, the orderly rushed me into the ward at a tremendous speed, as he was apparently off-duty officially. I had now arrived at the hospital where I least wanted to be a patient.

The newspapers on the day following the match were generally in the dark as to my exact fate. The *Sunday Telegraph* said: 'Hearn was detained in the intensive care unit of Leicester Royal Infirmary and his condition was said to be satisfactory.' But Vivian Jenkins was closer to the real situation when he wrote in the *Sunday Times*: 'Danny Hearn was carted off the field on a stretcher after making a tremendous tackle on his opposite number, MacRae. There was, too, disturbing news from the infirmary of a suspected spinal injury purely, one should add, as a result of the impetus and ferocity of his own tackle.' By late Sunday the situation was clearer and the headline in John Reason's report for the *Daily Telegraph* read: 'Brave Hearn on the danger list at Stoke Mandeville'. The hospital had issued a bulletin saying that I was 'suffering from serious spinal injuries and dangerously ill'.

I left the field when the match was only five minutes old and the performance put on by the Midland and Home Counties, after being reduced to only fourteen men, was nothing short of heroic. Their Coventry captain, Phil Judd, was playing in the match with an ankle the size of a balloon – I had seen it in the changing-room – but he knew that he might not make the England team if he did not play in this match. The All Blacks – remember they were regarded as the best team in the world – did win 15–3, but the final score was deceptive. Each team scored a try – ours was by my school colleague Lloyd – and the difference between the two sides was made up by a dropped goal kicked by first five-eighth Herewini and three penalties landed by McCormick. 'Never have I known a beaten side receive such an ovation as they left the field,' said the counties selector Tom Berry afterwards.

Unwisely, I thought, the selectors were influenced by the emotionalism of this display, and eleven of the side, including the entire pack, were chosen for the Test the following Saturday. In my opinion, it demanded too much of the players to play the game of their lives against the New Zealanders again within the space of eight days. And I think this was reflected in the result at Twickenham when New Zealand, who did not lose a game on the entire tour, crushed England 23–11. It was a sad end to Steele-Bodger's dream of producing an England side that would beat the All Blacks.

From *Crash Tackle*

No Fun – No Game

Gerald Davies and John Morgan

Gerald Davies is one of the greatest wing three-quarters ever to have taken the rugby field. He played 46 times for Wales and scored twenty tries for them; and five Tests for the British Lions, with three tries. He was born in a tiny village, Llansaint, overlooking Carmarthen Bay, and went from there to Loughborough where he studied PE, then to Cambridge to read English, and is now a rugby writer for The Times. His dialogue with fellow Welshman John Morgan tells us much about the evolution of the game to which he has given so much, and incidentally a good deal about him.

JOHN MORGAN What was it that made you determined to go on playing for so long at such a high level?

GERALD DAVIES What persuades a person to keep on playing and separates him from the rest who don't is mental, the psychological motivating factor peculiar to him. It's the vital ingredient which every talented player needs to have if he is to achieve his potential. Many players drop by the wayside because they haven't the tenacity, the nous, the inspiration or the motivation to want to go on. I remember my own earliest inspiration. There was a young boy in our village who won an Under 15 Welsh Schoolboy cap and brought his jersey and cap back to the village to be admired. And I wanted to emulate that. I failed to do it at Under 15, I managed it at Under 18. Then it got into my blood. Having achieved one thing, you want to go to the next, like getting a senior cap for Wales. Having got that first one, you don't want to be a one-cap wonder, the fate of so many, and by the time you have got several caps then it has become an addiction. There are several points during your career when you think about giving up, perhaps because of the pressure, because it is time consuming; perhaps you wonder whether all this effort in an amateur game is worthwhile. But in Wales the standing a Welsh player has in the community is a very seductive thing. And you thrill to the roar of the crowd.

JM Is the roar of the crowd very potent at the Arms Park? Does it deafen you?

TGRD You are only aware of it when the game is at a stop. When the game is in flow you are very rarely aware of the noise because you are concentrating on lots of other things, but you are aware that you are playing on your own patch and that everyone is there to support you. The crowd is an important element. There is a difference between playing in front of one man and a dog and playing in front of 60,000 people. Some say that this is an enormous pressure for players to bear, but it's a pressure that International players of the right calibre revel in. Jean-Pierre Rives has described it as the special ingredient. You come back for more.

JM Do you feel that you are bound to be playing better because that crowd is there?

TGRD Yes, it certainly gets the adrenalin going. For the first dozen or so games the only impression you get is of things happening very quickly. You can't remember details of games, just an overall impression, and before you know it, the game is over and done with. The longer you go on playing, the more you become aware of what is happening, and the more enjoyable the whole experience becomes.

JM So there is pleasure. If you write something that is satisfying and feel you have said what you wanted to say in an elegant manner, I think I understand that pleasure. So when you were in such a great team for so long, did you have a positive sense of aesthetic delight that you were with such gifted people?

TGRD I remember after I had got about a dozen caps a certain sense of dissatisfaction and even disappointment set in. I wondered was it worth it. The Welsh team wasn't performing all that well, we won a few games and lost a few. There was no sense of continuity, of knowing quite what we were up to. But then coaching came in and Clive Rowlands arrived and he, more than anyone, gave an identity to the Welsh team. Success came. And the success bred more success. At a crucial period this persuaded me to hang on. Not only was it a good thing in itself, but I was in the company of good men, of friends. We won the Triple Crown three times in a row and this captured the public imagination in a way that I had not known before, and that too was a driving force.

JM As a spectator in that period, I had the sense that people like yourself, Barry John, Gareth Edwards, Mervyn Davies and John Taylor, were playing international rugby yet looking as if you were enjoying yourselves. Did you have a sense then that you were enjoying it, and that there was almost an artistic, as well as a physical pleasure in being with people like that – men who were playing rugby of such quality that it was an extra element in the game?

TGRD Enjoyment was always important because that is the bottom line. Unless there is that element of enjoyment, I don't care how good a team you are or how competitive, if you lose that sense of enjoyment then rugby is not worth the candle. I think what has happened over the last few years is that the game has become more and more competitive, people have become more and more analytical about it, and coaching has tried to impose a certain way of playing without appreciating that in the end it is a matter of enjoyment. You got pleasure out of being in a good team and that gives a shared experience and enjoyment. But there is also within the team, as we played then, the player's contribution, which is something independent of the others, the self-satisfying kind of pleasure in knowing that you have performed well and that you were being allowed the opportunity to perform well. The wing can be a very isolated position, and if he doesn't feel as if he is contributing, then there can't be much enjoyment for him, however many times his team wins. Unless the individual player feels he has contributed to that win, he remains unfulfilled and empty.

JM I suppose the triumph you had with the British Lions in 1971 in New Zealand is regarded as the greatest achievement of any British team abroad. Was the actual touring fun? Or is the game such a preoccupation for the player that he doesn't really know he's travelling?

TGRD   No, we enjoyed the travelling, visiting places, meeting all sorts of people, going out to restaurants and so on. In Bleddyn Williams' day of course the Lions were away for six months of the year and two of those would be spent on board ship. Today things have tended to become a bit less leisurely and more intense, with the number of games played cut down as well. But rugby is still an amateur game and the great perk, for want of a better word, is the travelling, a broadening of the horizons which rugby football has given us. Of course there is the other side of the coin. There are those moments before a Test when you have a sense of fear. There are just the thirty of you, alone in a foreign and distant country, and the tension and pressure are at a peak. You begin to wonder what on earth you are doing there. There must be far more pleasurable things to be doing at the height of summer back home.

JM   Was it much fun playing, then? Did you actually enjoy being on the field?

TGRD   No question about it, yes I did. Back in '71 there was such a marvellous atmosphere in the team due to people like Carwyn James, John Dawes and Doug Smith. A game is not just a physical confrontation, it's a matter of techniques and skill, and also of attitudes. Attitudes coming from the top and from within the team. If the coach has a generous spirit which is able to instil a kind of fun in the players, that makes for a better game on the field than if he is tense and dour and oppressive. The crucial point about 1971 in New Zealand was that there was a great sense of fun and adventure. When you think of the players, you could never attribute adjectives like 'dour' or 'grim' or 'intense' to someone like Barry John or David Duckham or Willie John McBride. But though we had fun, there was also the common purpose, that serious objective which everyone wanted to achieve.

JM   Reading about the 1971 tour or any of the great matches, there is a tendency afterwards for people to analyse it as if it were all preplanned. You can look at the game as a rather incoherent mess with people just running around and it all seems pure chance. Nowadays people don't look at a match like that, as one did when young. They tend instead to consider it much more as something that has been preordained by the coach. The players are under instruction and carrying out orders. At international level do you play with both a very strategic and a strong tactical sense, or is it much more arbitrary?

TGRD   In a game with a ball the shape it is, it can't be other than arbitrary a lot of the time. But what you are hinting at highlights some of what is going wrong at the moment. Coaches feel they can plan a game. There is no way that you can plan a game. There are so many variables: the weather, obscure laws which a fallible referee has to interpret, the players themselves, and the scope of their individual abilities. These days we all subscribe to the ideal of playing expansive fifteen-man rugby. But you can't play like that all the time. You have to achieve what you can with the players you have facing the opposition you have. The pattern of play can't be dictated before kick-off. To distinguish between strategy and tactics: strategy is something you determine in a general sense before the game starts; tactics is what happens on the park. The cleverness of the players in the 'seventies was that there was sufficient confidence in the player in each position to determine the tactics as the game evolved. Gareth Edwards or Barry John or Phil Bennett would know when the ball should be moved or when it should be kicked.

JM Barry used to tell me that he would look at you out on the wing and if he thought you were looking a bit cold, he'd let you have the ball!

TGRD That's typical of his lovely arrogance – the majestic arrogance of the outside-half.

JM But seriously, in that period it used to strike me as an observer that the backs didn't get all that much of the ball; that what happened was people like you or Barry or Gareth or Phil or JPR would frequently make something out of practically nothing. The moments which were decisive were very often the unexpected moments of individual brilliance. The excitement was in never knowing what was going to happen next.

Having said that, this season international teams seem to have exhibited an almost spectacular stupidity. When we saw the Australians play Wales, for example, the visitors played a very intelligent game. They had very good forwards and they had the ball and knew what to do with it. Scotland and England played Australia subsequently, and they must have seen the Welsh match and what happened. Yet when Australia played Scotland, Scotland went and committed all the mistakes Wales had made. Surely someone in Scotland must have said we mustn't play like this against the Australians because we have seen what they did to Wales. Yet they still went out at Murrayfield and played into the Wallabies' hands as if mesmerized. Surely that is not an example of the bad side of coaching so much as a failure of intelligence?

TGRD Yes, and there aren't that many clever people around at the moment. You do need to analyse the play of your opponents, and these days the coach has taken too much responsibility for this on himself. But when it comes to the sharp end, the most important person is of course the captain, because he is the one on the field. It's the captain who can encourage and instil those qualities needed to beat the opposition. You can have a broad strategy, which the coach ought to have analysed somewhere along the line, but it is the captain and the players on the field who determine how to win the game.

JM When you played for Wales and the British Lions John Dawes was captain for a long period, and then there was Mervyn Davies. How does the captain on the field actually express his analysis to his team? Does he come over and say, look, we have to change our tactics here, boys? If he were a centre, would he go and tell the forwards they must do something different?

TGRD Almost certainly. There is a kind of dialogue. There's always a great deal of chatter among the forwards anyway about who should be doing what. But the key position is always at half-back. It's at half-back the pattern of the game is determined, regardless of where the captain is. I was fortunate to play at a time when Wales and the Lions were particularly strong in those positions. The captain didn't have much to say to them because the halves knew what to do and when to do it. This year Wales failed miserably to change tactics against Ireland at a crucial period in the last twenty minutes. The idea that Wales should persist in running the ball when they were being knocked down in midfield shows a lack of awareness at half-back. Running and playing a lovely expansive game is just one kind of tactic. But if you want to win, it may during the course of the game be necessary to vary the tactic; you may have to adopt, for the sake of argument, the Pontypool approach for a while in order to wear the other team down or show up their weaknesses.

JM Rugby of all games strikes me as being a team game. In rugby nobody can play well unless the team is playing well.

TGRD Certainly, the players are cogs in the machine of the whole team. But those cogs have their own hierarchy. While the prop forward may plough his lonely furrow, the outside-half is a princely figure who cannot possibly be considered on the same plane. His personality has to be different, as indeed does the full-back's or the wing's. A clever coach like Carwyn James recognizes these distinctions of personality and plays to individual strengths for the benefit of the team as a whole.

One of the perverse charms of rugby football is that the laws are so complicated the game is not clear cut in any way at all. Why does the scrum collapse? Whose fault is it? Why has a penalty been given? Why was it a free kick and not a penalty? What happens in the line-out? Was it a try under that great heap? Breweries have made their fortunes on post-match postmortems. The game gorges itself on all the talk.

JM Are you suggesting then that rugby players must be cleverer than other sportsmen because they need to master such complicated laws?

TGRD Far from it. I don't think many players know the laws. For my own part, I never actually read the rule book until very late in my life and that was only because I was captain of Cardiff and had to be sure of my ground if there was a point of disagreement with the referee. You have to have a legal mind to understand the laws. How many teams are there in Wales? About 900. How many of the players in those teams have actually read the laws? It must be a minuscule figure.

JM When we were down in the South of France looking at French rugby – and it was an entertaining and instructive trip – we had a very strong sense of the foreignness of the place. I wonder if more British clubs ought not to go and play more in Europe. They could afford to go more often to Holland or France than to New Zealand or Australia, after all. We have also heard on our travels about various players from Britain and the southern hemisphere who are now playing for French or Italian clubs and enjoying themselves immensely, and no doubt being rewarded. Should there be more of that?

TGRD Yes, if I have any regrets, and I don't like to look over the shoulder at what might have been, but I would have loved to have had the opportunity to play in France for a year, not only to get to grips with French rugby, but to learn the language. As you say, Australians do it, New Zealanders do it, some people from England have been doing it in recent years and I think it would be a good thing for Welsh rugby if players were able occasionally to move away from the Welsh environment, even if they only go to play for a while in Scotland or England. Welsh rugby has become very insular, and as a result we tend to become a little neurotic about it. We are not expansive enough in going out and meeting other people.

JM In the South of France it was clear that there were opportunities for young British players to have a very nice life and play a good class of rugby, and live in some style. It was a revelation to me and I don't think our young players are aware of what would be available to them. French players are certainly given preferential treatment, almost film-star status in the community. They are found jobs, flats, motor cars. You probably weren't aware of the fact but talking to the players in clubs and bars there, they could not believe you were not a millionaire. Because you were who you were and such a celebrated figure, they took it for granted that you, like so many French players we won't name, would be enormously rich. You would have a mansion and people would be coming to your house as a shrine, that kind of thing. It was a shock to them that you actually still need to work for a living!

TGRD We are coming round to the whole prickly question of amateur status now. My belief is that the game ought to remain amateur but that the regulations should be redefined in the simplest possible terms. Players ought not to be paid for playing the game. There are very many good reasons for this, not least that I think the players themselves enjoy the game as it is without the enormous pressures footballers have because their livelihoods depend on footballing success and they live in fear of failure. Another reason why I think it should remain amateur is that the laws are much too complicated! The best professional sports are games like snooker or golf, which are non-contact and everyone knows precisely what is happening. But rugby football is not like that. Since each man has his price, who is to say what dirty deed might not be committed at the bottom of a ruck for the sake of pieces of silver?

What need changing however are the laws of amateurism, enshrined in twelve pages in the law book. Why can't a player write a book and get some money for it? Why can't he sponsor something? It's these peripheral matters that need sorting out to give players the benefit. After all, the Unions rake in enormous sums in sponsorship for international and cup matches, and lots of money is ploughed into the game. But this doesn't make much sense to the man who plays week in, week out, at club level, and the Unions just don't realize that their money-making emphasis encourages similar ideas in the players.

When I was out in Hong Kong recently I spoke to Alan Jones, the very perceptive and articulate Australian coach, and he said what the players want is to be made to feel special. A sour note has been allowed to creep into our game because the Unions have shown a lack of generosity towards players. As Alan Jones said, why couldn't someone like Gould, their full-back, bring in some friends to the hotel and buy them a meal to thank them for their hospitality? The reason at the time was because he couldn't afford to do it. Why can't money be made available for something like that, or for entertaining wives or girlfriends?

I can remember when I was captaining the Barbarians against the Lions at Twickenham in the royal Jubilee year, Jean-Pierre Rives wanted to have a bottle of wine with his dinner. But the four Home Unions had allowed us a cask of beer, so he was told to drink that. Well, beer is not the beverage your good Frenchman is accustomed to drink with a meal, especially when he's travelled from France to play in a gala game. But we had to work quite hard to get that one bottle of wine for Jean-Pierre Rives. And there were the Home Unions proudly boasting of how much they were giving to the Jubilee Trust that year. Profit came first, instead of the players' welfare.

JM In England what struck me as odd was that there are players who are very good but have no interest in playing for England. They would rather play for their clubs, even small ones, than go and play for a big club and win an international cap. Now up until recently that seemed very unWelsh.

TGRD Yes, the curious development in Welsh rugby – the players who do not want to continue to play for Wales.

JM   It can't have happened before, can it? Not so pointedly, I mean, people saying I am not playing for Wales again?

TGRD   It must be a symptom of what is going wrong at the moment.

JM   But we spectators tend to think that those chaps who are great players are not actually touched by human emotions on the field. It can be very difficult for people who haven't played in front of big crowds or to a high standard to understand what is necessarily going on in the mind of the player. Is he nervous? Is he thinking that he has just made a mistake? If he's a full-back is he worrying about the wind blowing too strongly in his face? Is his old knee injury playing up? Nowadays, when you see a recording of yourself in a match, which is such a furious and excitable affair, do you remember the try just like it was?

TGRD   As far as individual games are concerned, I have only a general memory of what actually happened in each. I don't think I have the kind of mind to remember the details. Though someone like Mike Gibson could remember the actual minutiae of a game and talk you through particular incidents.

JM   Let's consider some tries where you side-stepped past people or went for the corner and it didn't look as if you would make it. In your mind at the time, was there a blind determination; or did you have a scheme for outwitting people? Or was it done out of instinct?

TGRD   Largely out of instinct. From my point of view the worst thing that could happen to me was to have a lot of time to think about something on the rugby field. I'm sure this is true for most players. With regard to my side-step, if you are in a very enclosed space, with lots of bodies around, you act instinctively. But there were occasions when perhaps I had fifteen or twenty yards to my next opponent. Then I had time to think about it and that did make me just a little bit nervous. However, I always feel the man with the ball holds the advantage and it's the other person who has to react. So it's a case of getting him into a situation where he has no time for second thoughts and is inescapably committed.

JM   And if you were in a defensive position, was that instinctive as well?

TGRD   No, in defence you have to think more about the other player – what would I be doing in that situation if I had the ball? You have to try and cut down the number of options for your opponent. You can veer him out to the touchline, or suggest by your own positioning that he ought to come back inside. You have to channel him to do what *you* want him to do. I can remember in the Second Test in New Zealand in 1971 facing up to Bryan Williams, a very formidable opponent and a lovely winger with speed and side-step, and a hefty fellow, too. He made about twenty yards on me in open field which really ought to put the defensive man in an awkward position. But I thought of the number of options he had open to him, and at the back of my mind I thought of the New Zealand attitude. Knowing that he was much larger than I was, I guessed that Williams would have been told, 'Run up to him and run over him.' And that's precisely what he tried to do. He simply ran straight at me and I thought, well, that's not good thinking when he has all his other options open.

JM   So you were able to stop him?

TGRD   So I stopped him, that's right. I just stood in his way and he trampled all over me. But he didn't get very far because the pack caught up with him.

JM   In the days when I played rugby, I never used to think that it was a peculiarly rough game or a dirty game, or even a particularly tough game. But today, viewing the game as a spectator, there looks to be a pugilistic element in it. Why does it look so much rougher now than it was to experience? Did you use to think to yourself, what am I doing here with all these other fellows punching each other and kicking each other and trying to hit me? What a daft way of endangering oneself, and for what?

TGRD   That is the great mystery. There was never a stage when I thought rugby was so rough a game that I didn't want to be part of it. Certainly there were odd things going on in the scrum, but I never thought it was a dirty game. I was caught at the bottom of a ruck or a maul sometimes, but there were only one or two instances in my whole career when anything untoward happened. Whether that was because there was some sort of gentlemanly understanding that forwards don't touch the backs, I rather doubt. But you're right, now I've stopped playing and started watching, it certainly does look rougher and tougher and more violent from the touchline.

JM   I broke a shoulder, a collar bone, a thumb and four ribs playing rugby. The four ribs were due to having a game in the Midlands for a team where the scrum-half was clearly demented. I was playing at outside-half and he kept on giving me the ball with about four blokes at the same time. That would never happen in Welsh rugby. But all that's a different thing from calculated violence and over-combative play. Should the authorities be dealing more firmly with that?

TGRD   Well, they do have a policy to a certain extent already, but it isn't followed through in as convincing a manner as it ought to be. If a player is sent off the field, he won't be open for selection for the national team. There are a very few thugs around the rugby clubs who can make the game disreputable. Generally speaking players keep to the laws. Speaking now as a back talking about forwards, I think the unspoken agreement that the forwards can get on with whatever they like and that punches are okay is wrong. In fact the thugs tend to use other means of expressing themselves, like studs and going for the eyes and the mouth and the nose. Though there are very few of those around, they do bring the game into disrepute.

JM   So what, then, do you feel is the peculiar appeal of the game?

TGRD   I loved playing it and I still love watching it. One of its unique qualities is the variety of people it gives a chance to. There are very few other outdoor ball games a chap the size and weight of a prop forward could play to a high level. I love the way it caters for all shapes and sizes from the lanky second row to the tiny winger, no bigger than a bar of soap. And then there's the social aspect which is a binding factor that brings people back every Saturday to play because they are with a bunch of friends. There's an eighty-minute period when they play, they combat the other team, which gives them a sense of identity, and at the end of the day both sides can still come together to socialize in the club house, and that is the binding factor of rugby.

JM   Do you find the experience of sitting there and *not* playing a saddening one? Does it make you melancholy that the years have gone and you are no longer on the fields of praise?

TGRD   No, and I don't have any sense of envy either. You know my philosophy. I don't keep looking over my shoulder. Having experienced successes and failures, wins and losses, you realize both are important. But in the end what is nice, of course, is to look back on a period of success. However, that period of my life is over now and, looking at the game today, I would just like the present players to experience what we experienced.

JM   But it wasn't just the success or the victory, was it? It was success in style?

TGRD   Style, yes. There was a lot of fun. The rugby player can train as much as he likes during the week, but his reward is to go out there and play and try to put into practice those things he has been taught. The coach can't do that. The only satisfaction for the coach is in winning. If the team doesn't win, the coach is dissatisfied. But for the player, win or lose, at least he has been out there trying to do something. That's the paradox – the curious blend of joy and achievement. Because there should be fun in the game. If there is no fun in rugby football, there is no game.

From *Sidesteps*

Where is our Neville Cardus?

R. D. Kernohan

The Scottish writer and former prop forward R. D. Kernohan published the next piece in Blackwood's Magazine *– now sadly defunct – in 1979. I would have gone all the way with him then about the grievous dearth of distinguished rugby writing; but as I hope we have shown in these pages, the picture is perceptibly changing for the better. Indeed when I discussed the question with him just before we went to press, he said he had noted the change himself; though he thought his basic premiss still stood.*

Why it should be so is still not totally clear; but I think the very intensity of rugby, the sizzling electricity with which it is played, makes it hard for the onlooker to recall it in tranquillity and quite impossible for the player. The heart-stopping dynamics dissolve as we look back on them into one kaleidoscopic blur.

So immensely enjoyable to play; so very difficult to write about, says Mr Kernohan of our game; and likens it to another human activity which is often written about, but seldom well. Have a look, though, at the three short pieces by Alan Watkins which follow it. Have we had our own Cardus all along?

It is a fact of life that some people prefer a round ball, large or small. There are even those who would give Cardiff Arms Park, Murrayfield and Twickenham a miss for the chauffeur-races now dignified as motor sport.

I told one of the dissenters that a son had given me Gareth Edwards's autobiography for Christmas, and that if I was good this year I might get J. P. R. Williams's new book on the greatest amateur game.

'Yes,' said the round-ball gear-changer, 'rugby's getting quite a literature these days.'

Was there really a hint of a sneer in his voice or was it in my sensitive imagination? If I have a feeling of guilt about my attachment to the game it is not because I am unavailable for domestic duties from October to March, unless there is frost. It's not because the house is like a sore-headed bear garden after Scotland lose, which means only too often. It isn't even because of allegations about shamateurs who do better out of the true faith than Rugby League professionals from their heresy. It's because I worry about the way rugby seems to lack the literature it deserves, and I wonder why.

Rugby is now part of the culture of people with great literary traditions. In Wales even a vote of thanks can sound like a passage from Homer. The line-out peel was developed in the land of the troubadours where Rabelais (whose influence is sometimes detected in the *après-ski* of the game) studied at Montpellier, near Béziers . . . Sir Walter Scott, so skilful at serving up Jacobite romances for dedicated Hanoverians, could have been as delightfully ambivalent in describing the clashes of the upper-crust Edinburgh clubs and the down-to-earth Border towns. And sound judges of literary form say there is good poetry in Afrikaans, and some hope for New Zealand.

Yet rugby lacks literature of the depth and variety that enriches cricket, golf and even angling. If you doubt that, tell me whose *Compleat Scrummager* will stand comparison with Izaak Walton, or who has written about the rugby country of the Borders or the Welsh valleys or the faithful enclaves of Northern England in the way that Edmund Blunden wrote about the cricket country of Sussex . . .

For that matter, tell me which of the very fine rugby journalists has moved beyond the reporting, the politics and the tactics of the game to the brave new literary world that has had such people as Pelham Warner, Neville Cardus and John Arlott in it.

Who can compete in this literary first division? Max Boyce? Perhaps he is the exception that proves the rule. Perhaps he is the hopeful natural talent that is in danger of being diverted by his popularity and his commercial success. For many a rugby man must have watched his television series, especially his raids down the blind side into England, and worried about whether the people's poet of the game was in danger of becoming just a very successful Welsh comedian. Did television producers and commercial managers tell him not to put in too much of the rugby stuff for the English audiences or the women? Did someone warn him off anything that might puzzle those not reared within sight of a rugby pitch and a Baptist chapel?

Certainly now that Max Boyce has found so lucrative a touch the sporting anthologies need never be so weak again where rugby is concerned. I have just consulted a very good one, with Damon Runyon on baseball, Hazlitt on prize-fighting, Sassoon on horseback, Wodehouse on 'the coming of gowf', the inevitable Hemingway, and a Scot who deserves his place in an anthology of cricket, A. G. Macdonell. But rugby is represented – or should it be misrepresented? – only by the house-match from *Tom Brown's Schooldays*. Now that certainly deserves its place in an anthology of rugby, but only in the way Leviticus deserves its place in the Bible: it is very interesting in the light of what comes after. But it is hardly the game of Jackie Kyle or Barry John, though I dare say that Andy Irvine would have had a go at getting through the mob on his own, usually trying the inside break.

Or take reference books, which are both a form of literature at their best and a foundation for literature. It is only in recent years that rugby in Britain has had anything like adequate reference books or a reasonable 'encyclopedia' of the game. In one case, unless my memory betrays me, the game is indebted to a firm involved in sporting sponsorship, and in the other to an immigrant New Zealander. Even now there is nothing in rugby that really matches *Wisden* in cricket – or which, like *Wisden*, provides a channel for the distribution of significant opinions about the game.

It may not be only Britain which has been lacking in this basic literature of rugby. Despite the vigour of French sporting journalism, not least in rugby, a French yearbook of the game I saw seemed good but no better than our own. And the last time I bought a *Wisden* was in South Africa, at a substantial premium on the British price, at the start of their rugby season and our cricket one. I bought it because even with the premium it seemed the best value in sporting books on the shelves in what from 1930 to 1965 was probably the greatest rugby country in the world.

I dare say some rugby-minded readers will tell me to forget about the anthologies and the reference books and to think instead of the quality of rugby journalism in print and on television: 'Never mind the books – get on with the game!'

As a journalist who writes only very occasionally about rugby I have an immense admiration for those who write about it regularly. Those of them who follow the British Lions can depend on me to buy their books after the tours – at least when the Lions have won. But the books – even with purple passages like John Reason's accounts of the 1971 Lions in the Wellington match and Third Test – are basically match reports. When the accounts try to go beyond that they are in danger of becoming political and even polemical journalism, which is a contribution to literature but not a foundation for it or a stimulus to its development. Read Reason's book on the 1974 Lions in South Africa and the parallel book by J. B. G. Thomas: it is hard to believe that the introductions are about the same tour, yet large areas of match report are almost interchangeable.

Rugby journalism is good and some writers like Bill McLaren have added new depth to it by making tactics comprehensible and interesting; but it rarely reaches the best cricket writing's insight into human relations, human frailty, and the relation of men to time, place, community and tradition. Yet rugby is as rich as cricket in such relationships and richer by far than some sports which are really little more than solitary vices.

The point about television has more force. Perhaps one of the reasons why rugby is slow to develop as rich a literature as it deserves is because of the quality and capacity of television rugby coverage – at a crucial time in the game's history.

The triumph of rugby in becoming a great world game has coincided with the dominance of television in our communications media and the technical mastery, especially by the BBC, of the problems of televising the game. It is a more telegenic game than real, pre-Packer cricket, or golf, with its small ball and slow motion. Unless we can get some close-ups of front rows in action, within or without the laws of the game, it is hard to think what dramatic improvements in presentation of the game itself are possible.

And for television the game's the thing. Compare the live coverage of a really good try – say the Barbarians' handling movement that started with Bennett near his own line and began the demolition of the All Blacks in 1973 – with the re-runs when we know what is going to happen. Something is lost. But compare the visual re-run with the results of the current commentators' obsession for having players 'talk us through' the try on television. Art is reduced to bathos. The poetry of motion, power and timing is reduced to something prosaic like this:

'Well, I picked up in our own twenty-five – I mean twenty-two – and just kept running. Then I saw wee Hughie come up outside me so I passed to him and he carried on and gave it to the Incredible Hulk – I mean Willie. Then he got stopped but somehow he slipped it back to Jimmy, but they had drawn in the defence so we had an overlap situation and Tommy missed out Archie, then beat the cover and sent big Hamish over in the corner.'

At the other extreme of television talk about the game I place Carwyn James and Cliff Morgan. Like the New Zealander Fred Allen, Carwyn James has enriched the technical literature of the game and, Plaid Cymru candidate or not, has earned the undying love of every British rugby patriot for what he did in 1971. But the kind of television coverage which he and Cliff Morgan provided this year on the history and evolution of the game was in its way a substitute – or should I say replacement? – for some forms of rugby literature. Maybe we got a cricket writer like Cardus because there was no broadcasting when he began, and a broadcaster like John Arlott because in his early days there was no televison and he had to give sight as well as insight to the 'blind'.

But perhaps I have been getting a lot of possession without putting points on the board. Why *does* rugby lack a literature to match the quality of the game, and of the people who play it or look at it, or back at it, with love?

First, a quick clearance of our own lines. It isn't because – as a few malicious spirits occasionally suggest – the game is played only by people who can scarcely read, never mind write, and whose idea of literature never gets beyond verses about being 'all right, in the middle of the night, finding touch together'. Counter-attack might suggest that, on the contrary, the trouble is that rugby men are too busy after their last no-side in being schoolmasters, or stockbrokers, or judges, or bishops, or civil engineers, or medical missionaries, or sheepfarmers. That obviously applied to Jackie Kyle; one of the joys of rugby journalism is that it doesn't apply to Richard Sharp.

The point is a serious one. Rugby is an amateur game – still is, despite some strains – and ought to remain one. Quite apart from the Unions' restrictive attitude about part-time journalism, the nature of the game means that players at every level have a lot to get on with at work and at home when they discover that the second forty minutes have got too much for them.

However, there are problems in the nature of the game as well as in the sociology of rugby. The intensity and patterns of play create problems that don't exist for the literary cricketer. You can construct elegant sentences while fielding at deep mid-wicket but hardly in the front row of the scrum.

In cricket it is often subtleties of individual skill and character which make the difference between two sides drawn from players of the same range of ability. The astonishing catch, the extra pace, the special guile, the elegant classic strokes and the brilliant unorthodox ones, are variations in a ritual. The apparent tedium of the game, which makes it unbearable to almost all Americans, can be relieved only by detection and reflection, and much in the literature of cricket is both detective and reflective.

Rugby can be dull, or frustrated by poor play or worse conditions, but it is never tedious. Far more has to be packed into a far shorter time, for even Sunday-league cricket is a leisurely business compared to eighty minutes of rugby, especially with the intensity and pressures of the top-class modern game.

Pressure is perhaps part of the problem. There are purple passages in rugby even at the highest level – the 1971 Lions against Wellington, the Barbarians of 1973, the Welsh demonstration this year in the last quarter against England, when J. P. R. Williams went off, that a great team spirit and tradition matter more than the greatest players. But for the most part winning rugby is a matter of pressure, though to stand up to attack after attack can itself put a form of pressure on the opposition. Pressure forces errors, not just bringing penalties but simple tries after more spectacular attacks have only just been frustrated short of the corner flag. Errors are forced – and very often what television commentators unkindly call 'unforced errors' are the result of well-disciplined pressure.

Recognition of the power of such pressures accounted for the success of 'percentage rugby', with its limitation of opportunity for error, in the bad old days of indiscriminate kicking into touch for territorial advantage. They are probably even greater in these days of intensive coaching and squad training. But it is hard to write about them, especially in the match reports which are still the basic form of rugby journalism. Why does a full-back who has apparently perfected his stance and position suddenly prove vulnerable again to the high ball? Why does a flanker who knows better get caught palpably offside? Why does a three-quarter who has picked up balls off his toes or over his shoulder suddenly drop a vital pass?

It may be that only those who have played at the level of Mike Gibson or Sandy Carmichael can write adequately about the game in their grade of near-perfection. But the fact is that rugby is a hard game to write about seriously at every level of honest attainment and modest competence. One way to write well and amusingly, no doubt, is to pretend to no attainment and complete incompetence; but writing about 'Coarse Rugby' bears the same relation to the literature rugby deserves as a hard-fought Rugby League match, enlivened by Eddie Waring, bears to a modern but classical Wales v. France match on a hard ground at the end of the season to decide the *Tournoi des Cinq Nations*. The coarser encounter may be fun, but it's not the real thing.

If any reasonably literate player or ex-player wants to discover the problem let him try to write about 'My Greatest Match'. We all have one. Mine is of an obscure Oxford league game in which, because promotion was at stake, our opponents fielded (quite legitimately) a member of their college who usually played at a far higher level: Paul Johnstone, the 1951 Springbok wing. But my memory is mainly of a lot of hard scrumming to deny the other side the possession that he could have exploited.

If you don't have much time to think while it's all happening, there's an obvious problem in relating and analysing it all afterwards. You can go for such subjectivity and literary imagination that the other twenty-nine players would fail to recognize the game or agree that they played in it – in which case a literary talent might be better employed in writing about an entirely imaginary game. Or you can write about what actually happened, as you remember it, and risk inclusion in an anthology of sporting boredom.

Rugby, so immensely enjoyable to play, is very difficult to write about. If this were not such an eminently respectable magazine I might even compare it to another act which, although now often written about, is rarely written about really well.

Of course if anyone wants to be the D. H. Lawrence of scrum and line-out by all means let him try. But I suspect that it may be the community and mood of the game and the less physical encounters of the players that make the best literature – which is perhaps also the case with the other act I didn't mention. For example, it was after an RAF cup-tie near the Lawrence country that, when we had been battered to defeat, a senior NCO honoured me with words of qualified praise: 'You played quite well, sir, and got stuck in at them. I didn't think you had it in you after the way you played before.' And he was right. There are mysteries of motivation which need someone like Jung to explain – not Freud, I think, for he would have produced some odd theories about the oval ball.

J. P. R. Williams, it is said, is applying himself to the medical problems of sport, and in Wales that must mean of rugby. I wonder if the literature of the game would not be immensely enriched if others of his calibre applied themselves to the history, the politics, the sociology and the poetry of the game.

I enjoyed Gareth Edwards's book, but one thing it taught me is that some kinds of literature really do require emotion recollected in tranquillity, and perhaps that maturity of emotion which comes with years. Is it because men can play cricket far longer, and play golf till their eighties, or fish for ever, that the other sports have a deeper literature?

Perhaps now that television has meant a vaster audience there will also be longer memories and a bigger market for the kind of rugby book that cannot be written till long after retirement. Arthur Smith might have had the nature for it if he had been spared. Tony O'Reilly might try it some day. Bob Hiller can talk on television as if he might have it in him. I sometimes find hints of it in Norman Mair's journalism in *The Scotsman*.

Or is what I'm looking for really there all the time – perhaps on sale in Welsh by Llanelli newsagents and only awaiting translation? Or in thesis form in some New Zealand or South African university library? Or buried in the thousands of intermittent words from the good rugby journalists, like John Reason and Terry McLean, and waiting to be edited and anthologized? For if the written word can capture the speed of Larwood, the efficiency of Bradman, the grace and power of generations of batsmen, can it not immortalize the things that marked out Barry John and Cliff Morgan? Take even players who are still at or approaching their prime and whose final status we cannot determine. There is that scissors-like action which seems to give Gareth Davies an extra ten metres in his tactical kicking, or Irvine's capacity (which can lead to fallibility) for working out the next move even before he has properly started the present one. And there was, among the recently retired, the personality which David Duckham and Gerald Davies expressed in speed and swerve.

But perhaps I ought to look in Langholm, the isolated, shut-in Border town away from all the rest, where they play a wet-ball brand of shut-in rugby. Can Hugh MacDiarmid really have been raised there and not left something for the anthologies? I suppose it is worth looking, not least in the Border and Welsh local papers, but the search is more likely to yield a few gems than an Aladdin's Cave.

(I thought one of them turned up this year in the Melrose Sevens programme when an old Langholm player wrote about what sevens tactics and needs can do to equip players for the full game. His name was Hector Monro, and I hope he does as well as Minister for Sport.)

As an amateur sport rugby has limited the scope for commercial spin-off from the game. As a comparatively young game compared with cricket it has also emerged at a time when English literature was not having its finest decades and when popular literature was partly replaced, first by radio and then by television. The game has been organized with great devotion, integrity and caution, not always with great imagination, and perhaps this mood has affected writing about the game.

There have also been times when many rugby men have been in danger of accepting the low valuation that some pseudo-intellectuals and pseudo-aesthetes have put on them and their game. They have also at times seemed in danger of countering malicious and dictatorial political interference in their private activities – for example, over tours to and from South Africa – with growls of inarticulate rage rather than a reasoned defence of the loyalties and values of the game and the civil liberties of those who enjoy it.

But perhaps the great expansion of rugby and enjoyment from it will create a broadly based and very diversified literature, which in time will produce the classics that no one can write to order. Rugby, after all, is the most vivid demonstration of the claim that sport is the sane man's substitute for war. Surely we ought in time to have the equivalent of our pontifical memoirs of the great commanders, the letters and diaries of the literary privates, the classics that can emerge when a literary subaltern reflects on his survival or a philosophical general on his defeat. And for Clausewitz, read Carwyn James.

Maybe if we all think more about the game we enjoy, and seek words to express the pleasure it gives us – not forgetting our thanks for the Blessed William Webb Ellis – we shall find that the scores are bound to come.

From *Blackwood's Magazine*

Part-Time Cardus

Alan Watkins

Alan Watkins is the distinguished political correspondent of the Observer, *where he is required reading for anyone remotely interested in politics and indeed for countless more who are not. He has written a number of books, notably a memorable set of cameos of his friends and contemporaries called* Brief Lives *and more recently* A Slight Case of Libel, *a most inspiriting account of the libel action he won against the Labour MP Michael Meacher against all the odds. However, he has another life as a sporting columnist of rare originality and insight. He derives his love of rugby from his father, a schoolmaster who taught in Ammanford, a small town in Carmarthenshire, and had played as a forward for London Welsh before the war. Here are three examples of Alan's work: an enchanting memory of going to the Victory International of 1946 as a thirteen-year-old boy with his father; a sharp and knowing look at the hitherto unchronicled world of the rugby bullshitter; and a cool summary of the state of play in rugby's biggest crisis: paying players. Who says we have no Cardus?*

Lloyd-Davies Knew my Father . . .

There was no television in those days. If you wanted to see the international, you had to go there. For the England and Wales match, as for all internationals, my father always wore his best suit. He also wore a hat, a heavy overcoat, leather gloves and, depending on the weather, a silk or woollen scarf. Though he was by no means sympathetic to communism – quite the reverse – the general effect of his outfit was to make him resemble a large but politically obscure member of the Politburo who was about to take the salute at a parade of tanks. In fact he was a Welsh schoolmaster who, while neither vain nor pushful, felt he had standards to maintain. He would no more have gone to the match with a leek and a red and white scarf than he would have appeared in front of his class with a false nose. I was expected to be correctly attired likewise, even if less splendidly.

The first match we saw together was not, strictly speaking, an international. It was the Victory International of 1946 for which no full caps were awarded. We travelled from Tycroes in Carmarthenshire to Cardiff in a hired single-decker bus (there were few coaches then). Also on the bus was another son of the village, Hugh Lloyd-Davies, in his pilot officer's uniform, who was playing for Wales at full-back.

Lloyd-Davies was an exciting though unpredictable performer who, a year later, was to win the university match for Cambridge by kicking two penalty goals. On this occasion he did not have the happiest of afternoons. Two pre-war English players, Jack Heaton and Dickie Guest, both of Waterloo, effectively won the match for England, Heaton with his cross-kicking and Guest with his elusiveness. Indeed, Guest was a wing in the class of Peter Jackson or Gerald Davies who, but for the war, would surely have won more than his thirteen caps. He twice went round Lloyd-Davies to score.

We could see because we were standing by that right-hand corner flag. Despite my father's correctness of dress and demeanour, we never sat in the stand but always stood in the 'field' or the somewhat superior 'enclosure': partly because stand tickets were hard to come by, partly, I suspect, because my father did not believe in throwing his money around and partly, I suspect also, because he would have considered it 'spoiling' to show me relative luxury at too early an age.

After the match we came on Lloyd-Davies, now back in his RAF uniform, behind the stand. My father, an old London Welsh forward of the years immediately after the First World War (though he would emphasize, that he had been 'lucky to get into the team'), was stern with the young full-back. 'I could see,' he said, 'that you were looking at his face, not his legs. It was his legs that went round you, not his face,' he added, to leave no misunderstanding about his views on correct play by a full-back.

At this and subsequent matches, we had a ritual. We did not eat before the match, but afterwards had a substantial tea. The menu was unchanging and suited the tastes of both of us. We had fish and chips, cakes (or 'pastries' as my father called them) and a pot of tea. He was always emphatic with the waitress about the need for a pot of tea; a cup each was not good enough. Thus fortified, we would walk to the headquarters hotel. This was almost certainly the most important part of the day for my father and partly accounted for his best suit. He was able to enter the hotel with confidence not so much because of any renown as an old player (he was, as I have said, modest about his past abilities) as because of his friendship with Aneurin Jenkins, a Cardiff schoolmaster and a member of the Cardiff Rugby Club.

Jenkins was by now a widower with no immediate family who lived in lodgings: the Cardiff club was not only his home but virtually his life. Like many of his type, he took a keen, even obsessive interest in rugby politics. He was a great obtainer of tickets, forecaster of selections, nodder and winker and putter of fingers to the nose. He knew not only players, members of the great post-war Cardiff side, but also administrators, even the selectors, 'the Big Five' themselves.

The year after the Victory International was that of the first full post-war match between England and Wales. This was also a time of one of the great recurring Welsh outside-half controversies. It was not simple. Should the outside-half be Glyn Davies of Pontypridd, later of Cambridge University, one of the classic, darting Welsh outside-halves? Or should it be the more utilitarian Billy Cleaver of Cardiff, 'Billy Kick' as he was called in West Wales?

But this choice did not exhaust the dispute. For there was Bleddyn Williams, also of Cardiff, to consider. Bleddyn was acknowledged to be a great centre three-quarter even then. But might he not turn out to be an even greater outside-half? In other words, was outside-half Bleddyn's true position? Or was it not? On this occasion, in 1947, the selectors decided it was. Bleddyn played outside the equally great Haydn Tanner, with Cleaver and Jack Matthews, also of Cardiff, in the centre. This combination was known in the public prints as 'the Cardiff triangle'. It was widely expected to beat England on its own. Alas, it failed. Bleddyn suffered a muscle strain in the first few minutes and, though Wales scored two tries to England's one, Wales lost because the late Nim Hall dropped a goal.

Afterwards Jenkins, my father and I were sitting in the lounge of the hotel. Two Welsh forwards, Rees Stephens of Neath and George Parsons of Newport, had somehow attached themselves to our party – or we had attached ourselves to them. Quite what these young men made of having to converse with two middle-aged schoolmasters and a thirteen-year-old boy with a balaclava helmet was difficult to say, but they were civil enough. Then Jenkins espied one of the selectors, David Jones (Blaina), who was always called 'David Jones (Blaina)'. Jenkins invited him over. 'So the mighty triangle didn't come off,' my father said to him. 'We live and learn,' said David Jones (Blaina).

Thirty-six years later, however, I shall not be mingling with the great. I shall be sitting before the television set, not wearing my best suit.

From *The Times*, February 1983

Tackling Rugby's Phoneys

For the last few days, the rugby news and comment in the papers has, quite properly, been about the international selectors and their choices for the coming championship. As a change, I should like to discuss people who claim that they were members of various more or less distinguished teams in the past – in other words, rugby bullshitters. For some reason, this form of boasting, romancing or fantasizing is more common among rugby followers than it is among those of other sports. Notice that I do not use the word 'lying'.

Your true rugby bullshitter is not, usually, a liar in his daily existence. He is often a model citizen. The chap who claims he had a trial for Swansea in 1957 is commonly a person who would tell an untruth, if he told one at all, only to the Inland Revenue.

Incidentally, the claim of having had a trial, as distinct from having actually played in the team, is a sure sign of the authentic bullshitter. First, such claims are difficult to check. Second, they indicate a becoming modesty – 'didn't make it to the first team, I'm afraid' – which, so the bullshitter vainly imagines, lends a verisimilitude to his claim.

Not that confirmation is always easy even when claims to membership of the first team are made. First-class rugby provides no record of players comparable to *Wisden* in cricket. This is one reason for the relative popularity of rugby bullshitting. Another reason is that the activity is tolerated, even accepted up to a point. As John Young, the former Harlequins and England wing, and English selector, once put it to me: 'When someone says that he was with Waterloo before the war, we don't ask too many questions.'

A political, or lobby, correspondent I knew claimed to have played centre for the Quins. Despite his excessive weight and thick spectacles, he had, so I was told by common acquaintances, been a good hockey and cricket player in his youth. So his claim was not entirely impossible, though it still struck me as implausible. Moreover, I had regularly watched the Quins during the years, the mid-1960s, in which he would have turned out for them. I could not remember either his name on the programme or his form on the field.

In fact, I remembered who the centres were for the period in question. They were Tim Rutter and Bob Lloyd. And my acquaintance from the House of Commons lobby was certainly neither of these. Though I was not obsessed by the matter, I mentioned it to a friend, a former Quins player, later a club selector. He had no recollection whatever of my chum. If he had played even for the third team, he said, he would have remembered him.

Then there was the case of the former Labour MP who was standing at a by-election in Wales a few years ago. His campaign literature stated that he was a keen rugby follower who had played for Llanelli. I could not remember him at all. My colleagues who were covering the contest, however, accepted his claim uncritically. By polling day, he was being depicted as a cross between Albert Jenkins and Barry John. Perhaps justly, he lost. But I never summoned up the courage to ask him straight out whether he had really played for Llanelli.

Even the *Dictionary of National Biography* is not exempt. In his contribution on the author, editor and MP Frank Owen, Michael Foot states that Owen won a Cambridge Blue. But this is not confirmed by the records of the time.

Perhaps the best comment was made by Dylan Thomas, in 'A Story': 'I played for Aberavon in 1898,' said a stranger to Enoch Davies.

'Liar,' said Enoch Davies.

'I can show you photos,' said the stranger.

'Forged,' said Enoch Davies.

'And I'll show you my cap at home.'

'Stolen.'

'I got friends to prove it,' the stranger said in a fury.

'Bribed,' said Enoch Davies.

From *The Independent*, January 1988

The Players are Restless

I was talking to a senior England player earlier in the week. He was saying that, sooner or later, the question of payment for players had to be faced. He did not actually use the word 'professionalism'. He did not need to use it, because it did not accurately express what was in his mind. He did not – does not – want to be a professional, in the sense of a young man who earns his whole living by playing rugby. He is, as it happens, a highly intelligent chap, who is also lucky enough to have an interesting and fairly secure job.

He was perfectly prepared to put in the six or seven days or evenings a week on which the England management insist, even though this disrupted his social life. They had, he thought, no choice; in modern rugby, training of this intensity and on this scale was necessary. But he did not see why he, and others less fortunately placed, should not receive some recompense for their trouble and effort.

At the same time, players see large sums of money going into the game from commercial concerns. I am no great lover of sponsorship, especially when (as Frank Keating demonstrated in a television programme a few months ago) it deprives genuine supporters of tickets which ought to be theirs. But sports sponsorship is essentially no different from guaranteed backing and block-booking at Covent Garden. No one suggests that opera singers should not be paid. In fact they are paid a great deal, way beyond the dreams of a Jonathan Davies.

The argument is not simply that players see this money being expended for purposes of commercial advertising and corporate public relations, and ask: why should some of it not be winging its way in our direction? Why does the RFU secretary, Dudley Wood (whom God preserve), go on so about putting money back into the game? What is this abstract entity called 'the game'? We, after all, are the game, or a good part of it, the reason why the sponsors are prepared to dish out the money in the first place.

A few years ago a well-known sports equipment company entered into an agreement with the Welsh Rugby Union to supply boots to the national team. Some members of the side objected, not so much because they were not receiving a cut of the money involved (though that certainly rankled), as because they did not care for being dictated to. Ray Williams, who was then still part of the higher echelons of the WRU, said that the players would be wearing the boots in question whether they liked it or not. A deal had been struck, a contract entered into, and the boots were as much part of the team's regulation equipment as the red jersey. When this kind of thing can happen, the sport has become professionalized – or, if you prefer the word, commercialized.

Let me draw an analogy. Even the finest hotels have, in their public areas, glass-fronted alcoves displaying expensive jewellery, bottles of scent, silk scarves, wrist-watches. No one really objects to this arrangement. Yet not even the most hard-pressed gentlemen's club would adopt or tolerate a similar arrangement, however much money there was to be made out of it. The reason is as obvious as the distinction is clear: a hotel is a commercial concern intended to make money for its shareholders, whereas a club by contrast, is a voluntary association intended to provide for the comfort and stimulation of its own members. The hotel, in other words, is unashamedly professional; while the club is proudly amateur. Rugby Union football has long ceased being a club and is now a hotel. Unfortunately the secretary has neglected to tell the members.

From *The Independent*, February 1989

A Fine Disregard

It was Norris McWhirter who suggested to me that there might well be an interesting correlation between awards for gallantry and rugby internationals. He was right; no fewer than three Irish internationals have won the VC, and Arthur Harrison, the England forward who won three caps in 1914, gained a VC at Zeebrugge posthumously in 1918. Remarkably enough Tommy Crean, the Irishman who won his VC in the Boer War, went on to win the DSO in 1915. If we look outside the internationals we soon see that the pattern continues. Two other naval rugby VCs were Rear-Admiral Sir Tony Miers, who won his in the submarine Torbay in 1942. He had played for London Scottish, Combined Services and Hampshire and had trials for Scotland. Commander John Linton won a posthumous VC in the submarine Turbulent in 1943. He played for the Navy, Combined Services and Hampshire and had trials for England. Then there was Lieutenant-Colonel Blair Mayne, who played for Ireland in the late 1930s and won no fewer than four DSOs between 1939 and 1945. Yet another Irishman, Lieutenant William Kenny, who played for Leinster, won a posthumous VC for gallantry in Afghanistan in 1920. Just one further point: every one of the men chosen for the heroic but suicidal raid at Zeebrugge was handpicked for his athletic prowess. The full details that follow need no further comment from me or anybody else.

Awards for Gallantry won by International Players

	England	Ireland	Scotland	Wales	Australia	NZ	SA	Total
VC	1	3	–	–	–	–	–	4
DSO	38	15	9	3	5	2	–	72
DSC	5	–	–	–	1	–	–	6
MC	37	14	13	8	5	7	2	86*
DFC	7	2	3	1	3	–	–	16
AFC	2	–	1	–	–	–	–	3
AM	1	1	–	–	1	–	–	3
DCM	1	1	1	2	1	1	–	7
MM	1	1	1	–	–	3	–	6

A Bar to a medal has been counted as a separate award.

* In cases where a player was capped by two countries the award has only been included once in the total column.

The Victoria Cross Holders

Johnston, Robert
Born: 13 August 1872, Laputa, Co. Donegal, Ireland
Died: 25 March 1950, Kilkenny, Ireland
Serving as a captain in the Imperial Light Horse, Robert Johnston was the first of four rugby internationals to be decorated with the Victoria Cross. On leaving King William's College, Isle of Man, he joined the Wanderers club and played in the Irish pack twice in 1893, being on the losing side against both England and Wales. In 1896 he went on the British tour of South Africa, when one of his team-mates was Tommy Crean, who also won a VC in the Boer War.

Johnston won his award in the action at Elandslaagte on 21 October 1899, when he rushed forward under heavy fire at point blank range to rally his men and enable a decisive flanking movement to be carried out. He was later promoted to major and served as commandant of the Prisoner of War Camp at Meath in 1914–15.

Crean, Thomas Joseph
Born: 19 April 1873, Dublin, Ireland
Died: 25 March 1923, London
Surgeon Captain (later Major) Tommy Crean was educated at Clongowes College and after joining the Wanderers club he played in the forwards

nine times for Ireland before going on the British tour of South Africa in 1896. Also in the tour party was Robert Johnston (see above) and, like Johnston, Tommy Crean later served in the Imperial Light Horse.

Crean was decorated for his action at Tygerkloof on 18 December 1901 when, although wounded himself, he continued to treat the wounded under heavy fire from only 150 yards' range. He stayed with his men until he was hit for a second time and it was, at first, thought that he had been mortally wounded. Fortunately, this was not the case and he went on to win a DSO in 1915. He also won the Royal Humane Society Testimonial for saving life at sea. He later enjoyed a distinguished medical career and there is a Memorial to him at the Roman Catholic Cemetery at Kensal Green.

Harvey, Frederick Maurice Watson
Born: 1 September 1888, Athboy, Co. Meath, Ireland
Died: 24 August 1980, Calgary, Alberta, Canada
The third Irish international to win a VC was Lieutenant (later Brigadier) Frederick Harvey of Lord Strathcona's Horse of the Canadian Expeditionary Force. At Guyencourt on 27 March 1917, he was leading his troop, which had already suffered heavy casualties, when they came under fire from a machine-gunner in a wired trench. Lt. Harvey jumped from his horse, ran for the trench, jumped the wire and shot the machine-gunner.

Harvey, who also won the MC and the Croix de Guerre in the 1914–18 war, was educated at Portora Royal School and Ellesmere College and won two Irish caps. His international appearances were at fly-half and full-back, and he was the only one of the four international VCs who was not a forward. Like Johnston and Crean he played for the Wanderers, thus giving the club the remarkable record of having three of their members win the VC. Harvey later settled in Canada, where he died one week before his ninety-second birthday.

Harrison, Arthur Leyland
Born: 3 February 1886, Torquay, Devon
Died: 23 April 1918, Zeebrugge, Belgium
Arthur Harrison is the only English international to win the VC and the only one of the four internationals to have been decorated posthumously. Educated at Dover College and the RNC Dartmouth, he was a career naval officer and played his rugby for United Services, Portsmouth, winning two caps in the England pack in 1914.

Lieutenant-Commander Harrison won his VC on 23 April 1918, when he was in command of the naval storming parties which had been given the task of silencing the enemy guns at Zeebrugge. Early in the attack he had his jaw broken and was rendered unconscious when struck on the head by a shell. On regaining consciousness he resumed command and continued the attack, but he was immediately hit again and died instantly.

England

Boer War

F. Bonsor, DCM	Army
R. F. A. Hobbs, DSO	R. Engineers
R. O'H. Livesay, DSO	R. West Surrey Regt
R. H. Mangles, DSO	R. West Surrey Regt

1914–18

A. H. Ashcroft, DSO	South Staffs Regt
A. F. Blakiston, MC	R. Field Artillery
L. G. Brown, MC	RAMC
J. Brunton, DSO, MC & Bar	Northumberland Fusiliers
V. H. Cartwright, DSO	R. Marines
E. L. Chambers, MC	Northumberland Fusiliers & KOYLI
V. H. M. Coates, MC	RAMC
G. S. Conway, MC	R. Garrison Artillery
A. O. Dowson, MC	Rifle Brigade
J. H. Eddison, MC	R. Field Artillery
L. F. Giblin, DSO, MC	Australian Forces
C. O. P. Gibson, MC	Northumberland Fusiliers
A. L. Harrison, VC	Royal Navy
H. C. Harrison, DSO	S. African Siege Battery
B. A. Hill, DSO	Ordnance Dept
F. J. van der B. Hopley, DSO	Grenadier Guards
P. D. Kendall, MC	King's (Liverpool) Regt
C. N. Lowe, MC, DFC	R. Flying Corps
A. H. MacIlwaine, DSO, MC	R. Field Artillery
W. E. Mann, DSO	R. Artillery
F. W. Mellish, MC	S. Afr. Artillery (Also capped for S. Africa)
L. P. B. Merriam, MC	Rifle Brigade
E. R. Mobbs, DSO	Northants Regt
E. Myers, MC	West Yorkshire Regt
C. J. Newbold, DSO	R. Engineers
R. C. W. Pickles, MC	R. Engineers
W. N. Pilkington, DSO & Bar	South Lancs Regt
C. H. Pillman, MC	Dragoon Guards
H. L. Price, MC	South Wales Borderers
J. A. Pym, MC	R. Artillery
J. A. S. Ritson, DSO & Bar, MC	Durham Light Infantry
A. D. Roberts, MC	Welch Regt
W. L. Y. Rogers, DSO	R. Horse Artillery
R. O. Schwartz, MC	KRRC
H. J. H. Sibree, MC	R. Norfolk Regt

F. le S. Stone, MC	King's Own Hussars
A. D. Stoop, MC	R. West Surrey Regt
F. M. Stout, MC	20th Hussars
P. W. Stout, DSO	Machine Gun Corps
F. B. Watson, DSO	Royal Navy (Also a bar to the DSO in WW2)
S. H. Williams, DSO	R. Field Artillery
W. C. Wilson, DSO & Bar, MC	Leicestershire Regt

1939–45

A. R. Aslett, DSO	King's Own Royal Regt
R. J. Barr, MC	Army
J. J. Cain, MM	Irish Guards
D. A. Campbell, DFC & Bar	RAF
R. S. L. Carr, MC	Manchester Regt & King's African Rifles
G. J. Dean, MC	R. Tank Regt
W. Elliot, DSC	Royal Navy
R. A. Gerrard, DSO	R. Engineers
R. G. S. Hobbs, DSO	R. Artillery
P. C. Horden, AFC	RAF
T. F. Huskisson, MC & Bar	Duke of Wellington's Regt
D. A. Kendrew, DSO & 3 Bars	Leicestershire Regt
R. M. Marshall, DSC & Bar	RNVR
J. O. Newton-Thompson, DFC	RAF
A. L. Novis, MC	Leicestershire Regt
E. I. Parsons, DFC	RAF
A. D. S. Roncoroni, MC	Army
K. A. Sellar, DSO, DSC	Royal Navy
G. M. Sladen, DSO & Bar, DSC	Royal Navy
J. W. R. Swayne, MC	RAMC
C. C. Tanner, AM	Royal Navy
G. A. Walker, DSO, DFC, AFC (1956)	RAF
F. B. Watson, Bar to DSO won in WW1	Royal Navy
R. H. G. Weighill, DFC	RAF
P. B. R. W. William-Powlett, DSO	Royal Navy

Other Theatres

W. B. Hynes, DSO	Royal Navy (Sea of Marmora in 1920)

R. A. Buckingham: BEM (1942) for gallantry while serving with the Civil Defence.

R. F. A. Hobbs, who won a DSO in the Boer War, was the father of R. G. S. Hobbs, who was similarly honoured in the Second World War.

F. M. Stout and P. W. Stout, who were both decorated in the First World War, were brothers.

Ireland

Boer War

T. J. Crean, VC	Imperial Light Horse (Also DSO in WW1)
R. Johnston, VC	Imperial Light Horse
W. W. Pike, DSO	RAMC

1914–18

M. Abraham, DCM, MM	R. Field Artillery
C. A. Boyd, MC	RAMC
E. D. Caddell, MC	RAMC
E. F. Campbell, DSO	Chaplain's Dept
S. B. B. Campbell, MC	RAMC
F. Casement, DSO	RAMC
T. J. Crean, DSO	Imperial Light Horse (Also VC in Boer War)
W. A. Cuscaden, DSO	Infantry Brigade
E. C. Deane, MC	RAMC
C. C. Fitzgerald, MC	Army
F. M. W. Harvey, VC, MC	Lord Strathcona's Horse
R. Hemphill, DSO	RAMC
F. P. Montgomery, MC	RAMC
C. T. O'Callaghan, MC	10th Hussars
J. P. Quinn, MC	RAMC
T. T. H. Robinson, DSO	RAMC
A. W. P. Todd, MC	RAMC
W. Tyrell, DSO & Bar, MC	RAMC

1939–45

C. V. Boyle, DFC	RAF
H. C. Browne, DSO	Royal Navy
A. B. Curtis, DFC	RAF
J. H. Gage, MC	Army (Also capped for S. Africa)
R. B. Mayne, DSO & 3 Bars	Army
C. F. G. T. Hallaran, AM	Royal Navy
C. O'N. Wallis, MC	East Surrey Regt
H. H. C. Withers, DSO	R. Engineers

Other Theatres

R. Roe, MC	Chaplain's Dept (Aden in 1967)

Scotland

Boer War

J. J. Gowans, DSO	R. Field Artillery
W. G. Neilson, DSO	Argyll & Sutherland Highlanders

1914–18

G. B. Crole, MC	R. Field Artillery
M. R. Dickson, DSO	Argyll & Sutherland Highlanders
J. Dobson, MC	Army
D. G. Donald, DFC, AFC	RAF
W. T. Forrest, MC	KOSB
R. A. Gallie, MC	Glasgow Yeomanry
C. M. Gilray, MC	Rifle Brigade (Also capped for New Zealand)
A. L. Gracie, MC	60th Rifles
F. Kennedy, DCM	Army
A. A. B. Lindsay, MC	RAMC
E. G. Loudon-Shand, MC	KRRC
H. Martin, DSO	R. Field Artillery
R. M. Scobie, MC	R. Engineers
J. N. Shaw, MC	Army
A. T. Sloan, DSO	R. Field Artillery
L. M. Speirs, MM	Army

1939–45

G. H. Gallie, MC	R. Artillery
K. I. Geddes, DFC	RAF
D. J. Macrae, MC	Army
C. L. Melville, DSO	Black Watch
R. K. Millar, DSO	R. Engineers
R. W. F. Sampson, DSO, DFC	RAF
C. M. Usher, DSO	Gordon Highlanders
F. A. Wright, MC	Army

R. A. Gallie and G. H. Gallie, who won MCs in the First World War and the Second World War respectively, were father and son.

Wales

1914–18

D. B. Davies, MC	Welsh Guards
B. S. Evans, MC	Army
W. T. Havard, DSO, MC	Chaplain's Dept
H. T. Maddock, MC	Machine Gun Corps
W. J. Martin, DCM	South Wales Borderers

E. Morgan, MC	Brecknock Regt & R. Engineers
F. Palmer, MC	Army
T. W. Pearson, DSO	R. Field Artillery
J. J. Wetter, DCM	South Wales Borderers

1939–45

W. H. Clement, MC	Welch Regt
B. T. V. Cowey, DSO	Welch Regt
L. Manfield, DFC	RAF
B. E. W. McCall, MC	Welch Regt

Australia

Boer War

S. B. Boland, DSO	Queensland Contingent

1914–18

A. C. Corfe, DSO & 2 Bars	West Kent Regt
B. D. Hughes, MC	R. Dublin Fusiliers
T. J. Richards, MC	Army
C. Wallach, MC	Army
W. T. Watson, MC & Bar, DCM	Aust. Imperial Forces (Also DSO in WW2)

1939–45

E. G. Broad, DFC	RAF
R. Rankin, DFC	RAF
W. T. Watson, DSO	Papuan Infantry (Also MC & Bar & DCM in WW1)
W. G. S. White, DFC	RAF
W. V. Wilson, DSC	Army

Others

H. W. Baker: Albert Medal for bravery for rescuing surfers from drowning

New Zealand

1914–18

H. E. Avery, DSO	NZEF
R. R. Fogarty, MM	NZ Rifle Brigade
W. M. Geddes, MC	NZ Field Artillery
C. T. Gillespie, MC	NZ Field Artillery
C. M. Gilray, MC	Rifle Brigade (Also capped for Scotland)
W. S. Glenn, MC	NZ Field Artillery

| C. McLean, MM | NZEF |
| J. H. Parker, MM | NZEF |

1939–45
W. Batty, DCM	6th Field Regt
M. M. N. Corner, MC	Army
J. Finlay, MC	25th Infantry Batt.
J. L. Griffiths, MC	19th Infantry Batt.
J. R. Page, DSO	26th Infantry Batt.

South Africa

1914–18
| F. W. Mellish, MC | SA Artillery (Also capped for England) |

1939–45
| J. H. Gage, MC | Army (Also capped for Ireland) |

Compiled by Ian Buchanan

Showdown

Godfrey Smith

We had meant to end the book here; but thought we would hold it open to see what happened when England played France at Twickenham in the last round of the 1991 Five Nations Championship. We thought it might be a day to remember; and we were right.

It turned out to be one of the greatest games ever played at Twickers, and it included probably the most magical try ever scored there. It earned England their first Grand Slam in eleven years, and made a fitting exit from the Five Nations Championship for Serge Blanco, the footballing genius from Biarritz who runs, say his team-mates, as if he is walking on snow without leaving any tracks. It was the game that had been dubbed – not altogether seriously of course – the greatest Anglo-French confrontation since Agincourt.

Alan Watkins, the political pundit and rugby sage, had put £100 on France to win at 7 to 2, and few lovers of the game are shrewder. The French saw it in more romantic terms. 'We have,' said the Toulon coach Daniel Herrero, 'the right to dream.' So it was a privilege to be there. In the week before the game, a pair of tickets with a face value of £20 each were fetching on the black market a whopping £1,000. There were precious few sellers.

Saturday 16 March dawned damp and drizzly, with a soft, mild south-westerly spreading scudding clouds and just a little sun peeping through between them. Happily, though, the threatened rain held off in the morning so that the traditional Twickers festivities could unroll in the car parks. Monster inflatables shaped like bottles of bubbly guided guests to several of the cars; a giant ballooning hand floated over another, fingers raised rudely in the air. Laura Ashley tablecloths decked with daffodils held langoustine and lobster; here a *boeuf bourguignon* seethed busily; there a majestic game pie awaited incision; the barbaric aroma of barbecues beguiled the nostrils.

There was a Rolls-Royce bearing the number plate TOF1; there were berets from Bresse and Barbour jackets from all over England; there were placards pathetically held aloft with the inscription: 'One ticket desperately needed – genuine supporter.' Even as kick-off approached, the black market price was still £175. Those who couldn't pay it made for the nearest television set. The fortunate 59,000 with tickets packed every seat in the place.

The 120-strong band of Christ's Hospital School played the national anthems. Every English player bellowed out the words of our stately old dirge. When the band played the *Marseillaise* – most vivid and martial of all anthems – not a French player's mouth moved. Maybe too much was going on behind the designer stubble and the sweatbands; maybe they just didn't hear. Call the clichés, mix the metaphors, empurple the prose – it was as nail-gnawingly tense as that.

Rob Andrew kicked off high and north; the French tried a daft little over-quick drop-out, were charged down, and lay over the ruck. Les Peard, the Welsh referee, gave England a penalty. Hodgkinson drilled the ball neatly between the posts. A minute and a half had been played; England were three points up. Three minutes later the French were penalized for the same offence; this time Hodgkinson missed – giving notice that this was not to be one of his metronome days; though he would kick well enough.

Next the French cut the line-out – thus giving notice in their turn that their two beanpole locks, Michel Tachdjian and Olivier Roumat, were not to be over-awed by the towering presence of Paul Ackford and Wade Dooley. Roumat indeed, best line-out jumper in France, was to have a goodish afternoon; Tachdjian a fruitless one. It ended early when he hobbled off with the recurrence of an old leg injury. For all he contributed, he would have been better employed cooking up a storm for France's ultra-smart Racing Club, where he doubles as player and chef. England's forwards in any event far outgunned the French pack in experience, with a daunting 196 caps to 91; the French backs in contrast had three times as many caps as the English – 302 to 91.

It was next the turn of Winterbottom, most durable of Yorkshire farmers, to lead a mighty maul that came within inches of scoring, but the move ended in another penalty to England, just pulled right by Hodgkinson. The English half-turned to arrange themselves for the 22 drop-out when Blanco, from behind his own goal line, and with a sublime disregard for the accepted wisdom, began his historic run. Now we saw what Mesnel meant when he said that as Blanco took the ball, the force seemed to flow with him. He passed to Philippe Sella, who slipped it to Didier Camberabero, son of the great Guy who played fourteen times for France. Didier is famed for his kicking, and now we saw why. He ran, chipped ahead, gathered his own kick, then as the English closed on him, saw wide open space to his left, and tapped the most exquisite cross-kick into it. The ball bounced perfectly for Philippe Saint-André, who raced between the English posts as Jeremy Guscott's despairing tackle just brushed his ankles. Camberabero slotted the conversion almost contemptuously, France led 6–3, and e'en the ranks of Tuscany could scarce forbear to cheer. For they had seen a piece of pure French legerdemain that lasted 17.25 seconds in all. 'Do not bother telling me how some old codger scored a better try in some half-forgotten game years ago,' wrote Stephen Jones in *The Sunday Times* next day. 'It was one of rugby's wondrous moments.' He was surely right.

Now Roumat tackled high and Hodgkinson had the chance of another kick to level the account. He missed, but no matter: Rob Andrew, cool and magisterially in control at stand-off (seldom was a position on the field more aptly named), was given exemplary service by his scrum-half Richard Hill after a glorious rumble by the white juggernaut of an English pack, and slotted a sweet drop-goal. Seventeen minutes of the game had been played and the score was 6–6.

Now it was the turn of the French to take a penalty shot at goal. Camberabero struck the ball well but missed. Twenty minutes gone, and still 6–6. Laurent Cabannes, the fifth French member of the elite Racing Club, who back home take the field in pink bow-ties and drink champagne at half-time, now showed less than elite manners. He lifted a knee in tackling Rob Andrew, and was warned by Les Peard. Andrew, unshaken, lifted a towering up-and-under, the French killed the ball under their own goal, and this time Hodgkinson made no mistake. He planted the ball squarely between the posts, and the first strains of the new English anthem, 'Swing Low, Sweet Chariot', echoed round the terraces. England 9, France 6.

Rob Andrew could do no wrong today; he found a soaring left-footed touch, but the French counter-attacked and pinned Hodgkinson to the floor. In extremis he did a most unskilled thing; he passed the ball into touch. This is a penalty offence and Camberabero made no mistake. Twenty-six minutes had gone and the score was 9–9.

Mike Teague, the rumbustious Gloucester builder, broke out of a seething ruck and set up an English movement that looked too flat for comfort. Yet the ball spun from Andrew to the intruding Hodgkinson to the unstoppable Underwood. He gave Lafond the outside, handed him off with deceptive ease, and whistled over the French line like the RAF pilot which on weekdays he is. Hodgkinson had no problems, and the score was 15–9 with 31 minutes gone.

Hill kicked with inch-true precision; tempers flared; the French were penalized. That blunder cost France another three points and England led 18–9. Hodgkinson slewed his next penalty attempt but no matter, Blanco was now being submerged in a deluge of up-and-unders. In a contest of such fury, the miracle was that no one was at all seriously hurt; Dooley had to have minor attention to his head, but was restored. The England pack was increasingly dominant. The massive props Jeff Probyn, the Bath furniture maker, and Jason Leonard, the East End carpenter, who said his Mum would not come to watch in case her little boy was hurt (he weighs in at 16 stone 8) were as solid as the Pillars of Hercules. Between them Brian Moore, that improbably shaped solicitor, hooked immaculately. Teague and Winterbottom raged round the base of the English scrum, disrupting movements and charging down kicks. Ominously for France, Blanco, heroic but alone, was drowned time and again by the rolling white forward wave. The line-outs gave fairly equal distribution, but England had the quality ball, and in the rucks and mauls there was no contest. An idiotic newspaper headline spoke of another Waterloo; it was hardly that, but one phrase from that old scrap between France and England surfaced in the memory: 'La Garde recule'. Such was the horrified word that ran round the French army when they saw for the first time Napoleon's elite troops go backwards; there was a touch of that now about the French forwards. Half-time: England led 18–9.

Still hungry, England piled it on; but Simon Hodgkinson sliced a penalty attempt and Rob Andrew's second bold drop was just shy of the upright. France missed a penalty too, but Cecillon of Bourgoin came on for the injured Tachdjian and seemed at once to infuse the French with new energies. Camberabero hit the English post with yet another penalty shot but then chipped ahead from broken play under the English goal. Carling leaped high to catch it but missed; and Camberabero touched down, but ironically, from the simplest of positions, failed to convert his own try. Still, out of nowhere, out of short commons and scant ball, the French had fashioned a second marvellous score, and the account now stood at 18–13 with seventeen minutes of the second half played.

Now there was another great England forward roll led by the Leicester barrelhouse Dean Richards. Teague got a bang on the nose but the blood was soon staunched. The French were caught blatantly offside and penalized. Xavier Blond – known throughout France as Monsieur X – was rash enough to grab the referee's sleeve in protest. However Les Peard was so manifestly in charge of the game that he felt no need to send him off, as he might well have done. Indeed, the clash between law and anarchy, chaos and order, was one of the most riveting aspects of this game. When the English cut their line to three – Ackford, Dooley and Richards – all three were police officers; not so much a line-out as a cop-out. A fourth policeman, Nigel Heslop, was playing on the English right wing. Indeed even the referee was a sergeant driving instructor with the Gwent Constabulary. To all this majesty of the law, the French had just one reply: Gregoire Lascubé, their loose head prop, is a detective.

Hodgkinson made no mistake cashing in on Blond's misdemeanour, and with 23 minutes of the second half played, England led 21–13. By now it was pelting down, and Camberabero's next penalty attempt with a greasy ball from the left touchline failed honourably. With a minute of full time left, England were still sitting on their comfortable 8-point lead. Then, the French fashioned another miracle. Berbizier launched a sweeping movement down the left side, sent the ball to Sella, who gave it to Blanco, who worked it to Mesnel, who shot past Hill in a reprise of the move by which Underwood had outwitted Lafond, to score in the corner. This time Camberabero's conversion went gloriously over, and suddenly it was 21–19 and still anyone's game. The French rashly conceded another penalty and Hodgkinson took his time but missed. Two minutes of injury had been played when Les Peard blew his whistle and pointed to the centre. Blanco tucked the ball under his jersey and sprinted from the field with his instant pregnancy. The English converged on their heroes and carried them off shoulder high. They all – players and spectators – sang 'Swing Low, Sweet Chariot' as if there would be no tomorrow. The electronic display board flashed its congratulations and announced that Grand Slam ties and T-shirts could now be ordered. They were not, be it noticed, already made, as they had been the previous year at Murrayfield, when England blew the Grand Slam. They would not, twice running, be guilty of hubris, the old Greek sin of pride that comes before a fall. Not on your nelly.

Michael Parkinson wrote next day that he looked back at the stadium as he left, music still ringing and lights still flashing, and for a moment felt it might take off like the space-ship in *Close Encounters*. It was as dreamlike as that. It was Michael too who drew up the list of opposing qualities shown by the French and the English that day: Wind/Earth; Blaze/Smoulder; Colourful/Monochrome; Imaginative/Pragmatic; Devil-may-care/Dogged; Plumed cavalry/Shire horse; Maigret/PC Plod. The pairings beguile, but the last one surely falters. The true antithesis is surely between Maigret and Morse – beer-drinking, music-loving, outwardly po-faced, inwardly romantic. No team that played with the passion England displayed could fairly be dismissed as plodders. They had been accused of having the technology but lacking a soul. They had shown they had both. They had snapped out of pudding mode and played out of their minds.

'The English are great gentlemen – after the game,' observed Blanco. 'Rugby is joy because it stems from friendship. It is pleasure because it is everything which unites man on the sporting field. You can only get results if you feel good together, if you appreciate each other. I would even say if you love each other.

'Of course,' he added just before the game, 'we shall need some moments of madness. I hope it will be a fête of rugby.' It was.

Acknowledgements

'The Sweet Thanks of Four French Tarts' by Robert Sloman was written especially for *Take the Ball and Run*. 'Four Great Twickers Tries' are reprinted from *Touchdown* published by the Rugby Football Union. 'The Greatest International Try of All' by Ross Macdonald is reprinted from *The World of Rugby* published by Elek Books 1967. 'Hymns and Arias' by Max Boyce is reprinted by permission of Maxbo Entertainments Ltd. 'A Welcome in the Valleys' by Richard Burton is reprinted from *Touchdown* published by the Rugby Football Union. 'There's Beautiful' by Alun Chalfont is reprinted from the *New Statesman*. 'The Last Place to be a Wallaby' by Godfrey Smith is reprinted from the *Sunday Times*. 'The Pontypool Front Row' by Max Boyce © 1975 is reproduced by permission of Ardmore and Beechwood Ltd trading as Ambleside Music, London WC2H OEA. 'The Making of Gareth Edwards' by Bill Samuel is reprinted from *Rugby Body and Soul* published by Gower Press 1986. 'The Day Gareth was Dropped' by Max Boyce is reprinted by permission of Maxbo Entertainments Ltd. 'The Shoulder-High Chivalry of the Vanquished Welsh' by A.L. Gracie is reprinted from *The Game Goes On* published by Arthur Barker Ltd 1936. 'The Broken Heart of Jack van der Schyff' by Reg Sweet is reprinted from *Pride of the Lions* published by Howard Timmins, Cape Town 1962. 'Did Deans Do It?' by William Scott is reprinted from *The World of Rugby* by Ross Macdonald published by Elek Books 1967. 'JPR, the Threes, and the Sevens' by Carwyn Jones is reprinted from *JPR* by JPR Williams published by HarperCollins 1979. 'The Majesty of King John' by John Reason is reprinted from *The Victorious Lions* published by Rugby Football Books Ltd. 'The Zap! Zap! Zap! of David Campese' by Evan Whitton is reprinted from the *National Times* (Australia) and *Amazing Scenes* edited by Daniel O'Keefe published by John Fairfax Library 1987. 'I, Charles Fry' by C.B. Fry is reprinted from *Rugger, the Man's Game* by E.H.D. Sewell published by Hollis and Carter (The Bodley Head) 1944. 'The Lifelong Regret of F.E. Smith' by John Campbell is reprinted from *F.E. Smith* published by Jonathan Cape 1983. 'The Priest with a Passion' by Alex Potter and Georges Duthen is reproduced from *The Rise of French Rugby* published by Reed Books, a division of Octopus Publishing Group (NZ) Ltd. 'The Rigorous Reign of Jacques Fouroux' by Steve Bale is reprinted from the *Independent*. 'Black is In for All Black Skippers' by Norman Harris is reprinted from the *Sunday Times*. 'The Fine Art of Bob Hiller' and 'The Genius of Carwyn James' both by John Reason are reprinted from *The Victorious Lions* published by Rugby Football Books Ltd. '9 – 3' by Max Boyce is reprinted by permission of Maxbo Entertainments Ltd. 'In a Dark and Secret World' by Mike Burton and Steve Jones is reprinted from *Never Stay Down* published by Queen Anne Press 1982. 'With What Result I Know Not' by M.H. Bloxham is reprinted from *The*

Meteor. 'Football Company v. Harlequins' is reprinted from the newspaper collection of Mr E.P. Vacher of Gypsies Club now in the library of the Rugby Football Union at Twickenham. 'A View from the Land of the Forward Pass' by Bob Donahue is reprinted from the *International Herald Tribune*. 'Goodbye to Glory' by Terry McClean is reprinted from *Goodbye to Glory* published by Pelham Books © Terry McClean 1977. 'How They Gave Luck a Chance' by Chris Greyvenstein is reprinted from *Springbok Saga* published by Don Nelson Publishers, Cape Town. 'Blood, Toil, Tears and Sweat': the extracts by John Mason and Michael Calvin are both reprinted from the *Daily Telegraph*; Steve Jones' piece is reprinted from the *Sunday Times*. 'For Ireland, Boys!' by Frank Keating is reprinted from *Up and Under* published by Hodder & Stoughton Ltd 1983. 'A Great Day for the Irish' by David Walsh is reprinted from the *Sunday Tribune*. 'The Art of Coarse Rugby' by Michael Green is reprinted from *Coarse Rugby* published by Hutchinson. 'The Unacceptable Face of Rugby' by John Reason is reprinted from *The Victorious Lions* published by Rugby Football Books Ltd. 'The Referee Everyone Wants' by Steve Bale is reprinted from the *Independent*. 'Lesser Breeds Without the Law' by Michael Green is reprinted from *Even Coarser Rugby* published by Hutchinson. 'I am an Entertainer' by Max Boyce is reprinted by permission of Maxbo Entertainments Ltd. 'Altogether Now' by Leo and Jilly Cooper is reprinted from *Leo and Jilly Cooper on Rugby* by permission of the authors. 'Shout, Crowd, Shout' by Richard Llewellyn is reprinted from *How Green was my Valley* published by Michael Joseph Ltd © 1939 the Estate of Richard Llewellyn. 'Tuppy and the Red-Haired Bounder' by P.G. Wodehouse is reprinted from *Very Good Jeeves* published by Hutchinson. 'Wee Jaikie Wins the Game' by John Buchan is reprinted from *Castle Gay* published by Hodder & Stoughton 1930. 'Bread, Cheese and Beer' by A.G. Macdonell is reprinted from *England, Their England* published by Macmillan 1933. 'A Game for Gods' by Eric Linklater is reprinted from *Magnus Merriman* published by Jonathan Cape Ltd by permission of the Peters, Fraser & Dunlop Group Ltd. 'The Day that Someone passed to Lowe' by P.G. Wodehouse is reprinted by permission of the Trustees of the Wodehouse Estate. 'Crash Tackle' by Danny Hearn is reprinted from Crash Tackle published by Weidenfeld & Nicolson Ltd. 'No Fun – No Game' by Gerald Davies and John Morgan is reprinted from *Sidesteps* published by Hodder & Stoughton Ltd. 'Where is our Neville Cardus?' by R.D. Kernohan is reprinted from *Blackwood's Magazine*. 'Part-Time Cardus' by Alan Watkins: 'Lloyd-Davies Knew my Father' is reprinted from *The Times* February 1983 © Alan Watkins; 'Tackling Rugby's Phoneys' January 1988 and 'The Players are Restless' February 1989 are both reprinted from the *Independent* © Alan Watkins.

Every effort has been made to trace the holders of copyright material used in this anthology. We apologise for any omissions in this respect, and on notification we undertake to make the appropriate acknowledgement in subsequent editions.

Thanks, Chums

First, I must yet again thank Colin Webb, managing director of Pavilion Books, for dreaming up the idea for this book. His spring of obviously good ideas never seems to dry up, and it is to him entirely that I owe the pleasure this anthology has given me to put together.

I must now thank a number of very good friends in the rugby world. There are few more friendly human beings than the great freemasonry of rugby writers, and they have been prodigal in their help. First, my thanks to Steve Jones, rugby correspondent of *The Sunday Times*, who prepared a magisterial reading list for me which forms the backbone of this book. Warm thanks too to Norman Harris, now of *The Observer*, and to my old friend Nick Mason, now of *The Guardian*, both former colleagues from *Sunday Times* days. The brilliant Michael Green gave me much kind and expert counsel and also lent me a number of valuable rugby books. I was also lent books by Alan McQuillan of Cirencester RFC and by Geoffrey Hughes, who read about my assignment in a Twickenham programme and generously offered me valuable items from his enormous rugby library. Peter Gifford, then chairman of Minety RFC, was most helpful over the rugby songs.

I am also much obliged to Bob Donahue of the *International Herald Tribune* for help with French rugby and his own uniquely American view of our sport; to Leo Cooper, who gave up playing only the other day at fifty; and to Norris McWhirter, who so kindly suggested compiling the gallantry statistics among rugby internationals which make such fascinating reading. I am also much indebted to Ian Buchanan, a seasoned sports statistician, for doing the hard research on which those gallantry lists are based.

Former international players like Andy Ripley and Gerald Davies were most supportive, and I owe a great debt of gratitude to Dudley Wood, secretary of the Rugby Football Union, who was good enough to see me himself and to introduce me to Rex King, who guards the museum, library and archives at Twickers so zealously.

Yet again I must thank my old friend and colleague Oscar Turnill for putting my untutored words through the fine mesh of his skills; not only is he a prince among editors but also a former hooker himself – an invaluable attribute in editing a book like this.

Finally I must thank my daughter Amanda, a long-term aficionado of the game, who has brought her customary zing to this compilation. Without her I should still be struggling to put it together.

Godfrey Smith

Index of players

The Grumpy Queen

Valerie Wilding
and Simona Sanfilippo

Evans

There was once a grumpy Queen.
Because the Queen was grumpy,
everyone else was grumpy. The castle
was a gloomy place.

The gardener was so miserable his sunflowers drooped like sad soldiers.

The cook was miserable, so the food looked like mashed mud. The servants never had tasty dinners so they were always grumpy.

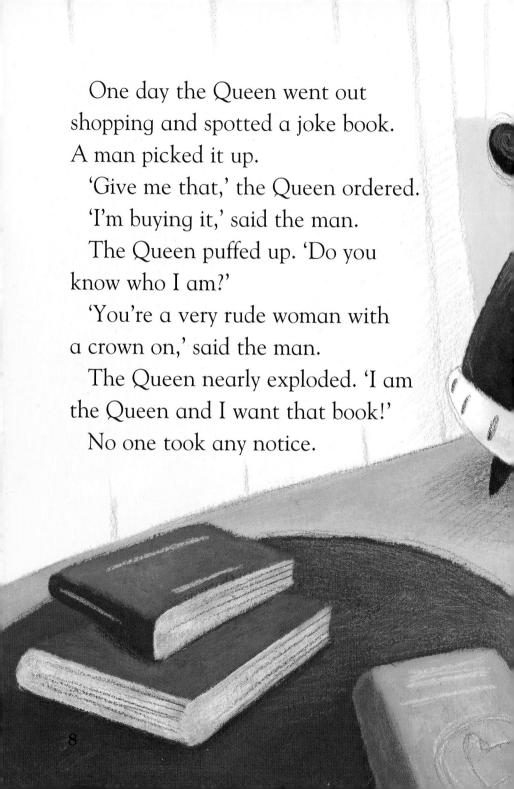

One day the Queen went out
shopping and spotted a joke book.
A man picked it up.

'Give me that,' the Queen ordered.

'I'm buying it,' said the man.

The Queen puffed up. 'Do you
know who I am?'

'You're a very rude woman with
a crown on,' said the man.

The Queen nearly exploded. 'I am
the Queen and I want that book!'

No one took any notice.

The Queen stomped to an ice cream van and pointed.

'Give me a Strawberry Coconut Fizzywizz,' she said.

'We're out of them,' said the ice-cream seller. 'What about a Choco Bom-Bom?'

The Queen screwed up her eyes. 'I want a Strawberry Coconut Fizzywizz.'

'All gone,' said the ice-cream seller.

'Do you know who I am?' roared the Queen.

'You're a very cross woman with a bright red face,' said the ice-cream seller.

The Queen stamped home.

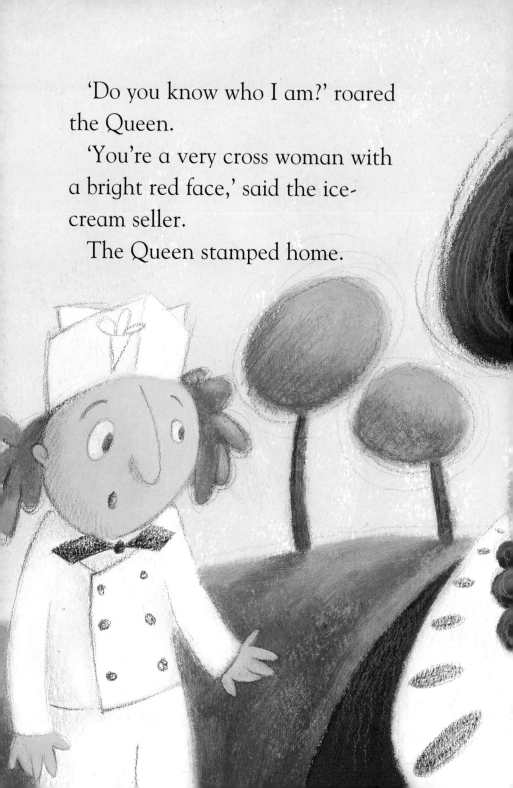

The Queen roared, 'I want a joke
book and I want an ice-cream!'
Everybody rushed to get them for her.

15

Every bookseller within fifty miles sent a funny book. Packs of ice-creams were sent, to sweeten her temper.

But by the time everything was delivered, the Queen had forgotten all about the joke book and the ice cream.

'What's all this clutter?' the Queen bellowed, 'get rid of it!'

The servants gave the books and
ice-creams to their children. They
settled down to read in the garden,
and in the castle corridors.

18

19

The Queen drifted about, grumbling.
She heard giggles everywhere. In the
gallery she found a curly-haired boy.

'What's everybody laughing at?' she
demanded.

The boy licked his lips. 'The books,
Your Majesty. They're funny. Here,
have mine. I've finished it.'

The Queen sat down to read. The boy
brought her a strawberry cornet.
'Thank you,' said the Queen. 'Yum.'
She read the funny book for a while,
and made herself jump every time
she chuckled.

The gardener trudged by, head down.
'Good day, Majesty.'
'Lovely day,' she said, and he was
so surprised he fell in the fishpond.

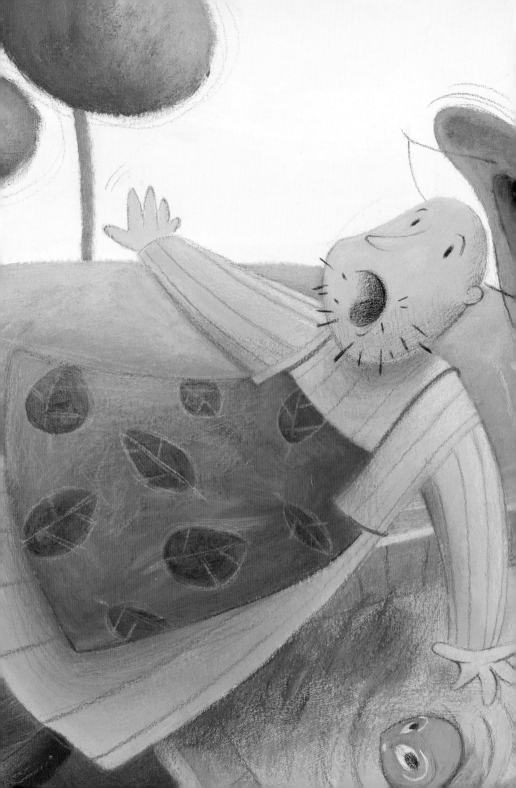

The gardener told the cook the Queen was happy. The cook didn't believe it, and came to see. She smiled at him so nicely that he said he'd make a special dinner.

'How kind,' the Queen said.

The cook was so surprised his hat fell over his eyes.

Suddenly everyone was smiling.

'Why is everybody cheerful?' she
asked the boy.

He grinned. 'Because you're
not grumpy!'

'Oh!' she said.

The Queen liked not being grumpy. She liked seeing everyone smiling at her, and being friendly, so she ordered chocolate pudding and lemon fizz for everybody, and decided never to be grumpy again. Ever.

Why not try reading a Spirals book?

Megan's Tick Tock Rocket by Andrew Fusek Peters,
Polly Peters, and Simona Dimitri
ISBN 978 0237 53342 7

Growl! by Vivian French and Tim Archbold
ISBN 978 0237 53345 8

John and the River Monster by Paul Harrison
and Ian Benfold Haywood
ISBN 978 0237 53344 1

Froggy Went a Hopping by Alan Durant and Sue Mason
ISBN 978 0237 53346 5

Glub! By Penny Little and Sue Mason
ISBN 978 0237 53461 5

Amy's Slippers by Mary Chapman and Simona Dimitri
ISBN 978 0237 53347 2

The Grumpy Queen by Valerie Wilding
and Simona Sanfilippo
ISBN 978 0237 53459 2

The Flamingo Who Forgot by Alan Durant
and Franco Rivolli
ISBN 978 0237 53343 4